GET YOUR LIFE BACK

A Twelve-Week Journey to Overcome Stress, Anxiety and Depression

FINDHORN PRESS

GET YOUR LIFE BACK

A Twelve-Week Journey to Overcome Stress, Anxiety and Depression

Mary Heath

FINDHORN PRESS

Published in 2015 by Findhorn Press, Scotland

ISBN: 978-1-84409-677-0

Edited by Jacqui Lewis
Illustrations by Jane Delaford Taylor
Cover Design by Richard Crookes
Interior Design by Damian Keenan
Printed and bound in the EU

Published by
Findhorn Press
117-121 High Street,
Forres IV36 1AB Scotland,
United Kingdom

t +44-(0)1309-690582
f +44(0)131-777-2711
e info@findhornpress.com
www.findhornpress.com

CONTENTS

Week 12

In Conclusion

Disclaimer

· · · · · · · · ·

THE INFORMATION IN THIS BOOK is given in good faith and is neither intended to diagnose any physical or mental condition nor to serve as a substitute for informed medical advice or care.

Please contact your health professional for medical advice and treatment. Neither author nor publisher can be held liable by any person for any loss or damage whatsoever which may arise from the use of this book or any of the information therein.

Dedication

To my loving husband Ray,
without whom this
would not have been possible.

Introduction

· · · · · · · · ·

WE ARE NOT BORN WITH STRESS, anxiety or depression. So why are so many people suffering the unpleasant symptoms and effects of such conditions? The answer is simple – life! As we make our journey through life with all its ups and downs, twists and turns and stresses and strains, we collect large amounts of baggage that can lie heavily on our shoulders and on our minds, weighing us down; slowing us down. We feel overwhelmed; find it difficult to function normally and to perform our daily duties. If we are not adept at handling this baggage we can crumble and fall under its weight. Some of us collapse, break down or have to stop because we can't go on any further, any longer. It engulfs our minds and emotions.

It also manifests itself physically. Stress affects every organ and gland in the body. It is estimated that between 75% and 90% of patients visiting their doctor are suffering from stress-related ailments. It plays a large part in many conditions such as headaches, high blood pressure, heart disease, diabetes, asthma, arthritis and digestive and skin problems.

A great amount of research has now proven, and it is now recognized, that the mind and body are not two separate entities; the body and mind are *as one*. They work together.

On reflection it is easy to understand how this is true. You only have to think of something that makes you sad and your body will produce tears (we don't *tell* ourselves to cry). Crying is the body's way of releasing emotion. Under a microscope, tears of sorrow, grief, laughter and joy all look very different. In fact almost every emotion has its own unique and distinct type of tear; and tears from peeling an onion look different from emotion-based tears. If you are mentally and emotionally distressed your body will pick up the message and react accordingly.

Many clients I have worked with found that once they began to practise their coping strategies and were able to manage their stress, they felt not only mentally and emotionally better, but also physically better. If you have physical conditions, pay attention to what happens to those conditions once you start working your way through this book.

Stress also has a huge impact on industry and commerce throughout the world. Stress is a major problem in British workplaces; according to the Health & Safety Executive stress costs the British economy an estimated £3.7 billion each year. The American Institute of Stress reports that stress costs the USA more than $300 billion annually. The European Union estimates that work-related stress affects at least 40 million workers in its fifteen member states and that it costs the European Union at least €20 billion annually. The World Health Organization reports that globally at least 350 million people live with depression, stress, and anxiety. It is the leading cause of disability worldwide, yet only about 25% of the world's population have access to effective treatment for stress and stress-related disorders, such as anxiety and depression.

Depression often starts at a young age and affects women more commonly than men. One to two out of ten mothers have depression after childbirth. It affects not only the person with depression, but also their loved ones.

Almost 1 million people worldwide take their own lives each year. Suicide rates have increased by 60% over the last forty-five years. For every person that commits suicide, twenty more make an attempt. Hence, many millions of people are affected or experience suicide bereavement every year. Suicide occurs across all ages and, in 2012, was the second-largest global cause of death among 15–29 year olds.

Many people think that stress is not a mental health condition, and in many cases it isn't. It is perfectly normal to feel stressed at the end of a busy working day; and if, after some rest, relaxation and a good night's sleep, you recover and have little or no problem doing it all over again the next day, that is normal too. However, when stress turns into something that completely overwhelms you and you begin to suffer physical, mental and emotional symptoms that don't get better, then it becomes more serious. If you don't seek help and your stress develops into anxiety, panic attacks and other anxiety disorders, it is even more serious. If you have no means of counteracting this stress and anxiety, and you reach break point or burn out, depression is often the next stage – if indeed it hasn't materialized already. Put all these issues together and you have a mental health condition that is not only severe but is often serious enough to mean hospitalization.

If you do seek help, your doctor may prescribe medication. However, this is often a trial and error situation until you find one that suits you, and this can take weeks or even months. Doctors themselves may be overworked and suffering from stress. One of their problems is that they rarely have enough time to spend with their patients. Even if they do have the time, they may not have the necessary skills and coping strategies to teach their patients how to manage their stress. In many countries counselling or psychotherapy is offered but there is often a long wait for this kind of treatment, if it is available at all. In the meantime, with little help and support, the condition can escalate. There is another problem too: often people who suffer from stress, or stress-related conditions, do not go to their doctor to seek help. They wrongly believe that they will, or should, be able to *pull themselves together* and *get over it.* They may also perceive it as a weakness and feel ashamed or guilty that they cannot cope. They might soldier on stoically, doing their best to keep going, but in time they are likely to worsen and suffer burnout or breakdown. They hit the proverbial *brick wall*, which stops them in their tracks and makes them unable to function normally. It is at this point that help is often forced upon them: they are by now so unwell that recovery can be difficult and a lengthy process. Unfortunately, on top of the stress and depression, because the pressure has gone unrelieved for so long, they can find themselves living in a whirlwind of emotions such as fear, anxiety, resentment, guilt and regret. Feeling bad can become habitual and it can be very difficult to escape from its troublesome clutches. Getting stuck in this nightmare scenario can be frightening and debilitating.

If you have been through something similar yourself you may give yourself a hard time because you blame yourself for everything that has happened. The outcome of feeling weak, helpless and unworthy of being helped results in a lack of confidence, which in turn causes you to achieve less and less. Your perceived failure creates a lack of self-compassion, low self-esteem and low self-worth and it is at this point that depression is almost inevitable. Without the right kind of help and support the depression deepens. You may feel as if you are living in a deep black hole; you can try to climb out, but the sides are slippery and you are just about hanging on with your fingertips.

It was seeing so many patients in such bleak scenarios that led me to decide to write this book.

Get Your Life Back offers help to those who are in the situation described above, or similar, and who do not have the benefit of first-hand, personal treatment and therapy. This book is a simple, but wide-ranging resource for anyone who needs help quickly, but who chooses, for whatever reason, not to seek personal or professional assistance. It is also the perfect aid to prevent everyday stress escalating into a more serious condition.

Many years ago when I desperately needed help myself, apart from medication, there was no help available. Coping strategies were a thing of the future. If there had been a book, like this one, I know I would have benefitted enormously from it. At the time, I didn't know anything at all about stress or depression and I don't think I had even heard of it, let alone understand it. I was left alone, completely in the dark and not knowing what to do to help myself. Not everyone was sympathetic, and I don't blame them – they didn't know what was happening to me or how to help me either. *Pulling myself together* was my only option!

Since then, and for many years, I have thought how unfortunate it is that we are not taught the basic skills and coping strategies for life. At school I was taught a wide variety of subjects, some of which I never used again, but why did no one ever teach me how to deal with difficult relationships, major life changes, how to cope with bereavement, financial problems or ill health? Why are we, as children, not taught the most important lesson of all: how to manage the rollercoaster of life in all its many guises?

I was happy to learn, however, that since I was at school (which was a very long time ago!) things have changed for the better. There are now some schools that teach relaxation, meditation, mindfulness or yoga. Living life at the tremendously fast pace that we do, though, there is still room for much more improvement in this area. My hopes and aspirations are that stress management and other life skills will eventually be on the curriculum of every school in the world! Until then, I am confident that this book will not only benefit parents and teachers, but also enable them to pass on these much needed coping strategies and skills to future generations so that they too can live life to the full without the struggle and hindrance of stress, anxiety and depression.

My own journey began when, at the age of twenty-three, I suffered post-natal depression after the birth of my first child. Although it was quite severe and debilitating, I did eventually recover but continued to suffer occasional mild bouts of depression. When I had my second baby I suffered post-natal depression again. It wasn't quite as bad this time but it went on for a long time and although I continued to take medication, it didn't help at all. I also suffered quite a few physical and psychological problems, most of which were diagnosed as psychosomatic illnesses (illnesses of the mind), but I was offered no help whatsoever. Trying to hide how I felt from my family put even more pressure on me: I wrongly assumed that it was best to keep as much as I could to myself. Of course, looking back I now recognize that my body was reacting to the stress that I wasn't dealing with either mentally or emotionally. One day, when I was feeling particularly low and in despair, a concerned friend suggested that I start attending yoga classes. I wasn't keen at first but I was desperate. It was the seventies and there was nothing else to help me, and I was determined not to get any worse. Shortly after that excellent piece of advice I attended my very first pranayama yoga class, and that was the day that changed my life for ever.

The first thing I learned was to live my life one day at a time, to live in the present moment and not to dwell on the past or the future. This was the first principle of the philosophy of yoga. (Mindfulness is the more fashionable term for this concept these days!) I felt as if the teacher had somehow got to know all about me and my worries and fears and was speaking directly to *me*. After the talk at the start of the class, we were taught how to breathe correctly. I was shocked to discover how quickly and shallowly I was breathing, but very soon picked up how to breathe slowly, deeply and from my abdomen. The physical exercises followed, which were very gentle and enjoyable, and at the end of the session we were asked to lie down and relax. Surprisingly, I found this part incredibly difficult and the teacher suggested that I was so stressed and anxious that I needed to take these yoga classes seriously! She clearly recognized how much stress I carried about with me and how much I had needed yoga to come into my life.

I remember that first class, thirty-six years ago, as if it was yesterday. I never looked back after that. I went on to learn so much more and week by week I became better, stronger and stronger and much more positive in my outlook. I continued with my twice weekly yoga classes and eventually I was asked to train as a teacher. I had one-to-one training sessions with my teacher, or guru, and after two and a half years I taught my very first pranayama yoga class. Before very long I was teaching several classes a week; I was privileged, over a period of thirty years, to help many hundreds of people to gain peace of mind.

Many of my students came to me suffering from stress, and recovered, just as I had all those years ago. I became more and more interested in the subject of stress and in 1991 I joined the Solihull Natural Health Group, which offered talks and workshops on a whole range of complementary therapies, natural medicine and alternative techniques. When I attended a workshop on stress management I knew immediately that this was to be the next stop on my journey. I trained with the International Stress Management Association in London and was soon delivering courses in stress management at the psychiatric hospital where I had been teaching yoga for many years. The courses were so successful that I was soon running several sessions a week. This led to me devising and delivering courses in positive living, which were both very popular and beneficial to the patients.

However, I didn't stop there. I decided that it would be useful to do more training, and my next project culminated in gaining a qualification in counselling at the University of Coventry. Over the next few years I became a bit of a course enthusiast and trained in all sorts of disciplines and all manner of therapies including: Cognitive Behavioural Therapy (CBT), Neuro-Linguistic Programming (NLP), solution-focused therapy and personal development. I also achieved diplomas in life coaching and energy field healing and, finally, I qualified as an advanced practitioner in the Emotional Freedom Technique (EFT). With my toolkit well and truly stocked to the brim, and all my experience in the field, I was in the very fortunate and rewarding position of being able work as a freelance stress management consultant, counsellor, life coach and complementary therapist. I worked for many years in mental health in both the private and public sector, as well as in industry including some large blue chip companies and organizations.

During my career I applied every therapy, skill and technique I had learned and acquired, much of which I now pass on to you here.

Although a book cannot provide a tailored care plan to suit all readers' individual needs, as working with individual patients or clients can, you will find here a comprehensive and eclectic selection of simple, easy-to-follow coping strategies, tools and techniques that anyone can learn and from which anyone can benefit.

It was difficult to know what to put in the book and what to leave out, but eventually it evolved into a twelve-week course. I chose twelve weeks because over my career, this has been the average amount of time it took for my patients and clients to recover.

Recovery times did vary; it very much depended on how much time, effort and dedication each individual put into their recuperation. The more *you* put in and the more time you spend in practice, the sooner you will *Get Your Life Back!*

There are many self-help books including many on the subject of stress. This book, however, differs from others in that it includes techniques and practices for overcoming a wide range of conditions including stress, anxiety, panic attacks, depression, phobias and low self-esteem.

It also differs inasmuch as it brings together in one book a diversity of skills and techniques selected from a range of therapeutic disciplines.

The reason for this is due to the fact that every one of us is a unique individual, whose journey is also unique. With all our different experiences and many different personality types, characteristics, opinions, values and beliefs, we are bound to need, and to respond to, a variety of skills, systems, approaches and techniques.

I like to think that everything in the book is useful, informative and therapeutically beneficial for *all*; even if you find that one particular strategy or skill isn't perfect for you, it is still worth learning and taking on board. We are constantly changing, in a constantly changing world, and being flexible now may benefit you in the future.

How to get the most
out of this book

· · · · · · · · ·

IDEALLY YOU WILL WORK your way through the book systematically, one day at a time in the order it is presented. If you follow the advice and guidance, do both the physical and mental exercises, practise all the forms of relaxation and meditation and take on board the importance of setting and achieving your goals, not only will you recover and *Get Your Life Back*, you will also soon discover a new way of living that will be more balanced, happier, healthier and more fun!

The book is organized into twelve weekly sections. On each and every day of each week you are guided through the process of acquiring the necessary strategies, skills, tools and techniques that will ultimately result in you overcoming what is currently making your life too difficult: the stress or anxiety that controls your life, the depression that prevents you from functioning normally, the low self-esteem and lack of confidence – whatever it is you need to work on.

I have structured the book as a step-by-step guide that allows you to advance at your own pace according to your own method of learning, capability and time allowances. Of course, it isn't essential that you spend exactly a day on each day's activity as it is presented here. You may want to spend longer than a day on one particular subject but be able to work through more than one topic in a day. For example, you can practise your breathing exercises three times a day as well as doing your relaxation and setting your goals for the week. Some of you may want, or need, to spread the contents out more liberally, perhaps even spending more time than twelve weeks.

It is perfectly possible to use the book to suit your own individual needs and preferences, but do make sure that you don't lose the necessary momentum and motivation. If this does happen, just remember what made you start the book and the outcome you wanted when you started. You can be flexible to suit your lifestyle, but do try to stick to a fairly strict routine and try not to go longer than two or three days maximum without doing something.

Remember, *it is important to take things in the order they appear in the book*. In particular, the pranayama breath control exercises are meant to be practised one at a time, moving on to the next only when you have mastered each of them. The relaxation and meditation exercises are also progressive, each one becoming slightly more advanced as you work your way through the book. The correct thinking passages also need to be used in the order they are presented here in order to gain full understanding.

You may, alternatively, like to dip into the book, opening it at a random page to seek inspiration for the day. This is fine if you are not particularly aiming to use the book as a twelve-week course but simply want to gain some insight and information on its various coping skills and strategies.

Good luck with your journey! I sincerely hope you find the peace, serenity, strength and joy you have been seeking and hoping for.

Now go and start your exciting journey. This day could be your first day of freedom and a new way of life!

Getting Started

· · · · · · · · ·

1. Your Workbook

MANY OF THE EXERCISES in this book require you to write things down. You will need a workbook (a notebook or exercise book) to do this. It will be useful for you to be able to look back on some of the material or details you have been writing down.

You will use your workbook to score yourself on a weekly basis on a self-assessment rating scale and to assess and check your progress, or help with your goal-setting.

You can also use it as a journal to write anything you feel like writing: how you are feeling each day; what you have done, achieved or feel good (or bad) about. It is also a very good idea to write down anything that you are worried about or things that are concerning you. If anything or anyone has made you angry and you can't easily discuss it, write that down too. You will feel better and less angry once you get it all off your chest and down on paper.

Keep your workbook by your bed at night so that if there is anything on your mind that is keeping you awake, you can write that down too. You will find that once you have transferred the thoughts out of your head and on to paper, you will fall asleep more easily, more quickly.

2. Your Commitment

"Commitment is an act, not a word."
— *JEAN-PAUL SARTRE*

You have already made your first positive commitment by purchasing this book. When you made the decision to do so there must have been a very good reason for it. Maybe you are suffering the effects of stress, anxiety or depression. Perhaps you are finding life difficult to cope with and need some help or guidance. So it's great that you have now begun to take responsibility for your health by finding how you can make improvements and by learning the appropriate and necessary coping strategies.

You may have needed some help for quite a while but you weren't ready before now, before today. Learning to manage and cope with stress can feel daunting, and often people just don't know where to start. The good news is that you *have s*tarted and you will soon be making some positive changes, one day at a time and at your own pace.

Commitment to making any important and beneficial change is just one of the key ingredients to success. Another key ingredient is imagination. If you are able to imagine how you would like to be and how much better you could feel in the future, you will find that your enthusiasm, dedication and commitment will soar!

When you commit to something, I mean really, really commit, you will have a far greater chance of sticking with your cause and seeing it through to the end. Unfortunately however, *reading* this book alone will not get you to where you want to be! But if you fully commit, not only to reading the book but also to following the advice and performing and practising the exercises, you will succeed in *getting your life back* and becoming the new you.

Committing fully to something, anything, involves doing four things:

1. SETTING A GOAL · You need to write your goal down and you need to write it in the present tense, as if you have already achieved it.

FOR EXAMPLE: *"I commit myself completely and am now reaping the benefits of reading this book. I am enjoying practising the exercises every day. I am calm, relaxed and now in control."*

2. VISUALIZING YOURSELF EXACTLY HOW YOU WANT TO BE · Do this every morning when you wake and every night before you go to sleep. Also do it whenever you remember to and when you experience any moments of stress or low mood.

3. MAKING THE DECISION TO CHANGE YOUR LIFE · Make a conscious decision now to learn these life-enhancing skills to help you overcome your stress, anxiety and depression. Decide to become the person you *really* want to be. Decide to work hard at this. Decide to do whatever it takes. Those of you who have taken exams at some point in your life will know that without hard work, study, dedicated practice and determination you may not pass. The good news is that this course doesn't have an examination at the end of it, but it will change your life for the better if you adopt the right attitude and make the right decisions.

4. TAKING RESPONSIBILITY · This involves taking responsibility for your own health and well-being and realizing that as you are an adult no one else can do it for you. Yes, you may need help, support and encouragement from others, and you will also need to take responsibility to ask them for whatever it is you need from them, but only *you* can do what *you* need to do. Start today, now, to believe in yourself. You really *can* do this. You may be keen to take responsibility to help yourself for the sake of someone else, perhaps a loved one who worries about you or takes care of you. So start today, not only to help yourself but also to take the pressure off those who are close to you.

I have seen many hundreds of people in my career, some in the depths of despair, some who had experienced the unimaginable, some who felt that they were right at the bottom of the dark pit of life, but they found the ability to climb up the slippery slope, one step at a time, and get to the top. They did it by using some of the tips and techniques found in this book; but first, they *all* made a firm commitment to help themselves.

3. Your Creation

"A journey of a thousand miles begins with a single step."
— *LAO TZU*

YOU HAVE ALREADY TAKEN THE FIRST STEP of your journey towards making positive changes in your life. So let's begin immediately with the *next* exciting step.

Find a chair and a place to sit comfortably, somewhere you will not be disturbed for the next half hour or so. When you are ready, in your own time, take three slow deep breaths and with each breath you breathe out, relax. Now, slowly try to relax your whole body; your face, your neck and shoulders, your back and tummy, your arms and your legs. Just allow your body to sink into your chair. Feel your chair supporting your whole body so you can just let go. The more your body relaxes, the more your mind will relax too. The more your mind relaxes, the more creative you will become when, in a moment, you begin to invent a whole new you – a you without the shackles of stress, anxiety and depression!

When you are ready to begin, start by imagining what kind of person you would like to be – sometime in the future. Imagine yourself at a point in the future when you have fulfilled your dreams and achieved your goals and aspirations.

Take your time now, and consider the following questions. You can write the answers down in your workbook, if you already have one.

1. What kind of person will you be?	
2. What will you be doing differently?	
3. How will you be behaving differently?	
4. What kind of attitude will you have?	
5. Where will you be and who will be with you?	
6. What will you have achieved?	

7.	How will you feel?
8.	Which qualities will you possess?
9.	In what other ways will you have changed?
10.	How will you recognize the new you?
11.	What is the first thing you will think when you wake up in the morning?
12.	What will you be doing that you couldn't do before?
13.	How will other people recognize how you've changed?
14.	What will they like about you now?
15.	How will they feel about you?
16.	What would they say to you?
17.	Why will they be proud of you?
18.	Why will you be proud of yourself?

This is where it all begins, in your imagination. Your mind is much more powerful than you might think; it has the ability to change everything, and every change you want to make will begin with a single thought. Everything you do starts with a thought. Everything that you have achieved in your life began with a single thought. Think about it! Even reading this book began with a thought to do so. Thinking is therefore vitally important. Or, more accurately, how you think. Your mind is so powerful that it has the ability to affect how you feel, what you do, how you behave, and all of your outcomes.

Your subconscious mind (which contains everything you have experienced in your life so far) is much larger than your conscious mind. You naturally draw on your subconscious mind when it comes to finding answers or making decisions, solving problems and finding solutions. However, if many of your past experiences were negative, there is a possibility that many of the choices you have made so far in your life have also been negative. Thankfully, the opposite is also true. It's a little like filling a glass with water and finding that when you come to drink from it, all you get is water! However, if you continuously pour champagne into the glass of water, the water will spill out and be replaced with champagne. In other words, whatever you put in is what you get out. Therefore, once you start to have more positive thoughts about yourself, your life, and your world, you will override the negatives, and the positives will supersede them. Your subconscious is therefore much more likely to generate what you want, rather than what you don't want.

So, from today, start to develop your positive attitude. Think about the positive new you. Keep returning to the questions above and the answers you gave.

Whenever you think of something new to create, write that down too. Remember, it must all be positive, and try too to be as descriptive as you can be. Open up your mind, and just let it flow. Just keep writing. Be imaginative, inventive and creative. Decide now who you want to be and what kind of life you would like to be living. Be excited about your potential. Decide now to be happy, healthy, at peace and successful. Believe in yourself, your ability to change and the power of positive thinking!

Welcome to the New You!

4. Your Self-Assessment

Your ability to cope with stress

0	1	2	3	4	5	6	7	8	9	10

0 = not able to cope at all; 10 = able to cope very well

Recreate the table above in your workbook. Mark your score as you feel you are today, and make a note of today's date. You can just go with the first number that comes into your mind but it must *feel right*. It would be unusual for someone to give themselves a score of zero, but if you feel that this is your score, it may well mean you are not coping at all, to the point of not being able to get out of bed in the morning, and should probably not focus on working with this book at the present time. It might indicate that seeking professional help, would be the best idea. I would suggest that you need to feel you can give yourself a score of 2 or above to be able to concentrate and put the advice into action.

At the opposite extreme, a score of 10 would also be rare. If you already feel you can give yourself a score of 10, I would suggest that you only need to read this book to make sure you maintain your high score and your ability to cope well with life. Your score will probably be somewhere in between these two extremes; you will be working towards increasing your score as the weeks go on.

Think about what score you would like to give yourself in twelve weeks' time. Be realistic. To reach a very high score would be good, but even if you increase your score by just a few points you will have made very good progress.

Now assess how stressed you feel and mark it on the scale line below, along with today's date.

Stress Levels

0	1	2	3	4	5	6	7	8	9	10

This chart works in the opposite way to the previous one.

A SCORE OF 0 = VERY LOW · This means you deal with and manage stress very well. In fact it is rare for someone to score a zero as everyone has – and needs – some amount of stress in their life; it's what motivates us and enables us to perform effectively. A score of 0 or 1 can also indicate that there isn't enough going on in your life and that you are in danger of becoming bored, lethargic and frustrated.

A SCORE OF 10 = VERY HIGH STRESS LEVELS · This indicates that you need a lot of help and support in addition to using this book.

If you are very stressed and perhaps also suffering from anxiety, your score will be high. The aim is to watch your stress levels reduce week by week as your ability to cope increases. As you work through the book, enter your scores at the end of each week on the chart below. Do not be alarmed if your coping ability score goes down one week. Sometimes, because there is quite a lot to learn, you may feel a little under pressure and your ability to cope may just slip a little. This is perfectly normal and nothing to be concerned about. Just watch your ability to cope scores increase and your stress levels go down as you work successfully on your exercises and directions.

Your Weekly Scores

Weeks	1	2	3	4	5	6	7	8	9	10	11	12
Coping Ability												
Stress Levels												

Well done! You have now completed your initial assessment and are ready to take the first step in your Twelve-Week Journey to Overcome Stress, Anxiety and Depression.

Week 1

. . . .

Week 1, Day 1
» *PHILOSOPHY* «
One Day at a Time

"Yesterday is gone. Tomorrow has not yet come.
We have only today. Let us begin."
— MOTHER TERESA

IF YOU ONLY READ THIS ONE PAGE, discard the rest of the book and start from today living one day at a time, I can assure you that your life will change for the better. This sounds like a sweeping statement, and you may find yourself disbelieving it, but throughout my career I have found the principle of living in the moment, which comes from yoga philosophy, to be the very best, most rewarding, most effective piece of advice ever given to anyone anywhere.

From this day forward you will endeavour to live just one day at a time. Yes, it's as simple as that. No marathon to run, no lengthy report to write, no heavy-duty physical exercise (unless you want to, of course!). All that is required of you is to live today fully, as if it were your first day and your last. Try to focus on everything that you do, no matter how mundane. Attempt to concentrate on each moment as it presents itself to you. Be aware, checking frequently that your thoughts are not dwelling on the past or racing ahead to the future. If you find that they are, STOP – and gently bring your attention back to the present, focusing on where you are, what you are doing and what is happening in the here and now.

Acknowledge the benefits of living in the present moment; know that each moment you have today is in itself very precious. Think about it – you only have each moment once. You only live your life one day at a time. Why spend so much time dwelling on the past or worrying about the future, when all you have is the present, and you will never have that "now" again? Cherish it, live it fully, be glad that you have it. Even if you are not particularly enjoying it, even if you are in pain or living through difficulties, simply try your best to face the reality of it. Face it with a calm still mind (you will shortly learn how to do this), because if you do you will be able to cope with it much more easily, thus moving into the future with strength, dignity and hope. Resolve to do this each and every day. Remember this is a new beginning. Start now. *The time is now. This is your present!*

Living for the moment can be the most effective and quickest way of relieving stress and anxiety. If you think about it, most of your anxieties are about the past or the future.

"Oh if only I hadn't done this or that, I really regret not having done so and so... " "Life was so much better then." "If only I could go back and change things." "I'm dreading..." "What if that happens?" "What if it all goes wrong?" "What if it all falls apart?" "Will I ever be happy again?", "What if..., what if..., what if...?"

And so on. Can you imagine what these thoughts do to you over a period of time? How miserable and unhappy or stressed and anxious you would become. Remember that your way of living in the past has led you to this day, to where you are now, to how you feel now and to what you do and how you do it. Each and every thought you have is stored in your subconscious, and that in turn makes you who you are today. If, therefore, you continue to have similar negative, pessimistic, self-defeating thoughts, feelings and actions, your future outcome will be the same. What you put in, you get out. If you continue to do what you're doing, you'll continue to get what you're getting!

The important thing is to realize and remember that you can't go back into the past, turn the clocks back and put everything right. You can't wipe out certain memories and change the decisions you made. Similarly, you cannot go back to a time in your life when everything was (or you think it was) a bed of roses. So why waste energy, bringing yourself down by allowing these thoughts and fears to fester and affect you so badly today? It doesn't make any sense and it certainly doesn't help.

The answer is to stop these thoughts that don't belong in the present. The past has gone and the future is not here yet, so prepare responsibly and positively for the future by living positively in the here and now. Think about this again; it is worth emphasizing – the more negative thoughts you have by dwelling on the past or future, the more negative you become, not only in the present time but in the future also; conversely, the more positive you are, the more positive your future will become.

That's not to say that you must never think about the future. Of course we need to make plans, set goals, feel excited about something lovely that's about to happen sometime in the future – but leave it there and return to reality, the present moment. Concentrate on the time that you have *now*. Similarly, of course there are times when we need to recall something from the past, or indeed when we enjoy thinking about happy events that took place in the past, and that's fine – just don't stay there! The time is NOW and you can never have the now back. There is no rewind button in reality!

If you're thinking that the here and now, your reality, is really terrible, the only answer is to try your best to remain positive. Believe a little more in yourself and try to believe that things can get better. Nothing lasts for ever. Turn to the new you that you created earlier and visualize yourself being that person, leading a full and happy life in the not too distant future. Remember that nothing ever stays the same; life is a constantly changing programme. Every day is different, every day something new happens. It is possible for you to grow stronger and stronger each and every day instead of becoming weaker or more and more depressed. If your circumstances don't change for the better on their own, make them change. Begin to create the circumstances you want. Set your goals to ensure that your life will be better in some way in the future.

You will find many skills and techniques in this book to help you, and if you follow the advice and instructions, by the time you reach the last page you will hardly recognize yourself! Not only will you grow stronger every day and in every way but you will also be able to realize a happier and healthier way of living. You have already taken the first step towards becoming the new you, so continue now to live in the moment.

Week 1, Day 2
» BREATH CONTROL «
You Are as You Breathe

"When you consciously decide to breathe more slowly and deeply,
you alert your body to the fact that you want it to behave differently."
— ERIC MAISEL, PhD, psychotherapist, teacher, coach, author

Unbelievable! I can hear you saying it. How could this possibly be true? I know, it's amazing – but actually it is very true. Our breath is the director of operations. It keeps us alive every single day, every moment of our entire life! However, how you breathe determines how you live your life.

Have you ever been really anxious or panicking about something and someone has told you to take a deep breath? This is because it really does help you to calm down. Perhaps you automatically find yourself trying to breathe deeply in times of stress? This is your body telling you that if you breathe slowly and deeply, it will help you regain control and find peace and calm.

The fact is, the way you breathe does affect the way you think, feel, act, react and behave. The opposite is also true! Your thoughts, feelings, actions and behaviour express themselves in how you breathe. It's a two-way street. You may not have noticed it or even heard of this before, but from today try to become aware of that happening. You will soon start to *use* your breath as an ally or best friend. You will be surprised just how much you will be able to depend on your breath in the pages to come. In some cultures the breath is known as the "Life Force" or "Chi" or "Qi". Your breath is the energy of life. You take your first breath when you are born and of course the last when you die. Without breath we have no life; in this sense it is easy to realize just how important breathing is to us, and yet most of us never even give it a second thought. Amazingly, we can spend years breathing incorrectly and suffering the consequences – mentally, physically and emotionally.

The symptoms of poor or incorrect breathing can be very unpleasant. As soon as we encounter stress – and unfortunately this can often even happen in early childhood – the physiology of our bodies automatically makes us breathe shallowly in order to deal with the perceived stress. If the stress doesn't go away, or it isn't managed or coped with effectively, it is possible for incorrect breathing to become habitual. What a pity that we are not taught this when we are young! If only we knew that we were harming ourselves. If only we could have been taught some very simple yet life-changing breathing exercises. If we had, we could have prevented many of the following symptoms and effects, which occur because of breathing incorrectly:

- Gasping, panting or catching of breath
- Headaches and migraines
- Chest pains and palpitations
- Light-headedness, dizziness and fainting
- Asthma and other respiratory problems
- Tingling and numbness in the scalp and hands
- Blurred vision
- Lack of energy, tiredness, exhaustion and lethargy
- Aching and painful muscles
- Digestive upsets

Identify your own symptoms from the above list, tick them off and note them and the date in your workbook. Check again in three months after you have been practising the breathing exercises that follow. You may see some changes.

Spend some time now trying to be aware of how you are breathing, especially if it is fast and shallow (high up in the chest) or if you have any of the above symptoms when you are breathing too fast or too shallowly. Make a note of your observations and reflect on them.

What were your findings? Were you surprised? Did you get a shock? I hope not, but it's true that many people do find that they are breathing too rapidly and/or too shallowly, and they probably have been for a very long time. The good news is that, here and now, you can learn how to breathe correctly and thereby transform a lifelong bad habit into something that will give you many health benefits – for both mind and body. Here are some of them:

- Induces and enhances relaxation
- Calms and stills the mind
- Controls and calms emotions
- Prevents anxiety, panic attacks and rapid breathing
- Softens and relaxes the muscles
- Aids concentration, meditation and other mental exercises
- Benefits the nervous system
- Aids digestion
- Increases blood and lymph circulation
- Improves sleep

How to Breathe Correctly

Here you will learn exactly how to breathe correctly. Some people might find this quite easy, others may need some practice, and for a few it may seem totally impossible. (These may well be the people who need it the most.) However, *everyone can learn how to breathe properly*.

When we are exposed to stress, and this can happen even at an early age, it causes us to start to breathe incorrectly, rapidly and shallowly. Unfortunately it is all too easy for this poor breathing to become a habit if we are not able to cope with or manage the stress effectively. As you have probably been breathing poorly for a long time, it may take you some time to master correct breathing. If you get agitated because you can't do it, you may make yourself anxious, which in turn will promote incorrect breathing and make the whole process harder. Therefore treat yourself gently and approach it calmly. If you do get agitated, just leave it until another time, but don't give up – it is very important that you persevere. It may help to attempt it after you have practised your relaxation on Day 7, which will calm the whole body, including your breathing.

When you are relaxed and lying flat on your back on the floor place your hands gently on your abdomen just below your navel. You should feel the automatic rise and fall of your abdomen, but if you don't, it means that you are not sufficiently relaxed. So try again when you do feel more relaxed, when you are more likely to be breathing correctly. Don't try to change your breath for the moment; simply allow your body to do the breathing for you.

NOTE: Always breathe both in and out through your nose when doing any of the breath-control exercises in this book.

Stay like that for a little while, until you become accustomed to how your body feels when you do breathe correctly – lying down can help with this, which is why I recommend doing this exercise in a lying position to begin with. Concentrate completely on your breathing.

Now take a deliberate long, deep breath in and use the muscles in your lower abdomen to make it rise further, pushing the tummy upwards towards the ceiling as if you are blowing air into a balloon. When you breathe out let the abdomen fall gently back downwards, like the balloon deflating. Don't just let the breath go; try to gently control it as it passes through the nose. Do this three or four times until it feels comfortable, but stop if you begin to feel dizzy. This could simply be your brain not being used to receiving all this oxygen, but you must not over-strain. Rest and then try again after a few minutes.

When you feel you have it right, sit in a straight-backed chair. Put one hand on your chest and one hand on your abdomen. Breathe as you would normally, without changing or forcing the breath, and pay attention to your hands.

If the hand on your chest is moving more than your lower hand, it means that you are breathing too shallowly. For effective breathing the hand on the abdomen needs to be rising and your chest expanding when you breathe in, and the chest and abdomen falling or sinking when you breathe out. However, the hand on your chest should only be moving slightly and your shoulders should stay fairly still. If this is not happening try – gently – to make it happen. If you have been breathing incorrectly for a long time, this might be quite difficult and take some time to correct. Don't worry. It is quite normal to find it difficult to change at first. Concentrate and imagine the air you breathe in is going into a balloon in your tummy (your lower abdomen) and making it rise or push outwards. When you breathe out again, let the balloon gently collapse and feel the tummy go down. Try to breathe slowly and deeply equally in and out.

Persevere and practise every day, several times a day. It will become easier and you will find that you become more and more relaxed, have more energy, sleep better and, generally, feel much, much healthier.

> **NOTE:** You are not expected to breathe like this all day long. This exercise, practised often throughout your day, will improve your breathing in general.

The 7/11 Breath-Control Exercise

When you are comfortable and at ease with slow, deep abdominal breathing, you may wish to try something more. If you are not yet ready to move on you can leave this exercise for another day and continue with the abdominal breathing exercise. The 7/11 Breath-Control Exercise is particularly good for calming down, lowering stress levels and alleviating anxiety and panic.

All you have to remember when you feel anxious or panicky is to breathe in for seven seconds and breathe out for eleven seconds, continuing until you feel calm and you have regained control. It sounds easy enough but when you come to do it it may prove to be a little difficult; however, practice makes perfect!

If you do suffer with anxiety and panic attacks it is important that you practise this when you are feeling OK, as it might be more difficult to practise it usefully when you are actually anxious. When you *are* anxious or having a panic attack, it will be easier for you to draw on this exercise because you will have mastered it beforehand and know exactly what you need to do. It can also act as a preventative if you use it as soon as you become aware that you are having anxious thoughts or feelings; you may actually be able to stop the panic getting a hold on you. If you practise four or five rounds, several times a day you might find that your panic attacks lessen anyway, Here's what to do:

> Remember, always breathe through the nose, not the mouth.
> Still using abdominal breathing, as in the last exercise:
> Breathe in for a count of seven seconds
> Hold the breath, just for a moment
> Breathe out for a count of eleven seconds (relaxing as you do so).

That's all there is to it, but if you find it difficult try breathing in for a count of five seconds and breathing out for a count of eight seconds. You can build up as and when you feel ready, until you can achieve 7/11.

Week 1, Day 3
» *DIRECTION* «
The Six A's of Serenity

To be in a state of serenity, or to feel serene, is an emotion that we all desire, aspire to or want to achieve. It is the opposite of feeling stressed or anxious, angry or being in turmoil: serenity is a feeling of utter calm and tranquility. It is absolute peace of mind and having a feeling that all is well.

The Six A's will lead you there.

1. AWARENESS · Be aware of who you are now, in this present time, what you are now and where you are in your life right now. Be aware of what makes you feel comfortable and what makes you feel uncomfortable. Be aware of your limitations, your weaknesses and faults. Be aware of what you can control and what you can't. But most importantly, be aware of your strengths, qualities, skills, abilities and achievements. Be aware of everything and everyone who makes you feel proud. Be aware of your surroundings, your circumstances and your environment. Be aware of those who love you, and why they love you. Be aware of your potential. Be aware of the progress you have made so far and what you need or would like to change.

2. ACCEPTANCE · Accept your limitations, weaknesses and faults (we all have them and that's OK) – but only if you cannot change them. Accept yourself for who you are – you are an important, unique individual; no one else is like you. We are all different, but in many ways we are all the same too. We are all equal and valuable, individual human beings.

Accept other people for who they are. They are also unique and valuable individuals but their qualities, skills, talents, strengths and weaknesses, faults and failures are different to yours. They have led a completely different life to you and their characteristics, qualities and values will not be the same as yours.

We need to accept everything that we cannot change or those things that are beyond our control. We cannot change or control other people. If we try, it will only create resentment, anger, disagreements and disharmony. Of course it is important to accept others for whom and what they are, as we would want them to accept us; however, we actually don't always have to *like* their behaviour or what they choose to do. Sometimes it is difficult to like everyone and maybe we don't have to, but accepting them will result in a more peaceful existence. It is tempting to judge people for their differences from us, but it is not for us to judge other people. Peace of mind can come from thinking and accepting that although people are different from us, they are not necessarily wrong.

3. ADJUSTMENT · If you are not prepared to accept something then – providing that it is within your control – you must change it. Change, however can be difficult as we are creatures of habit and we like the familiar. The unfamiliar can sometimes bring stress, so to begin with make only small adjustments. Set realistic goals and take one day at a time. Try to achieve something every day that will enhance the quality of your life, no matter how small the steps. Small steps are better than none at all, and every little step will ultimately lead you to your chosen destination.

4. ATTITUDE · One thing you *can* change is your attitude; it is always within your control. You are the master of your attitude because it reflects your own thoughts, feelings and approach to life. If you have a negative attitude, you need to work urgently on changing it; a negative outlook can be your downfall and lead to a negative outcome.

A positive attitude, however, will help you to succeed and achieve. It can bring you peace and happiness and also a life without stress, anxiety and depression. A positive attitude will increase your self-belief, confidence and self-esteem. If there is something you cannot change and this distresses you, change your attitude towards it and see the difference it makes. It may be difficult, but it is not impossible. Start by learning to let things go or asking yourself: "Does it really matter?" Take a few deep breaths to calm your mind and put things into perspective. Be on your guard for the negativity creeping in and catch it before it has a chance to influence and defeat you.

5. AFFIRMATION · An affirmation is a positive short phrase or sentence that you say, or think silently to yourself, over and over. It can change your feelings about yourself or the world around you. Your thoughts influence your feelings and your outcomes, so if you dwell on a particular thought and that thought is negative, your outcome will be negative. But if your thoughts are positive the reverse is true. Repeating your positive affirmations several times throughout the day, every day, will eventually change your feelings and attitude for the better. They will inspire you to become more positive and help you to become the person you yearn to be.

Repeat your affirmations with conviction, commitment, passion and belief, and repeat them out loud if possible. Shout them if you can! You will learn later in the book that we are programmed or conditioned by our belief systems. Some of our beliefs are detrimental, harmful and disempowering and cause self-defeating behaviour. Because they are deeply embedded in our subconscious they can sometimes be very difficult to change, but if we can challenge them and change them, it can be amazing how our lives can take a turn for the better, producing positive and more favourable outcomes. Applying positive affirmations helps to break down distorted and disempowering beliefs and assists in building and breeding new, positive and life-changing outcomes. Jump to Week 9, Day 6 for more on affirmations if you wish.

6. ACHIEVEMENT · If you follow the above steps you will be well on your way to achieving your aims and aspirations. You *can* change and enhance the quality of your life.

As you achieve more and more, you will become more and more positive – thus achieving more and more and getting off the vicious circle of unhealthy stress, anxiety, depression and failure. What you focus on is what you get more of!

Today, reflect on the above and when you have learned the Six A's and digested them fully, try to apply them to one of the issues you are troubled with at the present moment.

Answer the following questions below or in your workbook:

1.	What is it about me that I find difficult to accept?
2.	What do I want or need to change?
3.	What is it about other people that I find difficult to accept?
4.	What do I need to adjust?
5.	What affirmation can I repeat to myself that will help me make that change?
6.	What is it about my attitude that I need to adjust?
7.	What is it that I will achieve if I follow the above?

Week 1, Day 4

» *ORGANIZATION* «

Getting Organized

"If you fail to plan, you are planning to fail."
— *BENJAMIN FRANKLIN, Founding Father of the USA*

Today is the day for planning how you are going to excel at this course, create the new you and *Get Your Life Back*! Working through this book will lead to that happening, but first you need to be organized in such a way that nothing will prevent you from achieving your goals. Dedication, commitment and perseverance are all vital components if you are to succeed. It is therefore essential that your life is free from distractions as you work through the book on a daily basis.

You will need to prioritize your time and your energy. Of course, life being as it is, something totally unexpected could always turn up out of the blue and cause you to take a sideways step. If this does happen, don't panic! Accept and simply deal with the emergency, meet your demands with calmness, then return to your plan as soon as possible. However, you can of course continue to practise what you have learned so far. In fact, your breathing exercises will come in very handy if you are feeling frustrated because you have had to put some things on hold!

So, the plan to *Get Your Life Back* should look something like this:

- Identify the time in your day that is best for you to read or work with your book. Remember you only need to read one day at a time, if that's what you have decided to do. Try to read it at the same time every day so that you get into a routine.

- If it is a direction that needs some action, identify a time in the day when you will carry this out, unless you can do it immediately.

- If you have the space, identify a room where you will read your book, practise the breathing exercises, meditation and relaxations etc. If this room is untidy or cluttered it will not be conducive to relaxation. Spend some time, preferably today, clearing out everything that is of no use to you. Uncluttering a room is extremely beneficial. Throw away or give to charity anything that you no longer need, like or love. If you can't do this right now, plan to do it as soon as possible and write it down as a goal together with the day, date and time. Don't put it off.

- If you don't live alone, plan to inform whoever you live with what you are doing and why. Try to help them to understand what the benefits will be – for both you and them. Obviously when you become more relaxed, you regain control and your mood is better, they will benefit too! You may even want one of your loved ones to follow the programme along with you. Above all, ask for their help when you need it – they may need and want to help you and the gratitude you show them will make them feel as if they are contributing to you becoming well and *getting your life back*.

- Decide now that you will plan to do only the things you really *need* to do. In other words, if you have become aware that you waste time or energy doing things that you don't enjoy or don't really need to do, then plan to stop!

- Plan to succeed! Plan what to say to yourself if ever you become despondent or negative about what you're doing. You may be in the habit of thinking negatively about things. This is a common feature of being stressed or anxious and depressed, but you must be ready to challenge the old you who has these feelings. Rome wasn't built in a day, and the good news is that you really can achieve success if you follow the programme in this book and stick at it. Tell yourself that many hundreds of others have done so – and so can you! Tell yourself that nothing will stand in your way to becoming happy, in control and at peace with yourself, with others and with the world around you. Plan to believe in yourself! Remember to breathe slowly and use positive affirmations.

- Plan for failure! Yes, I know, it sounds ridiculous; but you are, after all, only human! No one is perfect, not even a perfectionist – in fact, perfectionists are often the ones who become more stressed than anyone else! Again, don't panic if things don't go according to plan – simply stop, take a few deep breaths, regroup and start again. It's OK! You are allowed to stray from the path. You are allowed to make mistakes – everybody else does, why not you? Accept that human beings do make mistakes – we are not infallible. Remember too that success often comes after several failures; you learn what *not* to do and how not to do it again. Just keep a positive outlook and visualize the future you want. Keep calm and carry on!

Week 1, Day 5

» *CORRECT THINKING* «

There is Power in Your Thoughts

"Whether you think you can or think you can't, you're probably right."
— *HENRY FORD*, industrialist and founder of the Ford Motor Company

Such a bold statement – but Henry Ford was absolutely right. Whatever it is you're thinking about, those thoughts will directly affect your feelings, your behaviour and your actions and outcomes. But where do your thoughts begin? Your thoughts are a result of the beliefs you formed when you were a young child. You would have taken in information from the environment you were in, from your family, teachers and other people you shared your life with. Some of that information will have been good, true and positive but some of it will have been negative, untrue and even harmful. But, when you are a child you don't think to question things; you simply accept and believe whatever you are told and whatever you experience. Some beliefs and values can stay with you all your life, but often as we grow older many of those beliefs, values and opinions start to be inappropriate or out of date.

We start to question things when we realize that others haven't experienced the same things that we have. We learn that others have had completely different lives, sometimes better, sometimes worse than ours. We therefore modify or form new beliefs and values as we journey through life, every step producing different thoughts, feelings and outcomes.

So our thinking processes start with what we believe about ourselves, other people and the world we live in, along with the experiences we have lived through along the way. So our beliefs determine our thoughts and subsequently our feelings. These then lead to what we do, how we behave and what transpires. Of course, it works the other way round too. In other words, how we behave and what we do feeds back to how we think and feel.

If your thoughts are negative, your feelings, behaviour, actions and outcomes are also going to be negative, and this creates a vicious circle.

Vicious Circle of Negative Thoughts

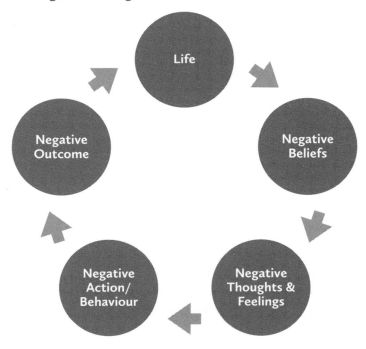

Here are some examples of how our thoughts and beliefs can influence our outcomes:

Negative thoughts and beliefs	Positive thoughts and beliefs
Can result in anxiety and panic	Can result in peace and calm
Can make you miserable, and unhappy	Can motivate you
Make you avoid or run away from things	Help you to make positive changes
Exaggerate reality	Help you to achieve your goals
Can cause you to worry about the future	Help you to make the right choices
Make you think you can predict the future	Can result in better relationships
Make you think you can read minds	Help you to make decisions
Can cause hostility, anger or aggression	Help you to find solutions
Cause low self-esteem	Increase self-esteem and confidence

Think about the information on this page, then for the rest of the day (and from now on) try to identify any negative thoughts you have. You may not be able to catch them all, so it may be a good idea to recruit someone else to point out whenever you are saying anything that could be construed as being negative. You then need to think about how you feel or felt at the time of having those negative thoughts.

If you are aware of any particular recurrent negative thoughts you have, write them down in your workbook. Try to become aware of the link between your thoughts and feelings; thoughts and feelings go together, so it follows that if you do not want to have a negative feeling, don't have a negative thought. If you want to feel good, think positively!

Week 1, Day 6
» *DIRECTION* «

Goal-setting

What is a goal? You may immediately think of a game of football. OK, so let's go with that. Why do footballers want to score goals? Well, that's simple – they want to win and they want to become successful!

Whoever scores the most goals for their team will not only feel great about themselves but will also be very popular. When they continue to win, it could lead to winning the trophy or being top of the league. Does the goal scorer gain anything on a personal level? Well, if the matches I've watched on television are anything to go by, they achieve exultation, triumph and great rejoicing, to say the least! They feel proud; they gain recognition, status, financial gain, excitement from the onlookers and adoration from their fans.

Scoring a goal in a game of football isn't always very easy though. First of all you have to know what you want, which goal to kick the ball into and how to get past the opposing team. These could be considered obstacles in your way. But, if you do your best, you have the support of those around you and you have the determination, the desire to win, the commitment and the belief that you *can* achieve, then you most likely will achieve.

So – although you aren't a football hero – the same applies to you. Setting goals increases your motivation and your will to succeed. You are much more likely to succeed at anything if you set appropriate goals; and additionally, studies show that if you write your goals down you are even more likely to achieve them.

In order to achieve your goals you also need:

- Desire
- Commitment
- Dedication
- Self-belief
- Vision
- Positive and strong emotion

So what is a goal in your own reality? A goal is something that you want or need. It is something that you aspire to and which will make a positive difference in your life when you achieve it. A goal is something that, when achieved, will enhance the quality of your life and give you a feeling of accomplishment, satisfaction, fulfilment and perhaps a sense of joy and pride in yourself. The achievement will increase your self-esteem, self-confidence, self-worth and your self-belief. It will motivate you, spur you on and encourage you to achieve even more. It will lift your spirit. Success breeds success. When you get a taste of success and achievement, you want more and you become determined to achieve more.

There are many different aspects and areas of your life where you might want to set yourself goals. This will be covered later in the book and by then you will have a better idea of which areas of your life need to be improved. But for now, focus on setting goals that will help you to reduce your stress and anxiety and help improve your mood and outlook on life. So let's start with something easy. Even a Premier League footballer has to start somewhere!

In your workbook make a list of everything you want to achieve in the next fortnight. You can include anything you like, anything that comes into your mind – as long as it is nothing major, like finding a new job or moving house. Stick to small, realistic and achievable goals. Examples might be: tidying a kitchen drawer; writing a letter you've been meaning to write; baking a cake; going to bed earlier; or taking some kind of exercise four times a week. Remember, a goal is something you want or something you need. It is *not* something you were going to do anyway, so don't be tempted to put down "cook dinner" or "go to work" if that's what you do every day.

Next, cross out the ones that are unrealistic to achieve in two weeks. Also remove anything that just isn't possible or that you are not committed to. Be honest. Try to leave yourself with around ten goals.

Now make a plan. Write beside each one how long it is going to take and write the day, date and time by which you will have achieved it.

Example Goal-setting Plan

Date	Goal	When	Done	Feeling
1 June	Tidy out the kitchen drawer with all the utensils & large cutlery (1 hr)	Sunday 5 10:30 am	Yes	Fantastic
1 June	Email Louise to thank her for Sunday lunch (10 mins)	Monday 6 9:00 pm	Yes	Relieved
1 June	Go to bed at 11.00 pm on Mon, Tues, Weds & Thurs every week	Mon 6, Tues 7 so far		Less tired
1 June	Paint the garden shed, buy paint on Saturday morning when shopping then start at 11.30 (2hrs x 3 days)	Saturday 11 Sunday 12 Monday 13		Very happy

When this is complete and you are happy and comfortable with your plan, close your eyes, take three deep breaths and visualize yourself having already achieved your goals. You will learn more later about how visualization is so powerful that it can help make your dreams come true!

Don't forget to make a note of how you will feel when you have achieved the goals. Each time you achieve a goal on your list, cross it out or put a big tick by it. Close your eyes and feel how good it feels! Then reward yourself in some way. You deserve it.

Week 1, Day 7
» *RELAXATION* «
Deep Relaxation

This is the first of six methods of relaxation. The idea is that you learn and practise all six different methods, and then you can choose which one or ones you prefer. If you want to jump ahead in the book to find the others, that's fine. You can even use a different one every day once you've learned them all.

So, this form of relaxation is probably the easiest for most people because it involves doing nothing! Yes, you read that correctly, *doing absolutely nothing* apart from lying down on the floor! However, do not underestimate the power of this relaxation. It is extremely effective and is particularly beneficial for eliminating anxiety. It relaxes both the body and the mind, both the conscious and the subconscious mind, all of which hold anxiety. It is the form of relaxation I used to get my life back all those years ago when I started attending yoga classes.

Choose a time of day that suits you best – obviously this will probably not be the middle of a busy day at work! If you do go out to work, do your relaxation when you get home and before you start cooking or eating or doing anything else around the house. Relaxing when you return home from a busy day helps you to detach from the pressures of the day. If you have children you may want to do your relaxation once they have gone to bed and the house is quiet. However, do not leave it until your bedtime as you may simply fall asleep; relaxation has different benefits to those of sleeping.

Tell whoever else is around what you are going to do and why. As you become more re-laxed the people you share your life with will probably notice this, so they too will benefit! You will need to switch off your phone and tell others that you prefer not to be disturbed. You also need to be warm, and in a slightly darkened room (but make sure it's not so dark that you fall asleep!). This applies to all methods of relaxation. So too does lying flat on the floor. You should not lie on your bed, because you may associate this with sleeping. Another reason is that for your body to relax completely your spine should be allowed to drop downwards towards the floor, lessening the natural hollow in the middle of your back. When this happens your organs and glands sit perfectly in your body, thus resting them completely and allowing your blood to flow perfectly through them, nourishing and sustaining them.

You can put a thick blanket, duvet or piece of carpet underneath you for comfort, and maybe a blanket over you for warmth. If you cannot lie flat because of discomfort in your back, put a cushion underneath your calves or put your lower legs up on a chair (so that your hips and knees form a right angle). A comfortable chair with a head support will suffice if it is not possible at all to lie on the floor. However, if you can you should persevere with lying on the floor; you will find over time that after just a few minutes of lying flat, your back will become much more comfortable as your spine adjusts and relaxes.

Start by taking three slow deep breaths and with each breath you breathe out, just allow your body to sink down towards the floor as you give yourself permission to relax. Tell yourself that you are ready to relax. Give the message to your body, firmly but gently, that now is the time to relax. Also tell yourself not to fall asleep. Then simply watch your thoughts as they gently come and gently go. Don't try to direct your thoughts, although this may be difficult to start with. Your mind may be busy at first, thinking about your day or what you must do later. This is OK; eventually the busy thoughts will slow down and you will find that your thoughts are just drifting off, coming and going of their own accord. This is perfectly acceptable in this form of deep relaxation.

Try not to hold on to any particular thoughts. If, for example, a decision you have to make comes in to your mind, acknowledge it, then just bring your attention back to the present. Take three deep breaths again and continue to let your thoughts just come and go. Watch these thoughts as if they were waves gently lapping on the shore, coming in and going out, or clouds drifting effortlessly across the sky. If you feel sleepy, open your eyes and continue to relax with them open. If you really can't help falling asleep it may be better to stop doing the practice for today and just get up. If you feel sleepy often when you try to do this practice, it could mean that you are not sleeping enough, or well enough, at night. If you are disturbed by sounds try not to attach yourself to them; again just let your mind wander. Eventually you will find that sounds do not affect you at all.

When your body is fully relaxed your mind also becomes relaxed and stress is eliminated – it is impossible to be relaxed and stressed at the same time. Your breathing and heart rate will slow down, your blood pressure will reduce, your muscles will become soft and your digestive system will work efficiently. All these changes cause the blood in your body to flow perfectly and to every part of your body. This is the opposite of when you are stressed, when blood is diverted to the muscles in your back, arms and legs, preparing you to flee or fight your perceived danger. You will learn more about this later.

When you are fully relaxed you may lose all sensation in your hands and feet and perhaps even in your whole body. You may feel detached from your body and feel as if you are floating or perhaps sinking down into the floor and becoming at one with it. This is quite normal and a truly wonderful sensation.

When you are ready to come out of your relaxation, do so slowly. Take your time and allow your breathing to return to normal as it will have become quite slow and almost unnoticeable. Roll over on to your right side and stay there a minute or two to allow your breathing and heart rate to return to their normal rate and flow. Sit up very slowly and stay sitting until you are completely ready to stand up and move around: do this slowly and when you are ready to continue with your day, you will feel calm, refreshed and re-energized.

At first you may only be able to relax for a few minutes. If you become agitated try taking some slow deep breaths, and if this doesn't work, get up slowly and try again later or the next day. This usually means that you are totally unaccustomed to relaxing, and shows that you are in great need of doing so.

Try to increase the time you spend relaxing until you are able to stay lying down for twenty minutes, half an hour or even longer. Perhaps once a week or once a fortnight you could find the time to relax for a whole hour. You will benefit enormously from this.

You may wonder why on earth you never did it before! Ideally you need to practise deep relaxation every day for the next two weeks, after which you will be introduced to a new method of relaxation.

If it is not possible to do it every day, relax for a minimum of four times in a week. Try to practise at the same time every day, and in the same room.

Week 1

» RECAP AND REFLECT «

Tick the box when understood, practised and achieved

 ONE DAY AT A TIME: Live each and every day one day at a time. Live each day fully as if it was your first and your last. Do not dwell on the past or the future. How are you finding this and how can you benefit from this philosophy?

 YOU ARE AS YOU BREATHE: How did you get on with the abdominal breathing? Did you find it difficult? How often will you practise? Do you realize now that how you breathe affects your life? Can you see the benefit? How did you find the 7/11 breath-control exercise? How will you be able to apply this exercise?

 THE 6 A'S OF SERENITY: How can you relate to this? What do you need to change? How do you think it will help you?

 GETTING ORGANIZED: Have you done any of this yet? If so, how did you feel once you had accomplished it? Have you any plans to continue? Why do you feel this is important? In what ways will it help you?

 THERE IS POWER IN YOUR THOUGHTS: Negative thoughts and beliefs determine our feelings, behaviours and outcomes. Identify your negative thoughts and be aware of the feelings that accompany them. Write down your most frequent and most powerful negative thoughts. Did you realize any of this before reading about it? How can you benefit from this information?

 GOAL-SETTING: Have you understood the importance of setting and achieving goals? Have you written your goals down and achieved any of them yet? If so, how did you feel when you did? Are you fully committed to continuing with this?

 DEEP RELAXATION: How did you find this? How long did you relax for? How did it help? Did you find it easy or difficult to relax? Why do you think that is? How many times this week do you intend to practise?

Now turn to your self-assessment rating scales and enter your scores for the end of Week 1.

Week 2

. . . .

Week 2, Day 1
» *AWARENESS* «
Reflection

WELL DONE! You have now completed the first week and are on your way to coping well and *getting your life back*. Take another look at the items in Week 1 and think about how they have affected you, what impact they had on you and whether you have noticed any change yet.

Answer these questions below or in your workbook:

1.	What have I learned so far?
2.	How do I feel today?
3.	What is it like for me to live in the moment or take one day at a time?
4.	How does living in the present feel?
5.	Why am I going to continue to take one day at a time/live in the moment?
6.	How did I find the breathing exercises/how have they helped me?
7.	What else do I need to do to find serenity?
8.	What would my life be like if I was a little more organized?

9. How would my life benefit if I was totally organized?

10. What would help me to be more aware of my negative thoughts?

11. Why is setting goals important for me?

12. Why must I write them down?

13. How did I get on with the relaxation? How did I feel afterwards?

14. How often will I practise the relaxation?

15. How will I benefit?

16. What is the most effective thing I have done since starting this book?

17. Has anyone I know benefitted from what I have done so far? If so, how?

18. What is my score out of 10 on the "Coping" scale?

19. What needs to happen for my score to increase by one point?

20. How will I feel when my scores have increased?

Week 2, Day 2

» UNDERSTANDING «

Understanding Who You Really Are

Do this exercise below or, if you are using your workbook, do it there. Write the day number, along with the date, at the top of the page.

Some of you may find this exercise more difficult than others. If you immediately think *"Oh I can't do that"* or *"I don't have any skills"*, just ignore that negative side of you, put it away, take a deep breath and try again. Take your time – and don't be embarrassed or feel silly. No one but you will be reading this. Well, not unless you want them to of course!

If you are still struggling after twenty-four hours, ask someone to help you. You may find that they are able to identify answers much more quickly than you are. If this is true, you need to ask yourself why that is. Think about what prevents you from acknowledging these personal points, or why it is that you cannot accept these positive truths about yourself.

Although I have asked for only three examples, you may wish to add more.

Date: /   /

Name three things that you are grateful for:
1.
2.
3.

List three or more of your qualities:
1.
2.
3.

Name three of your happiest times:
1.
2.
3.

Name three of your skills or abilities:	
1.	
2.	
3.	

What do you think your weaknesses are?	
1.	
2.	
3.	

What do you think your faults are?	
1.	
2.	
3.	

Name three of your major causes of stress:	
1.	
2.	
3.	

Name three ways you cope with your stress:	
1.	
2.	
3.	

Name three things you are proud of, or could be proud of:	
1.	
2.	
3.	

Name three people who love and/or respect you:
1.
2.
3.

What do people like about you?
1.
2.
3.

What do you like about you?
1.
2.
3.

List three of the changes you need to make:
1.
2.
3.

Give three reasons why you need to make some changes in your life:
1.
2.
3.

This has been an exercise in self-awareness. Hopefully, by examining these areas of yourself and your life, you can come to realize that not everything is bad, not everything is hopeless and that even though you have weaknesses and faults, that's OK; we all do. Now you are aware of them, and because you are aware of them, you will be able to make changes if that is what you choose to do.

Perhaps this awareness exercise has also helped you to realize that as well as some negatives there are indeed many positives. Have you ever stopped to think about the fact that you do have qualities, skills, abilities and strengths? Maybe not, but today I would like you to think more about the positive aspects about yourself and the fact that there are some good things happening in your life.

Also today I want you to keep remembering your positive aspects. Focus on them whenever you have a moment. Plant them firmly in your mind and keep returning to them whenever you catch yourself thinking or feeling negatively.

Remind yourself frequently that there are things that make you, or could make you, feel happy, proud and worthy of being loved, liked and respected.

Read the exercise you have just completed at least once every week.

Week 2, Day 3
» PHYSICAL HEALTH «
Exercise

*"If we could give every individual the right amount
of nourishment and exercise, not too little and not too much,
we would have found the safest way to health."*
— HIPPOCRATES

One of the most effective ways of managing stress, anxiety and depression is exercise.

EXERCISE:
- helps you to relax
- switches off the stress response
- makes you more alert
- helps you to sleep better
- reduces high blood pressure
- prevents coronary heart disease
- improves circulation
- tones up the muscles
- regulates your appetite
- improves digestion
- increases physical strength
- improves mental concentration
- increases confidence
- may improve intellectual capacity
- increases productivity
- balances body and mind

If you are not already taking adequate exercise, do so; you need a minimum of twenty minutes four or five times a week. Walking is the most effective and beneficial form of exercise for stress and anxiety. Swimming, cycling, dancing or other forms of aerobic exercise (those which increase your heart rate and breathing) are also acceptable providing you do not exceed your limitations. You must start off slowly and finish the exercise slowly. Warm up your body with some gentle stretching before you begin. While you are exercising, be aware of how your body feels. Harmonize mind and body: in other words, focus your mind on what is going on in your body. If your muscles are tense, try to relax them. Think about your muscles becoming soft. Check that you're not holding your stomach in; let it go loose and soft. If your shoulders are up by your ears drop them downwards – think "*soft*". Also check your face for tension – smooth out your forehead, unclench your teeth, let your jaw, tongue and the whole of your mouth relax loosely.

At the end of your exercise, rest. Lie or sit down and allow your breathing and heart rate to return to normal before you do anything else.

You will need to check with your doctor if you are very unfit, suffer with any physical ailments such as heart disease, or if there is a family history of heart disease, or other health conditions such as kidney disease, diabetes or arthritis. Also check with your doctor if you are a man over the age of forty-five or a woman over the age of fifty-five, or if you are pregnant.

If you haven't done any exercise at all for quite some time, start your exercise with perhaps only five minutes on the first three days, then increase it by five more minutes, and so on until you feel comfortable enough to work up to twenty minutes. When you are able to exercise easily for twenty minutes you can then work your way up to half an hour, but this may take some time. Remember, you are not training for a marathon; at this stage you are working on reducing stress levels. The marathon will take a little longer! Do not push beyond your limitations.

NOTE:
- If you are over forty-five and/or unwell and not used to exercising always check with your doctor before you begin exercise.
- Always begin slowly, warm up the muscles and slow down the pace at the end of the exercise.

- If you have very high stress levels and are at the stage of exhaustion or burnout do not do any vigorous exercise; it releases biochemicals in your body called endorphins and, although in healthy people these can improve psychological health as well as physical health, if you are already exhausted or otherwise vulnerable you could potentially become addicted to them. Stick to one of the more gentle forms of exercise like walking until you are fit and well again.
- Starting today, try to take some gentle exercise like walking.
- If you are not used to taking any exercise, start today with just five minutes a day, gradually increasing to twenty minutes for four times a week. Once you are fit and well you may feel like aiming for half-hour walks.
- Use your workbook to work out a plan and try to stick to a routine.
- If your motivation slips, think about the benefits and why you need to exercise. It will not only beat your stress and anxiety and help to lift depression; it also has the potential to prevent ill health, and help you to live longer.
- Recruit a friend or family member to exercise with you. This will help with your motivation and you can encourage one another.
- If you can join a class of some sort, this will help to increase social contact and lift your mood. Choose something that you enjoy and which makes you feel good.

Week 2, Day 4
» MANAGING STRESS «
One Thing at a Time

Constantly flitting from one job to another, whether at home or in the workplace, can cause mental overload. When too many demands are put upon the mind in a short space of time, it quickly becomes fatigued, weighed down and dull. It's a little like plugging too many appliances into one electrical socket: eventually you will blow a fuse, or even worse!

Do you start the day with good intentions to achieve a number of tasks, and at the end of the day you wonder where the time has gone because you haven't fully completed even one? Are there things left unfinished that you will have to go back to the next day? How does that make you feel? Possibly tired, frustrated and angry because you don't have any sense of achievement, and there are still things left unfinished. Starting everything again the next day is even more frustrating and you could be tempted to put it off until another time. Once you start to procrastinate, it is a very slippery slope to a low mood, apathy and hopelessness. Lack of self-confidence follows due to never having that sense of satisfaction from a good day's work well done. You may even lose the motivation to do anything; if you allow this to continue, before too long low self-worth can begin to set in.

The answer to this kind of stress or despondency is easy: simply do only one thing at a time! When you are completing your tasks focus only on the job in hand. Once again, harmonize mind and body. Detach from everything else and concentrate on the here and now, stay in the present. Focus, focus, focus! Always finish one task before going on to the next. Perhaps even sit quietly and practise some slow deep breathing in between tasks. This way you will accomplish everything more easily, more efficiently and make fewer mistakes.

Sometimes it may be possible to switch your phone off or ask not to be disturbed, but living in the real world, I know this may not always be realistic! So if you are disturbed, deal with the interruptions as they arise, with a calm manner and in a non-aggressive way. The person who is demanding your time may not know anything about your agenda. If it really isn't convenient for you, ask if you could get back to them at a time when you will be able to give them your complete attention and devote more time and energy to them. Once this has been done you can return to the job in hand and refocus. Remember, do not start another job before completing the one you are doing.

One of my yoga students once told me she would start to clean her house in the morning without any clear plan or idea about what she was going to do. At the end of the day she would look around her and realize that there wasn't even one room in the house that was completely finished. This really got her down and she would wonder what had gone wrong. It happened time and time again. She would begin to feel anxious and frustrated because she never appeared to accomplish anything completely. It wasn't that she *really* had to clean the whole house in one day; it was simply that she *felt* she had to. It was all self-inflicted stress.

What was going wrong was that she would start tidying in one room, take something from that room to the bedroom, make the bed, take something from the bedroom to the bathroom and while she was there she would clean the bathroom.

> The phone would ring and she would hurry down to the kitchen to answer it, staying chatting for half an hour. She would then begin to clean the kitchen floor as she was already there. This would go on all day; she would flit around the house from one room to another, never getting the satisfaction of completely finishing one room. By the time she was cooking dinner, she felt she hadn't done anything all day – even though she was exhausted!

After I explained this simple principle of doing one thing at a time, and reminded her of the fact that she was only human and therefore couldn't achieve everything in one day, she applied the advice – and she reported feeling much happier very soon. Doing one room at a time and sticking to it resulted in a great feeling of satisfaction. If she had to take something to another room she would not allow herself to be tempted to start another job there. She would tell herself that she could clean the other rooms on another day; but it was a great feeling to have one completely finished room in one day looking wonderfully tidy and spotlessly clean. Simple! Stress gone and time to relax!

Week 2, Day 5
» ANXIETY SOLUTIONS «
Change is the Answer

You may already have come to the conclusion that some things need to change if you are to overcome your stress and anxiety. Of course that is obviously easier said than done and you may wonder where on earth to start; but that's one less thing for you to worry about because that's where my help comes in!

As you continue to work your way through the book, you will see that there are many things you can change to help yourself and to enhance the quality of your life. Let's start with the following:

1. CHANGE YOUR THINKING · Everything begins with a thought, whether it's a panic attack, going to the shops, getting dressed, watching television or reading this page, as you are now.

You may not necessarily catch or notice the thought, but if you begin to feel anxious or become panicky, it will be as a direct result of a thought, or how you have negatively interpreted a situation.

I want to be clear that I am not talking here about Generalized Anxiety Disorder (GAD), also sometimes called free-floating anxiety or chronic worrying; if you suffer from this, you will feel anxious a lot, possibly twenty-four hours a day. The anxiety of this disorder is the result of a build-up of continuous and prolonged high levels of stress, negativity, worry and fear.

Here I am referring to acute anxiety, the kind that appears suddenly or without an obvious cause. If you think and believe that something is frightening, your body will respond immediately by going into the stress response, also known as the fight/flight response. This inherited and primitive reaction will cause your heart rate and your breathing rate to increase. You may begin to perspire or feel sick or shaky. You will experience anxiety that, if you are not able to control it, will result in panic. If you can catch, or very quickly identify, the negative thought that causes these unpleasant feelings and change it into a positive or more realistic thought, you will avert the anxiety and panic. Better still, if you retrain your mind not to have negative or worrying thoughts in the first place, you will prevent the fear, anxiety, panic and its consequences that may have ruled your life for a very long time.

We will address how to do this later. Just for now, accept that it *is possible to control your anxiety by controlling your negative or worrying thoughts.* Try to remember that it is your thinking, not a situation, that causes your anxiety.

However, I must point out that anxiety is a valid and perfectly normal emotion that we all have. It is a normal human response to anything that is considered a threat. You have already learned that it is often your imagination that brings with it the feeling of anxiety, but there are of course times when the threat is real and it is perfectly normal to feel anxious, afraid and even panicky. It is in these situations that the stress or fight/flight response becomes very useful; in fact it can save lives. Our very clever body has the ability to act quickly by, for example, slamming on the car brakes to avert an accident, or preparing us either to run away or to fight off an attacker. This response is designed to help us survive, and without it we might be in danger of being seriously hurt. We are able to respond immediately to the threat or perceived threat because of the massive and immediate changes that the response triggers in the body. You will find more on the fight/flight response in Week 6.

2. CHANGE YOUR BEHAVIOUR · Your thoughts can influence your behaviour; and it is also the case that changing your behaviour can influence your thoughts and thinking patterns. So, if you find yourself in a situation from which you would normally try to escape, instead stay put. Use your breathing exercises and your positive affirmations to help control your feelings of anxiety. You will eventually learn that you can stay in that situation, using your new-found coping strategies, and nothing bad will actually happen. This will lead to a change in your thinking. For example: you might think "*I stayed and nothing terrible happened; I was able to deal with it without running away.*" You realize that it was your thoughts and beliefs that caused the anxiety, not the situation. You will eventually overcome your anxiety and panic, thereby changing your behaviour and enjoying a better quality of life.

3. CHANGE YOUR LIFESTYLE · Changing your lifestyle doesn't mean you have to go and live in another country, change your job and go dancing every night! It can simply mean incorporating some healthy coping strategies into your daily routine. These might include:

- practising your breathing exercises every day
- taking some physical exercise at least four times a week
- thinking positively and using positive affirmations
- relaxing every day if possible, or at least four times a week
- cutting down on unhealthy substances such as alcohol and caffeine
- giving up smoking (if this applies to you)
- eating a healthy balanced diet
- getting regular quality sleep
- increasing your social life if necessary, or reducing it (if that applies)

One of my clients, a young man, was referred to me as a result of being diagnosed with generalized anxiety disorder and extreme agitation. He had some of the typical symptoms: trembling; increased heart rate and breathing; fidgeting; sleep problems; and he was unable to concentrate or sit still. He appeared to be in quite a bad way.

During his assessment he admitted to drinking four two-litre bottles of cola every day. I explained that excessive caffeine intake could be causing or contributing to his anxiety and agitation and asked him if he thought he would be able to cut down gradually, with an aim of reducing his intake to just two glasses a day. With this huge reduction it was possible that he might suffer withdrawal symptoms, so we worked out a mutual and acceptable desensitization plan for him to follow. He was due to see me again in a week's time to check on his progress. However, I had a telephone call from him the day before the appointment. He told me that not only had he cut down on drinking cola but he had stopped drinking it altogether. He told me he didn't want to follow the plan, so he just gave up completely. Thankfully he suffered no adverse reactions or side-effects and all his symptoms disappeared. He was feeling very well and there was no need for him to see me again!

NOTE: Caffeine is a stimulant and is the most popular and widely used drug in the world. It acts on the central nervous system to speed up messages from the brain. It is found in high quantities in coffee and tea, (there's even some caffeine in most decaffeinated coffee and tea) and very high quantities in cola and energy drinks.

There may be other things related to your lifestyle that you need or choose to change; it very much depends on your personal circumstances. Some of these may be more serious and will take longer to change. If for example you are in a job where the pressure is unbearable, you may wish to think about finding a new job. If you are in an unhealthy and unhappy relationship you may want or need to seek professional help. It is best to tackle these kinds of major changes once you are feeling stronger, better able to cope and have your stress under control. Too many major changes too close together will only push your stress levels higher.

Week 2, Day 6
» DIRECTION «
Accept or Change

"I can accept failure, but I can't accept not trying."
— MICHAEL JORDAN, *former basketball player*

Make a list below, or in your workbook, of all the things that are troubling you about yourself and your life. Make sure you put them under the appropriate column.

Change or Accept

The things I can change	The things I must accept

When your list is complete, look at your list of changes and decide which ones you would like to work on first. Don't try to change everything all at once; make a plan and set your goals appropriately. Some of these may be long-term goals, and this is fine, but put them in a diary or calendar so you don't forget about them. Once you have achieved something, don't forget to cross it off your list and commend yourself.

Next, look at your list of things you must accept. Write them down on a piece of card, perhaps as one-word cues or reminders. For Example:

> **I completely accept:**
> - the weather
> - the journey to work
> - my height
> - my mother-in-law
> - the neighbours
> - my past
> - my big feet

Keep this card close to you, in your purse, wallet, work bag or somewhere where you will often notice it. Eventually, whenever you feel yourself becoming distressed or worried about something over which you have no control, you will remember that your distress is pointless and that you must work on letting go those things that you cannot change. Breathe it away, use a positive affirmation and accept!

You can always add to these lists as time goes by. Always remember that if something is impossible to change, or is totally out of your control, acceptance is the only route to take if you are to live in peace and harmony without stress and anxiety.

Week 2, Day 7
» MEDITATION «
Counting Breaths

"If you want to conquer the anxiety of life,
live in the moment, live in the breath."
— AMIT RAY, *author and spiritual master*

Meditation is an ancient practice grounded in Buddhism – but you don't need to be Buddhist, wear an orange robe or sit in a full lotus position to practise it! It is for everyone and anyone.

As with yoga, it is non-religious and non-competitive. Today, meditation has become in the West a popular and favourable form of inducing a sense of peace and calm in mind, body and spirit. It has become more and more accepted in the last few decades, and its popularity has soared. Meditation goes hand in hand with yoga and indeed many aspects of yoga are based on meditation, but it can also be practised alone. More and more people are turning to this valuable and beneficial mind exercise as stress becomes more widespread and more of a problem. It is recognized not only as a spiritual system, but also as a useful tool for calming, clearing and stilling the mind. It is the art of focusing attention, contemplation, concentration and reflection.

There are many ways to meditate and I have given you a different method of meditation to work on every two weeks. We will begin with one of the easiest forms of meditation.

Sit comfortably on a chair, a cushion or a meditation block, or you can lie down on the floor as you did in your relaxation practice.

Begin by taking three slow deep breaths. Breathe in and out through the nose and start to focus on your breathing.

Don't change it; just notice it in your body. Watch and be aware of the gentle rhythm of the breath, coming in and going out, without any effort on your part, your body very cleverly breathing for you. Your breathing will gradually slow down and become more regular.

Remain like this for as long as you want to. There are no rules. If your mind wanders off, simply acknowledge it and, without force, gently bring your focus back to your breathing.

When you feel ready to move on, count the beginning of each in-breath. Start the count just as you feel the breath enter your nose.

When you reach a count of ten in-breaths, go back to one and start counting again. Complete as many of these circuits as you like. Again there are no rules, but try three circuits, or counts of ten, to begin with.

Next, when you are ready, count the end of each out-breath, as the breath finishes its journey through your nose.

Again, return to one when you reach ten.

The last part of this exercise involves counting the gap, or slight pause, between the out-breath and the in-breath. This pause comes at the end of each out-breath and before the in-breath begins.

Take a few moments to notice or find this pause before you begin the exercise. It may be just for a moment, but it *is* there. You will probably find that as you become more relaxed, the pause becomes longer.

NOTE:

- You can spend as much time as you like on this exercise; there are no time limits.
- Notice the benefits. Be aware of the calmness of your mind.
- If your mind wanders, just acknowledge this; there is no harm done, it is normal. Simply return your focus to the breath and the counting.
- Build this meditation into your daily routine and set this as one of your daily goals.

Week 2

» RECAP AND REFLECT «

Tick the box when understood, practised and achieved

 REFLECTION: The contents of the first two weeks are vitally important if you are to get your life back as soon as possible. Read the reflection page again to remember what you have learned so far. What benefits are you feeling? What has had the biggest impact on you so far?

 UNDERSTANDING WHO YOU REALLY ARE: Read this over and add any further observations. What did it make you think about? How did it make you feel? Were there any surprises?

 EXERCISE: How many times have you exercised this week? What are your feelings on this subject? What kind of exercise have you chosen to do? How will exercise benefit you?

 ONE THING AT A TIME: Is this something you need to do? If so, how have you benefitted so far? Will you find this easy to do or difficult? Why do you think that is? What else will help you to accomplish this?

 CHANGE IS THE ANSWER: Are you able to catch some of your negative thoughts? How important do you think this is for you? In what ways will it help you? Which aspects of your behaviour are you changing? Which items from the list are you going to change?

 ACCEPT OR CHANGE: Which changes from your list are you working on first? Do you need to add to the list? Have you become aware when you are stressing about something over which you have no control? Are you able to identify areas in which you have difficulty accepting? What do you need to do next?

 COUNTING BREATHS: Did you like this form of meditation? How did you benefit from it? How many times will you practise in a week?

Now turn to your self-assessment rating scales and enter your scores for the end of Week 2.

Week 3

. . . .

Week 3, Day 1
» *PHILOSOPHY* «

Worry Doesn't Help

"That the birds of worry and care fly over your head,
this you cannot change, but that they build nests
in your hair, this you can prevent."
— *Ancient Chinese proverb*

MANY OF US WORRY ABOUT SOMETHING; I suppose it's a human trait. Surprisingly, sometimes worrying can be a good thing. I bet you didn't expect me to say that! What I mean by it is that, if we worry about something, it can sometimes make us do something about it.

If you are proactive and can channel your worries to attempt to solve the problem, then worrying *can* be a positive thing: but only then!

Generally speaking, worrying gets us nowhere. There is no sense in it, and apart from your worries getting tangled in your hair, here are more of the pitfalls of worrying:

- It can make you anxious
- It can make you miserable
- It lowers concentration
- It is intrusive
- It stops you doing things
- It makes things seem worse than they actually are
- It can negatively predict the future
- It can induce stress and anxiety-related disorders

As well as the psychological effects of worry, there are also physiological symptoms such as:

- Stomach upsets
- IBS (irritable bowel syndrome)
- Headache
- Nausea
- Vomiting
- Palpitations (rapid heartbeat)
- Can contribute to other heart conditions
- Raises blood pressure
- Dizziness or light-headedness
- Breathing difficulties including asthma attacks
- Excessive sweating
- Lack of appetite or comfort eating
- Sleep loss and other sleep disturbances

Worrying also has a habit of causing lifestyle changes:

- Relationship problems
- Lack of social contact
- Problems at work
- Anxiety when leaving the house

Breathing exercises, relaxation, meditation and physical exercise are all excellent remedies for worrying. In addition, the following strategies are also beneficial.

- Remember to live one day at a time.
- Make realistic plans for the future, then leave the future alone.
- Ask yourself what are the actual facts about this worry.
- Tell yourself that there is no sense in worrying. It doesn't solve anything and nothing changes for the good because of worrying. All it does is make you unwell and worry more.
- Ask yourself "How can I solve this problem?"
- Do something about the problem, seeking help if necessary.
- Ask yourself "What is the worst that can happen?"
- Work on either accepting the worst or convincing yourself that the worst won't happen. You could be exaggerating or getting things out of proportion, making mountains out of molehills.

Next time you find yourself worrying shout "STOP!" to yourself (in your head, or out loud!). Take a slow deep breath in and out, then replace the worry with a positive statement such as "*I stay in the present moment and all is well.*"

You should also write your worries down. Transferring them from your head on to paper can be very releasing and beneficial. You could even have a worry book! If you tend to worry about things when you go to bed and they keep you awake, keep the book next to your bed. You can of course use your workbook for this too.

It may also help to set aside specific times to take positive action, or to question the validity of your worries. You could set some boundaries and just allow yourself five or ten minutes a day to think about your worries. When the time is up, make a firm, conscious decision that you must not worry again for the rest of the day. If there is a genuine problem, work on finding a solution in order to turn the worry into positive action. Keep the birds of worry from nesting in your hair! Later in the book, we will address how to challenge worrying and negative thoughts and beliefs.

When I was a teenager I suffered terrible migraines. My father's advice was to stop worrying about everything. He told me that I took life far too seriously and should learn to "loosen up". It sounded like good advice, and I knew he was right. I tried my best to stop worrying about everything and adopted a more balanced view of the things that I worried about. Before long my migraines had almost disappeared – but not completely. I still had one or two a year, and when I thought about it I realized that, sure enough, I had been worrying again, and it was the worry that had brought on my migraines. Later, in my early twenties, due to post-natal depression, I started yoga classes. In all the years since, I have only had two or three very minor migraine attacks.

Week 3, Day 2
» *PRANAYAMA* «
Unique Exercises to Control the Emotions

The yogini Sunita was a pupil of the celebrated Tibetan yogi Narainswami, one of only five exponents of pranayama yoga in the world at the time. After coming to live in England in 1959, Sunita recognized the need for this philosophy in what she called the "western rat race" and in 1962 founded the Yoga Relaxation Centre for Great Britain. Students came from all over the country and overseas to study not only the physical aspects of yoga but also relaxation, meditation, breath control and the philosophy of yoga – for many people, a new way of living.

Prana means breath control, yama means relaxation of the mind and yoga means unity, or harmony of mind, body and spirit.

The breath control exercises found at various intervals in this book are those taught to Sunita by her teacher Narainswami. When I learned them myself in the early seventies, along with the philosophy of yoga, they changed my life for ever. Not only did I find peace of mind, calmness and the ability to cope with life, I also went on to teach others that they too could overcome their struggle with life's pressures.

Not only did I teach pranayama yoga breath-control exercises in my yoga classes, I also taught these wonderful and unique skills to all my clients and patients, whether in hospital, community mental health clinics or in my stress management consultancy work. I cannot recall anyone who did not welcome them into their lives or benefit from them. Many people said to me that these breathing exercises alone were significant in helping them to recover and return to good health.

These unique breathing exercises, if practised well and regularly, can control emotions, calm the nervous system, quieten the mind and reduce or eliminate stress and stress-related disorders.

Before you begin, do the chest expansion exercise below to help the muscles in the lungs to expand and relax more easily:

> Place your arms across your chest with the palms facing down and your fingertips just touching. Now take the elbows back, drawing your shoulder blades together, until you feel a slight rebound, then return your arms to the starting position. Repeat this movement six times.

When doing the breathing exercises, you should ideally sit on a straight-backed chair or on the floor with your back straight and your legs crossed. If you choose instead to sit on the floor with your legs stretched out in front of you, place your palms flat on the floor beside you, but do not lean back on your hands. It is very important that your back is kept straight and your shoulders back, making sure that you are not slumping forwards. This position promotes good posture.

Practise slow deep abdominal breathing, as you learned to do in Week 1, Day 2, for one minute.

Now try the first exercise:

The Abdominal Muscle Control Exercise for Calming the Mind and Body

This exercise calms the whole body but particularly the digestive system; it eliminates butterflies in the tummy, tones the abdominal muscles and is also good for constipation.

Since it is the key to all the breath-control exercises that follow, you must practise it until you achieve complete control. This may take a little while, but persevere gently and be patient with yourself.

Remember to sit with a straight back and breathe normally throughout the exercise. Don't even think about your breathing, just focus on the tummy muscles.

The word "tummy", by the way, refers here to the muscles in the lower abdomen, below the navel.

Pull the tummy all the way in towards the spine and hold for a moment.

Then let the tummy all the way out again smoothly, if you can (this will come with practice).

Now divide that tummy pull into two equal divisions:

Take the tummy in halfway, pause, then take it right in.

Let it out gently halfway, then right out.

Now divide into three equal divisions:

Take the tummy in one third, two thirds and right in.

Let it out one third, two thirds and right out.

Try to establish a gentle rhythm.

Now four divisions:

Take the tummy in for one, two, three and four.

And let it out for one, two, three, and four.

With more practice you may be able to go on to do five and six divisions.

Try to get the divisions equal; this will also come with practice.

When you are able to divide into six divisions comfortably you can move on to the next exercise.

Combining the Tummy and Breath for Nervousness and Tension

> Take the tummy right in, hold it in while you breathe all the way in and out (always through the nose), then let the tummy out smoothly.
>
> Take the tummy in halfway, pause, then right in, and hold.
>
> Breathe in and out.
>
> Let the tummy out halfway, then right out.
>
> Take the tummy in one third, two thirds, right in. Hold.
>
> Breathe in and out.
>
> Let the tummy out one third, two thirds and right out.
>
> Continue with four, five and six divisions when you are able.

Only when you can do this without strain, try the next exercise. This is also for nervousness and tension. Slightly more control is needed, but it is also slightly more effective.

The Reverse Order – for Nervousness and Tension

> This time, breathe in first and hold the breath.
>
> Take the tummy right in and hold it in.
>
> Breathe out, keeping the tummy held in.
>
> Finally, let the tummy out.
>
> Now with two divisions:
>
> Again, breathe right in and hold the breath.
>
> Take the tummy in halfway, pause, then right in and hold.
>
> Breathe out.
>
> Let the tummy out halfway, then right out.
>
> Breathe in again and hold.
>
> Take the tummy in one third, two thirds and right in.
>
> Keep the tummy in as you breathe out.
>
> Let the tummy out one third, two thirds and right out.
>
> Carry on with four and five divisions, then six when you are able.

If you practise these valuable exercises every day, when you feel that you actually need them they will work more effectively to reduce or even eliminate your nervousness and nervous tension.

Week 3, Day 3
» *DIRECTION* «
Let It Go

Today, make a list in your workbook of all the things in your life that you regularly struggle to accept.

There may be things from your distant past that still haunt you or keep popping into your head uninvited, when you least expect it.

There may be memories that keep you awake at night; things you haven't been able to let go.

There are probably things that broke your heart, which you yearn to go back to and make better, or undo.

Past regrets that you just can't seem to shake off.

Bitter memories of people who hurt you, let you down, or disappointed you in some way.

You may be thinking that earlier in the book I advised you to let go of the past, that the past has gone and you can't go back there to change anything. You would be right of course! But I know just how difficult it is to do that, so if you still need help to let go, the powerful visualization exercises below will help you to overcome these difficulties.

It may help if you attempt these exercises after your daily relaxations, when your mind is already in a state of peacefulness.

Lie down on the floor and take three deep breaths. Try to relax and detach from everything except your breathing. From your workbook bring to mind the list of everything you find difficult to let go and, one at a time, imagine putting them into a black metal box. You can use a different symbol for each of them, or a label with a name or a picture on it, or an object that symbolizes the memory. When you have put them all in the box visualize digging a deep hole in the ground, then tossing the box into the hole. Cover it with earth, then stones or anything else you want to throw in! Imagine the heavy box sinking deeper and deeper, right down to the core of the earth until it is completely buried and perhaps even burned up by the earth's core of fire. Once you are content that the box has gone for ever, walk away knowing that it can never ever affect you again. Practise this visualization often until it has a positive effect on you.

Another exercise you can do is to imagine putting all the things you cannot let go into the basket of a small hot-air balloon – one small enough for you to hold in your arms, not one big enough to climb into! Visualize going to the top of a hill on a windy day. Feel the cool wind on your face and the earth firm beneath your feet. Notice the clear blue sky and the large orange sun above you. Look at the balloon with all the unwanted things in its basket. Listen to the sounds around you and, when you feel ready to let go completely, let the wind carry the balloon away and watch it as it drifts upwards into the blue sky, sailing higher and higher. Watch it getting smaller as it fades away into the distance. When it has disappeared into the clouds, imagine it flying even higher into space. Anything can happen in your imagination.

Practise this visualization often, especially at night if you are kept awake by negative thoughts. You can always devise your own method of letting go and freeing yourself from these burdens and attachments. Notice how different you feel when you have achieved this.

Your mind is amazingly powerful and, after just a little while of letting go, you will feel lighter. You won't even notice that you don't think about the burdens from your past any more.

When I worked in a small psychiatric hospital, I devised and facilitated a course called Positive Living for patients diagnosed with stress, anxiety and depression. Every week we would do something to help turn negative thoughts and attitudes into positive ones. One day I asked everyone to write down, on a very large piece of paper, their problems, difficult issues or whatever they were angry or worried about. I got them to use coloured pencils and I noticed that the patients who were depressed used black pencils and the ones who had an anger problem used red. Some wanted to borrow the large coloured marker pens I used for the flipchart. I told them they could write anything they liked on this piece of paper, as no one else would be reading it.

One asked if it was OK to use bad language! So in one session I gave them permission to write or draw anything they wanted. There was a frenzy of heightened activity in the room and we all ended up laughing and having fun. They loved the exercise and some of them asked for more paper as they had a lot more issues they needed to transfer out of their head and on to the paper!

Once we were done, with great merriment we went outside into the hospital grounds where I had prearranged for the groundsman to be standing by with a lighter. I instructed the patients to tear up their pieces of paper and toss them into the metal container the groundsman had found for us. They absolutely loved doing that, and when the groundsman set fire to the paper, there were hoots of joy and laughter. I don't think I had ever seen patients in a psychiatric hospital so invigorated!

Later we discussed this exercise in letting go. The patients all agreed that even though it was a physical thing they had done, the emotional freedom they felt was both uplifting and extremely therapeutic. When we laugh, endorphins, the happy hormones, are released into the body, causing your mood to lift. The patients may not have realized it at the time, but I knew that the laughter alone would have been extremely beneficial to them and would have improved their mood enormously.

Try it yourself – but be careful with the fire!

Week 3, Day 4
» *SELF-ESTEEM* «

A Lifetime of Achievements

Everyone has achieved something. However, not many people go around thinking about their achievements or successes in life. In fact any achievement can be quickly forgotten, especially if a person's self-esteem is low. Some people refuse even to acknowledge their achievements and are quick to dismiss them. If congratulated or praised, this kind of person quips "Oh it was nothing!" or "I could have done better", or "Well it was about time I did something good in my life!"

If this is you, perhaps it's time for some positive change in that department.

Today, you can start by making a list in your workbook of everything you have achieved or have been successful with in your life; everything you can remember. Start this exercise in the morning and then, throughout the whole day, try to recall more successes, and record these too. In fact this can be an ongoing exercise, where you add to the list every day. You may not realize it but you do actually achieve something every day. Maybe you just don't recognize, or acknowledge it as an achievement; perhaps because you take yourself for granted; or your negative thinking, low self-esteem or a misplaced belief tells you that you are incapable of achieving anything or doing anything right.

Your list of achievements doesn't have to be full of great things. They don't have to be academic achievements or running-a-marathon type of achievements. Go right back in time to your earliest memory of achievement or success. It could be learning to ride a bicycle or getting gold stars at school, playing a musical instrument, or making a friend.

Your list doesn't need to be in chronological order either. Just write things down when they pop into your head. You may want to recruit family members or friends to help; they may well come up with something that you have dismissed or forgotten about, or that you may not have perceived as an achievement yourself.

Don't allow negative thinking to get in the way, and remember, no one else need read your list, unless of course you feel proud enough to show it to them – and I sincerely hope that one day you will!

Once you have listed all the achievements from your past, try to get into the habit of listing everything you achieve each and every day. I have a feeling that you may need to buy another workbook for this! Also, ask yourself *"What made me proud of myself today?"* and list everything you can bring to mind.

NOTE: Once you have made your list of past achievements, instead of using your workbook for your daily achievements you may want to use a diary, and make the entries just before you go to sleep. It will help you to go off to sleep with a positive mind.

Week 3, Day 5
» *CORRECT THINKING* «
Thoughts and Feelings Go Together

Thoughts and beliefs are sometimes referred to as *"cognitions"*. These cognitions go hand in hand with your feelings, which result in your behaviour, actions and outcomes. You previously learned that if your cognitions were negative they resulted in negative outcomes. It is also true the other way round: positive cognitions produce positive outcomes.

You were asked to try to identify your negative thoughts and be aware of how you were feeling. If you wrote anything down then, refer back to it now.

Below are some examples of how *negative cognitions* can affect your feelings:

Negative Cognitions	Feelings
I'm really worried about going shopping today	Anxiety, worry, fear, panicky
Other people are better than me. I'm hopeless	Dismal, inadequate, sad, shy
I did a terrible thing and should be punished	Guilty, regretful, wretched
Nobody likes me. I always look so awful	Unhappy, low, woeful, fed-up

And now examples of *positive cognitions* and the resulting feelings:

Positive Cognitions	Feelings
I know what I'm doing and always do my best	Happy, confident, proud
Things will work out really well for me now	Positive, confident, optimistic
I am loved and respected by my family and friends	Loved, contented, at peace
I try my best to achieve something every day	Proud, satisfied, determined

Now write down your own negative and positive thoughts and related feelings. You might think it is impossible to capture your thoughts, but it is actually quite easy to do if you work at it and persist. Once you have identified some of your more common negative thoughts and feelings, work out what you could say to yourself to counteract them. For example:

"I'm really worried about going shopping today"

BECOMES: "I went shopping last week and nothing bad happened. I will use my breathing exercises to help me to stay in control and positive at all times. I know I can do it."
FEELINGS: optimistic, determined, confident, successful, safe

"Everyone is better than me - I'm hopeless"

BECOMES: "Everyone is different and everyone makes mistakes. I am equal to everyone and I always try my best."
FEELINGS: positive, confident, proud, assured

"I did a terrible thing and should be punished"

BECOMES: "I know I did wrong, but I am learning to let it go now. I have learned a great deal from my mistake. The past has gone, I forgive myself and today I know better."
FEELINGS: accepting, free, exonerated, at peace

Week 3, Day 6
» *DIRECTION* «
The STOP Technique

The STOP Technique was one of my most frequently used exercises for controlling negative thoughts and spiralling anxiety. Commonly used among therapists, it is one of the most simple, yet effective tools I have ever taught. If ever you spot someone wearing a rubber band round their wrist, you can pretty much guess that they are working through their anxiety using this technique.

First, find a rubber band that fits round your wrist comfortably – not too tight; there should be a bit of slack.

Practise the following technique several times. For your first attempt, do it on a day when your anxiety is at its lowest. This will help you to remember more, and know exactly what to do when anxiety strikes or you suddenly catch yourself in a stream of negative thoughts.

1. As soon as you become aware of the very first thought or feeling of anxiety (often it is a physical symptom such as shallow breathing, your heart pounding in your chest or sweaty palms), shout "STOP" and, at the same time, snap the rubber band on your wrist, just enough for it to hurt a little. This action will snap you into the present moment – you will be focusing now on your pain instead! It is also useful to imagine a STOP sign at the same time.

2. Then take a long deep breath in and hold for a moment. Breathe out slowly, counting down from 10 to zero. Try to relax and focus on the numbers as you exhale.

3. When you reach zero, form a mental image of a peaceful place (have one ready in your mind before you start the exercise). Let it be somewhere where you always feel, or felt, happy and relaxed, like a beautiful garden or sitting by a peaceful lake or a calm sea.

4. Then repeat a positive affirmation to yourself, such as "I am calm and relaxed and perfectly safe now" or "I am now calm, safe and in control."

If necessary repeat the whole process, but if you continue to feel anxious use the breathing exercises you have been practising too. They are very powerful and can soon bring you back to feeling normal again. The STOP Technique is also useful as instant first aid when you begin to feel anxious, or the anxiety is growing out of control. You can also use the STOP Technique if you are trying to control your negative thoughts, or when you are trying to give something up like smoking or comfort eating. You don't have to limit its use to feelings of anxiety either – it is also excellent for when you catch yourself worrying.

Week 3, Day 7
» *RELAXATION* «

Yoga Nidra

This means "Yoga Sleep". This practice induces a complete feeling of such peace and relaxation that it is like being in a peaceful sleep, although you are actually fully alert. It is one of the easiest relaxations you can do because it involves simply becoming aware of various parts of your body, one at a time. You do not have to move them or stretch them, but just contemplate them for a moment.

This form of deep relaxation has been around for centuries and can be traced as far back as 200 BC. Many forms of yoga include it in their practice and it was first introduced into Britain in the 1800s. The mindfulness movement uses this form of relaxation too, but call it the Body Scan.

It is best practised by listening to someone else reading the script in a monotone voice, or recording your own voice in the same manner.

There are eight stages of Yoga Nidra:

1. Preparing the body to relax
2. Introducing a sankalpa. This is a positive statement or affirmation, something you desire or aspire to with a feeling or emotion attached to it. Over time it forms and grows in your heart or mind. For example: "*Every moment brings me closer to peace of mind*" or "*My mind, body and spirit are as one.*" You should compose yours to suit your own individual needs, one that you can relate to personally.
3. Awareness of the breath
4. Focusing attention on the different parts of the body
5. Awareness of feelings or emotions
6. Visualization of sensory images
7. Repeating your sankalpa
8. The gradual return to full awareness

You should practice in your usual place of relaxation. Yoga Nidra is best done lying down on the floor as with the deep relaxation in Week 1, Day 7 with your body in a straight line, your arms by your sides with palms facing upwards, or down if that is more comfortable for you. Your arms and hands should not touch your body. Your feet should be shoulder width apart, relaxed and flopping outwards at the ankles. If this is in any way difficult, you can also do the relaxation sitting in a comfortable chair with your head fully supported and your feet flat on the floor.

Make sure you are warm and not going to be disturbed. This relaxation can take up to forty-five minutes or even longer, but you can shorten it to suit your own needs. In the script below you will see some dots (..........). This is where you pause and stop speaking for a moment. Where there are more dots (......................................), you pause for longer.

When you are completely comfortable, close your eyes softly and allow a feeling of peace and relaxation to come over you. Allow your body to sink deeply into the floor (or chair). Feel yourself being fully supported, your whole body sinking down into your support.

Now move your attention to your breathing. Breathe normally, allowing your body to breathe for you, the breath just coming in and going out.

Now repeat your sankalpa (affirmation) silently to yourself three times.

When you have done this, take your attention to your right foot .... your right big toe.......... second toe.......... third toe.......... fourth toe.......... little toe.......... the top of your right foot.......... the sole of your foot.......... your heel.......... ankle.......... lower leg.......... calf............ shin............ knee............ back of the knee............ the front of your thigh.......... the back of your thigh............ right buttock............ right hip............ right side............ under your right arm.......... your right shoulder.......... top of the arm.......... elbow.......... forearm.......... wrist.......... your right hand.......... back of the hand.......... palm of the hand............ thumb............ first finger............ middle finger............ ring finger.......... little finger.......... The whole of the right side of your body .... The right side of your body feeling lighter .... and lighter......................................

Now take your attention to your left foot..........your left big toe.......... second toe.......... third toe.......... fourth toe.......... little toe.......... the top of your left foot.......... the sole of your foot.......... your heel.......... ankle.......... lower leg.......... calf.......... shin.......... knee.......... back of the knee............ the front of your thigh............ the back of your thigh............ left buttock.............. left hip.............. left side.............. under your left arm.............. your left shoulder.......... top of the arm.......... elbow.......... forearm.......... wrist.......... your left hand.......... back of the hand.......... palm of the hand.......... thumb.......... first finger.......... middle finger.......... ring finger.......... little finger......................................

The whole of the left side of your body...................................... The left side of your body feeling lighter...................................... and lighter ....

Take your attention now to your lower back.............. the middle of your back.............. upper back.......... right shoulder blade.......... left shoulder blade.......... the whole of your spine.......... back of the neck.......... back of the head.......... top of the head.......... forehead.......... right temple.......... left temple.......... right eyebrow.......... left eyebrow..........

right eye.......... left eye.......... the space between your eyebrows.......... your nose..........
right nostril.......... left nostril.......... right cheek.......... left cheek.......... right jaw..........
left jaw.......... the space between your nose and the upper lip.......... the upper lip..........
lower lip.......... both lips together.......... inside of the mouth.......... tongue.......... upper teeth.......... lower teeth.......... chin.......... throat.......... right side of the neck..........
left side of the neck.......... right collarbone.......... left collarbone.......... right side of your
chest.......... left side of your chest.......... the middle of your chest.......... top of your
abdomen.......... navel.......... lower abdomen.......... right groin.......... left groin.......... pelvic
floor...
   The whole of the right leg.......... the whole of the left leg.......... the whole of the right
arm.......... whole of the left arm.......... the whole of your back.......... your whole torso..........
your whole face.......... your whole head.................................... your whole body..............
.... your whole body.................................... your whole body........................
....

Be aware of your breathing .... your heart beating ....
...... your digestive system.................................... your blood flowing through your body....
....
   Your whole body feeling light.......... as if you are floating ....
your whole body feeling heavy .... sinking into the floor ....
.... your body feeling cold.................................... your body feeling warm
....

Now visualize yourself standing in a forest.................................... touching the bark of
a tree.................................... taking in the scent of a single white rose...........................
.... a snow-capped mountain.................................... and a clear deep blue sky............
.... the sky at night with many bright stars.................................... the sun
as it rises in the sky at dawn.................................... the large orange sun setting on the
horizon.................................... sitting by a still, calm lake.......... a still calm lake.......... like
your body.......... and mind.......... still and calm.................................... still and calm........
....

Now repeat your sankalpa silently to yourself, three times....................................
.... Slowly become aware of your breathing.................................... your
surroundings.................................... slowly begin to stretch gently....................................
and sit up very slowly.................................... staying there for as long as you wish...........
....

Stand up very slowly only when you are ready. Move around the room slowly. Acknowledge how your body and mind feel now. Practise daily or whenever you are able until the
next relaxation appears in the book.

Week 3
» RECAP AND REFLECT «

Tick the box when understood, practised and achieved

 WORRY DOESN'T HELP: Have you been a worrier? Do you understand that it doesn't make any sense to worry? Have you been able to put this into practice yet? How difficult will this be for you? Are you trying your best? What will help?

 UNIQUE EXERCISES TO CONTROL THE EMOTIONS: Were you able to do these exercises? Are you practising enough? Can you feel them working yet? How many times a day will you practise? Have you used them when you have needed them?

 LET IT GO: Are you managing to let go of things yet? Have you used the visualization technique? How did you find it? If you have many things to let go, have you made a list?

 A LIFETIME OF ACHIEVEMENTS: Did you make your list of achievements? Were you surprised at how much you have achieved in your life? How did it make you feel? Continue to add to your list every day.

 THOUGHTS AND FEELINGS GO TOGETHER: Did you make your list of thoughts and related feelings? Have you managed to change your thoughts from negative to positive thoughts? How do you think this will help you? Continue to do this whenever you catch yourself with a negative thought or feeling.

 THE STOP TECHNIQUE: How effective have you found this? Have you benefitted from this exercise yet? Continue to practise until it works, then use it whenever necessary. In which circumstances or occasions do you think it will help you?

YOGA NIDRA: How did you find this? If you haven't found anyone to read the script for you, either record it yourself or learn the script and talk yourself through it. It does not have to be the identical words or sequence.

Now turn to your self-assessment rating scales and enter your scores for the end of Week 3.

Week 4

· · · · · · · · ·

Week 4, Day 1
» *AWARENESS* «

What is Stress and
Where Does it Come From?

"People are disturbed not by things, but by the views they take of them."
— *EPICTETUS, first-century philosopher*

EVERYBODY TALKS ABOUT IT. Almost every magazine has a feature on it and nearly everybody seems to suffer from it! But what exactly is stress? Can you really define it? Most people know when they're stressed and they might be able to tell you how stressed they feel, but can they tell you what it *actually* is and where it comes from? Why do different people get stressed about different things? For example: most people would probably be terrified of giving a speech in front of a large group of people, and if they really had to, they would say that their stress levels would go through the roof. However, there are those among us who actually thrive on giving speeches and are more than happy to talk in front of a very large audience. Some even feel very excited about doing so. So what's the difference between these people and those who would be stressed about it?

There are many definitions of stress but mine is:

Stress is an imbalance between perceived demands
and the perceived ability to cope with them.

Stress is an automatic reaction to *anything* that we *perceive* to be stressful. As you have already learned, because we are all different and have led completely different lives, what is stressful to one person is not necessarily stressful to another. Our experiences when we are young determine whether or not we will find something stressful in adulthood. Our personality type will also have an impact on our perception of things and therefore our outcomes. In other words, if you *think and believe* that something will be stressful for you, then it will be.

Suppose for example, when you were seven years old you had to stand up in front of the classroom and recite a poem – but you had forgotten to learn it. The result was that everyone laughed at you, mocked you, and the teacher reprimanded you. You burst into tears and felt very ashamed. You have always remembered this, and the feelings you felt about this unfortunate incident could cause you to feel very nervous about speaking in front of a group of people ever again. However, if you had a different attitude; if this event hadn't upset you and you were able to laugh about it later, the outcome might have been very different. In later life you may well not find speaking to a large group of people to be a problem.

So, if you believe that you can do something without feeling stressed or anxious, and that there is nothing to be afraid of, then you will be fine and you might even enjoy it! It all comes down to the experiences we've had in the past and how we dealt with them at the time. Remember, we form our beliefs about things when we are very young and these beliefs can stay with us for a very long time, maybe for life.

Here is another example that you may be able to relate to:

What if, when you were out shopping with your mother when you were a young child, you lost sight of her? You look all around the store but you can't see her anywhere. After a few seconds you become terrified that she has gone and left you alone. You start to believe that you are all alone and you will never find your mother again. You begin to cry, maybe scream . . . and then she appears, gives you a big hug and warns you never ever to wander off again. She tells you it is very dangerous and she could have lost you for ever.

You may not be able to remember this incident, but it has been registered in your subconscious and it may have contributed to you forming the belief that to lose someone you love would be terrifying.

Another example:

If when you were at school you weren't very good at mathematics and didn't do well in your exams, you may have grown up believing that maths is frightening and that you can't cope with it. Years later you may be in a job where you are expected to do the accounts or balance the takings at the end of the day. This will probably trigger the memory of not doing well at maths at school and switch on your stress response, causing you to feel nervousness and anxiety. As we don't perform well under pressure it is possible that you will make mistakes with your accounts or takings, therefore confirming your belief that you are no good at maths.

So generally stress occurs when a situation we encounter causes us to believe that we cannot cope with it. However, it is usually possible for us to cope with these difficult or even terrifying situations, but due to our negative thoughts and attitudes we just don't generally have enough faith in ourselves and don't perceive ourselves as being strong and capable. Unfortunately, there is another dimension to this issue: many of our coping strategies may not be helpful. They include avoidance, burying our head in the sand, running away or even taking unhealthy substances such as alcohol, caffeine, illegal drugs or misused prescribed medication.

As children no one teaches us how to cope with stress – in fact, the chances are that we are not even told what stress is! Our first encounter with it might be when we have to take a test at school and we don't know all the answers. The result is fear or anxiety, which in itself causes even more anxiety. We may feel our heart thumping, find it difficult to breathe and we won't know what's happening to us. We therefore become afraid that something terrible is happening to us – and we don't know what to do about that either! As we as children have no understanding of stress and haven't yet learned how to cope with it or how it affects us, it is easy to feel nervous, anxious, afraid and unprepared every time we are faced with any kind of adversity. Before very long, if the pressure continues and we still don't know how to cope with it, we begin to experience helplessness, hopelessness and despair.

It is important to point out that stress is not always or only caused by a major life event or trauma. Stress can be induced when we have an accumulation of too many demands or expectations put upon us, or lots of little problems mounting up, or occurring all at once. We also frequently put unrealistic demands on ourselves, on top of those from others. If we have a negative perception of these demands and subsequently feel that we are unable to cope, if we also lack support the imbalance between demands and coping strategies triggers the stress response. See "The Model of Human Stress" below.

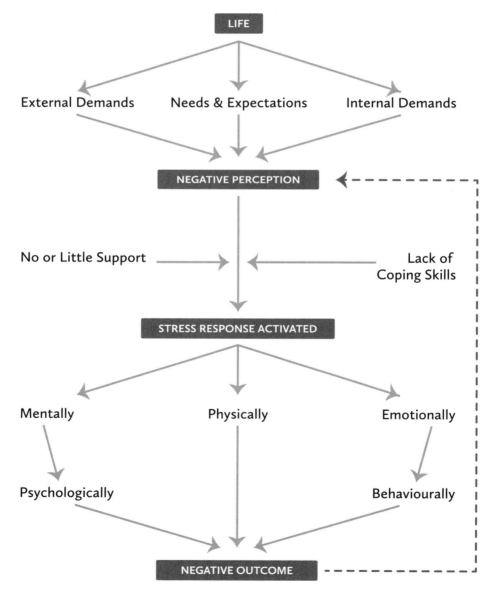

We have all inherited a primitive, automatic response from thousands of years ago when early man lived in fear of being attacked and killed by a wild animal or an unfriendly tribe. Our ancestors needed to be incredibly strong, physically fit, clever and resourceful in order to escape from or survive attacks. Faced with a threat, the body's chemistry and responses automatically and quite dramatically transformed, enabling primitive man to escape quickly or to stand and fight the attacker in order to survive. This survival reaction is called the fight/flight response or sometimes the stress response, and it affected every single organ and gland in the body.

When one of the senses perceived that an attack was imminent, a message was relayed from the sense organs to a small gland in the brain called the hypothalamus. This in turn sent chemical messengers to all other parts of the body, resulting in increased heart rate, breathing, sweating and muscle tension. All of these changes are designed to aid our chances of survival, by either fighting or fleeing.

Even though for most of us in the modern world, threats from wild animals and human enemies do not exist, this primitive part of the brain remains and the body mechanisms it controls still exist. It may be helpful for you to have an awareness of what might be triggering your stress or fight/flight response. This response can be triggered by external stressors, which include:

- Bereavement
- Own illness or that of a family member
- Divorce, separation, marriage or other relationship issues
- Financial difficulties/ pressures
- Pressures of work or conditions of work, deadlines, targets etc
- New job or change of job
- Redundancy
- Retirement
- Moving house

- Family pressures: parents, children, new baby, children leaving home
- Social events or family gatherings
- Speaking in public
- Problems with neighbours or friends
- Noise
- Car breaking down
- Traffic jams
- Public transport

In addition to the stressors outside of ourselves, we also have certain thoughts, feelings and emotions that switch on our stress or fight/flight response. These are called internal stressors and include:

- Anger
- Anxiety
- Apprehension
- Bitterness
- Depression
- Envy
- Fear
- Frustration
- Grief
- Guilt
- Impatience
- Irritability
- Lack of confidence
- Lack of control
- Lack of respect
- Low self-esteem
- Low self-worth
- Resentment
- Regret
- Worry

There are further pressures that can also contribute to increasing our stress levels. These factors are usually out of our control and are common among individuals already suffering the effects of stress. They are known as contributory factors to stress and below is a list of the most common.

1. TOO MANY MAJOR CHANGES · Too many major changes occurring too close together. For example: moving house, new job and new baby all around the same time or within a year. It isn't the change itself that causes the distress; it is the unfamiliar that we have difficulty with. We are creatures of habit just as other animals are; our brains are wired that way in order to ensure our survival. We all have habits and most of them are so automatic we hardly even notice them; many are extremely difficult to break. It is for this reason that we can find adapting to change very difficult.

When too many life-changing events happen very close together, adapting to all of them can easily push our stress levels sky-high. The stress occurs whether or not we have made the change voluntarily – even if we have, say, planned for a baby, or moved to a much-wanted new job, too many important events occurring too close together can still easily be perceived as pressure and we can find them too stressful to cope with. Post-natal depression is not only caused by a hormonal change, it is the result of massive changes in routine, habit, responsibility and sleep patterns.

One could argue that the hormonal changes are due to the chemical imbalance as a result of high levels of stress. If the changes are not of our choosing – such as bereavement, redundancy or illness – they can have a devastating effect, especially on someone who is already stressed and feeling that they are unable to cope with normal everyday demands.

2. CARING FOR OTHERS · Caring for others is something over which we may have little or no control. We may be in a situation where we have a duty or responsibility to care for someone else, like children or a sick or elderly relative. Whether or not you enjoy it and are happy doing it, there is nevertheless no escape from it. For some people it can just feel like relentless pressure, going on day after day without any respite. As the pressure builds up over a period of time, so does the stress.

3. SLEEP PROBLEMS · Sleep problems can cause stress or increase stress levels. If you are not having regular undisturbed sleep over a long period of time, you can start to feel not only exhausted but quite unwell and in danger of pushing yourself beyond your limitations. If you have sleep problems see Week 12, Days 1 and 2.

4. NOT ENOUGH TIME · Not enough time to meet demands. Too many things to do and not enough time to do them in is something I'm sure we are all familiar with at times! But when this goes on for too long and seems never-ending it can send you hurtling towards that brick wall. Doing one thing at a time, making lists, organizing and prioritizing can all help. You will also find that if you practise your breathing exercises, relaxation and meditation you will be calmer, your mind clearer and you may not worry so much about all the things you have to do. In this situation, building up your reserve of coping strategies is invaluable.

5. BEING BULLIED · Being bullied, manipulated or controlled can cause an enormous amount of stress; not being able to stand up to a bully, or someone who wants to control or dominate, puts a great deal of pressure on the victim. In addition there is the pressure of trying to hide it from other people; many victims wrongly presume that others will think they are weak or even that it is their own fault. The guilt, or perceived weakness of not being able to cope with it, or stop the bullying, adds a greater burden. Even if a person has no other stress in their lives, sadly it can still create lasting damage.

6. CHILDHOOD TRAUMA · Childhood trauma or adversity tends to stay with us for a very long time, if not for ever. It can manifest in many and diverse ways but mental health problems such as anxiety disorders and depression in later life are common.

So today – yes, you've guessed it – have a long hard think and make a list of all the things that cause your stress, and any issues that contribute towards your stress. They could be completely different from the factors above, but if you have one or more of the above major contributors you will need to do something to balance out the pressure.

Week 4, Day 2

» UNDERSTANDING «

Understanding the Stress Response

Now that we've looked at what stress is and where it might come from, let's take a look at what actually happens when we find ourselves in a stressful situation:

FROM PERCEPTION TO ILL HEALTH

A situation is perceived as being stressful, a threat or a challenge

↓

The fight/flight response is switched on automatically by the nervous system

↓

Chemical messages are sent and received by various organs and glands in the body

↓

Adrenalin and other stress hormones are released into the bloodstream

↓

Every organ and gland prepares the body to take action by fighting or fleeing from the attacker. We experience these changes as unpleasant physical symptoms that cause more anxiety and stress. More stress hormones are released into the bloodstream.

↓

Our state of alertness heightens and the reaction continues to prepare us to fight or run away

↓

We experience mental, physical, emotional, behavioural and psychological effects

↓

If the stress is prolonged and continuous and we do not cope adequately, we become ill

↓

We perceive this also as being stressful and the cycle begins all over again.

NOTE: If the situation is not perceived as being stressful or frightening the fight/flight response is not activated. The outcome will be positive, or realistic, and we carry on as normal.

The fight/flight response is automatically switched on when our senses are alerted to danger and the brain interprets the message from the senses as being threatening. However, the response does not switch off automatically and the symptoms and effects of stress will stay until you balance out your stress by applying coping skills and strategies.

Here are some of the most common effects of stress:

Physical Effects	Mental Effects
Breathlessness	Depression
Headaches	Nightmares
Indigestion	Lack of concentration
Muscle tension	Lack of initiative
Nausea	Lack of sensitivity
Palpitations	Memory problems
Weight loss or gain	Worry

Behavioural Effects	Emotional Effects
Apathy	Anxiety
Insomnia	Irritability
Increased drinking/smoking	Feeling guilty
Loss or gain of appetite	Feeling sad
Low productivity	Feeling tense or angry
Problems at home	Lack of motivation
Restlessness	Loss of confidence
Withdrawal	Mood swings

If you continue to feel stressed over a prolonged period, you can find yourself in a continuous state of alertness and a higher ongoing level of stress. On the next page you can find a list of potential outcomes and effects of long-term pressure and stress. Do you recognize any of these?

- A feeling of being overloaded
- Less creative and efficient
- Complete lack of concentration
- Unable to make decisions
- Generalized anxiety
- Anxiety disorders such as panic attacks, OCD (Obsessive Compulsive Disorder) and phobias
- Confusion
- Burnout (complete inability to work efficiently, lack of caring, physical symptoms, exhaustion, withdrawal from social events)
- Breakdown (complete inability to perform effectively, collapse, mental or physical illnesses)
- Depression (inability to cope, feeling of emptiness, hopelessness, withdrawal, lack of interest in anything)

The good news is that there are many ways of switching off the stress response, or preventing it being triggered in the first place, many of which we look at in this book. It is important for you to apply as many coping strategies as possible, especially if your stress levels are running high. However, the *major* coping strategies, listed below, are vitally important and you should put them into practice *every day*.

The Four Major Antidotes to Stress are:

RELAXATION

EXERCISE

SLOW DEEP BREATHING

POSITIVE LIVING

1. RELAXATION · Relaxation is the direct opposite of stress. You cannot be relaxed and stressed at the same time; they are at opposite ends of the spectrum. Many of the unpleasant symptoms and effects of stress will disappear if you are able to relax. None of the wonderful effects and benefits of relaxation will be felt when you are stressed. Going back to our primitive ancestors, once an early human had escaped danger and after he had expended energy in fleeing or fighting, he would rest until his body returned to normal. Only then would he continue his normal activities. Nowadays, however, "danger" or stress is perceived more in the form of pressures from family, friends and work; and these are often continuous and unrelenting pressures. This can mean that we don't have time to relax and allow for our bodies to return to normal.

2. EXERCISE · I have had clients who would run up and down the stairs a couple of times when they first become aware of their anxiety symptoms, and sometimes even in the middle of a full-blown panic attack. This burst of energy very often does the trick because they are mimicking primitive man fleeing from the sabre-toothed tiger or an unfriendly tribe. Because these days we don't spend a lot of time escaping from tigers, we need to find our exercise elsewhere. Exercising for at least twenty minutes, four or more days a week, will help to counteract the effects of stress by expending the negative energy that has accumulated as our body prepared us to take flight.

3. SLOW DEEP BREATHING · This also switches off the fight/flight response. When we are in the stress response our breathing automatically becomes rapid and shallow, enabling adrenalin and other stress hormones to circulate quickly around the body via the bloodstream. This action in turn creates the energy we need to escape the danger. If, however, we reverse this automatic reaction by breathing slowly and deeply, everything in the body returns to normal. We become calm, because slow deep breathing tells our body that we are in control and there is no need to release more adrenalin. If we practise slow deep breathing often, it prevents the stress response from kicking in and our body chemistry remains at its normal functioning range.

4. POSITIVE THINKING · Remember, everything begins with a thought. If the thought is negative, the brain picks up a negative message and sends further messages round the body to prepare us to face danger. The stress or fight/flight response switches on and, before we know it, even though there is no actual danger we are experiencing unpleasant symptoms and effects. Keep your mind positive and you will be surprised at how much better you feel.

In modern times when we experience a challenge, whether real or imagined, the fight/flight response is often only temporary. The threat is dealt with and, just as with primitive man, the body returns to normal. An example of this is when we hear a noise in the middle of the night and jump to the conclusion that someone is breaking into the house. Our internal alarm is sounded, our heart is banging in our chest and the hair on the back of our neck stands up. But then, we realize it's only the cat, and off we go back to sleep as if nothing has happened. This sort of sudden alarm is easily dealt with. But if you live in a stressful situation that you are not able to control, the fight/flight response may be constantly being triggered. It is very important therefore to keep these major coping mechanisms in your mind. Practise them every day. Remember they can act as preventatives as well as stressbusters.

Week 4, Day 3
» PHYSICAL HEALTH «
The Three Stages of Stress

1. HEALTHY STRESS · It is important to point out that some stress is healthy and can be good for you. We tend to think that all stress is bad and we really could do without it, but just think how life would be if we didn't ever have any stress. We might never bother to get up in the morning, we wouldn't run to catch the train and we wouldn't worry about whether or not we were able to pay the bills and meet those deadlines or targets. There would be little or no motivation at all to succeed or achieve, to stay safe or secure, happy and well. A little stress keeps us on our toes!

A positive way of looking at stress is that it often gets the job done. It helps us to achieve and accomplish things. It motivates us to do our best and be the best we can be. Stress drives us, it stretches us, motivates us and many people thrive on it. Some people even love a bit of stress so much that they invite more. This is fine, but only up to the point of remaining healthy and manageable.

Below is a list of the effects of healthy stress:

- Your general health is good and you feel well.
- You cope reasonably well with demands and pressures.
- You are able to solve problems and make decisions easily.
- You are able to concentrate well and your thoughts are clear.
- You appear approachable and people feel comfortable with you.
- You deal with change well and adapt easily.
- When overworked you are happy to delegate.
- You thrive and perform well under pressure, even asking for more.
- You are able to recover quickly from pressure, relax well and sleep well.
- You are able to enjoy a good social life.
- You take adequate breaks and don't feel guilty about it.
- You accept your own and other people's limitations.

If you cannot identify with more than five of the above it may be because you are experiencing unhealthy stress.

2. UNHEALTHY STRESS · If you recognize any of the following traits it could be time to make some positive changes:

- You sometimes feel tired and drained but not necessarily exhausted.
- You are able to make some changes but don't invite them.
- You procrastinate (put things off).
- You ignore your low energy levels and carry on regardless.
- You are still continuing to succeed and achieve but maybe lack energy.
- When tired you are able to recover reasonably quickly but not always.
- You are still assertive and can sometimes say no but not every time.
- You are able to sleep reasonably well but not always.
- You maintain a healthy social life but often turn down invitations.
- You are not feeling as well as you were.
- Occasionally you may feel as if something has to give.
- You are becoming irritable and sometimes lose your temper.

If this is you, you are probably just about coping, but if the pressure continues to increase at the same rate without any coping mechanisms you could be heading for exhaustion. Act now to start increasing your reserve of coping strategies.

Think about setting some goals in order to prevent the pressure increasing. Take a break, learn to be more assertive, relax more and practise the skills you have learned so far.

3. EXHAUSTION OR BURNOUT · If you've been running full steam ahead at a hundred miles an hour, without adequate breaks, for a long period of time, you may have already hit burnout, or the proverbial brick wall. If not, you may not be very far away from it, and if you display any of the following symptoms you will need to stop doing what you're doing, take a long rest and maybe get away from it all on a nice long relaxing holiday. You will probably need to seek help if you haven't already done so. This book will certainly help you, but some of you may also benefit from counselling or life coaching. You need to begin by seeing your doctor, who will be able to point you in the right direction, possibly suggesting counselling, psychotherapy or medication. Here are just some of the signs of exhaustion:

- You may think you are well but those close to you know that you aren't.
- You look, sound and appear very tired but find it difficult to sleep well.
- The pressures are excessive but you feel you have to carry on.
- The pressures cause you to become less effective, less efficient.
- Performance and productivity rates go down.
- You take on even more pressure because you can't say no.
- You see no need or have no time for relaxation or to increase fitness.
- It may be very difficult or even impossible to relax at all.

- You feel anxiety, anger, irritability, aggression and hostility.
- Sleep is inadequate and you wake up feeling exhausted.
- Your mind is set against change.
- You may increase your eating, drinking, smoking etc.
- Appetite is often lost and you don't always have time to eat.
- You may be depressed or getting very close to being depressed.
- You may experience feelings of hopelessness or helplessness.
- You may have thoughts and feelings of not being able to carry on.
- You may know you need help but are unwilling or too proud to seek it.
- You feel overwhelmed and powerless.
- You are unwilling to take or listen to advice from others.
- You may be thinking "I can't go on like this."

Week 4, Day 4

» MANAGING STRESS «

When the Pressure Becomes Too Much

If you can relate to any of the symptoms in the second and third stages outlined in Week 4, Day 3 above, now is the time to take things seriously, even if it means going back to the beginning of the book and, if you haven't already done so, applying the advice and using the exercises. You need to be relaxing every day, even if you can only manage five minutes at a time. If this is the case, find the time to have three or four five-minute sessions a day. When you feel you can relax for longer, gradually work up to twenty minutes or more once a day.

Now set some realistic goals based on how you can reduce the pressure, what you need to change, what you need to stop and how you can increase your ability to cope. For example:

- Cut down or stop working overtime.
- Do some relaxation every day without fail.
- Go for a twenty-minute walk before your evening meal.
- Arrange a weekly relaxing night out with family or friends.
- Don't take on too much at work if you don't have to.
- Take adequate breaks.
- Practise your breathing exercises several times a day.
- Learn to say no and delegate everything you can.
- Ask yourself "Do I really need to do this?", and "Am I pushing myself too hard?"

- Get organized: make to-do lists; do things in order of priority; clear out clutter etc.
- Use the STOP Technique to counteract negative thoughts and manage anxiety.
- If you are a perfectionist read Week 12, Day 4 and follow the instructions.

Start adopting some of the suggestions from the above list. However, don't put yourself under more pressure by attempting to put them all into practice at the same time!

Week 4, Day 5
» ANXIETY SOLUTIONS «

From Stress to Anxiety

In Week 4, Day 1, we saw that stress occurs when there is an imbalance between perceived demands and our perceived ability to cope with them. When pressure increases and becomes too much for us, our ability to cope must also increase if we are to function effectively. If we are not able to increase our coping abilities we become overloaded and may experience the added distress of anxiety. Anxiety is a symptom of too much unmanaged stress.

The graph below shows what happens to our efficiency and our ability to function effectively, according to how many demands are put upon us.

The Human Function Curve

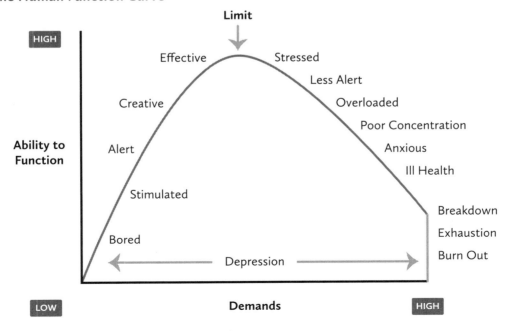

When there are no demands at all it is easy to imagine getting bored and lethargic, which can in turn result in unhappiness, despair, misery and ultimately a form of depression. As the demands increase we become more alert and stimulated. The right amount of pressure produces the best scenario where we are effective, creative and coping very well. However, no one is superhuman and although we might have good intentions and expectations for ourselves, those expectations can often be unrealistic, become difficult to deal with and cause the pressure to increase. If this happens, or we have an unexpected crisis, it is easy to become overloaded, overwhelmed, exhausted and unwell. This unpleasant and unexpected state can take many forms but very often it manifests as anxiety. The anxiety then has the potential to escalate. If it does, it may become too difficult to control and can result in our very first – and very frightening – panic attack. Other anxiety disorders such as OCD (Obsessive Compulsive Disorder) may also develop at this stage.

Push even further and we start to suffer ill health, which can be physical, mental, emotional or psychological. Eventually, if no action is taken to reduce the demands on us or increase coping strategies and resources, breakdown or burnout occurs. This can in one sense be a positive outcome because often it is only with this serious decline in health that we are forced to stop, seek help, and ultimately find a healthier life balance.

When we reach the point of breakdown, it is here that reactive or clinical depression is often diagnosed. We, in effect, swing over to the bottom left hand corner of the Human Function Curve Graph above where there are no demands or pressures to weigh us down, and this gives us the breathing space to recover. However, this is not a good or healthy place to be for too long. On top of the depression, we can start to suffer severe lethargy, low self-esteem, lack of confidence and lack of interest and succumb to complete inactivity and apathy. We are unable to meet any demands effectively, and do not have the energy, the interest or the motivation to achieve anything.

However, people do recover from this place of darkness and doom. It may take some time, a lot of support and lots of new coping strategies, but it can be done. Many doctors will prescribe medication and even exercise on prescription. You may also be offered counselling and/or a referral to a mental health consultant. Unfortunately, not everyone will have access to this extra care. However, everyone *can* learn, and adopt, all the necessary coping strategies found in this book, which will lead them to recovery and good health.

Try to work out what caused you to become over-stressed, anxious or depressed. Examine the Human Function Curve above and place yourself at the point where you are today or where you were when you started this book. Mark it with today's date so that when you come to the end of the book you can identify your improvement. This will help you to acknowledge the work and effort you have put in to make that improvement.

Today, sit quietly and refer back to the list in Week 4, Day 4. If you haven't already set your goals, do it now. Also try to become aware of the demands that you think put you under too much pressure. Work out which of your pressures were too difficult to cope with, and which pushed you out of control. Decide what you need to *stop doing*. Make a decision as to *when* you will stop and write it down as a goal with a date and time attached to it. Next, decide what you need to *start doing.* What else can you do? What do you need to *change*? Look at these examples below:

What do I need to stop?

For example: doing too much; taking on too much when you know you are at your limit; doing too many things at once and too many things to help other people; working late or without a break; taking work home; staying up too late; drinking too much alcohol; eating junk food.

What do I need to start?

For example: relaxing and meditating every day; using the breathing exercises; doing more physical exercise; having more fun; taking more breaks; saying no to the demands of others and recognizing that you too have needs to be met.

What do I need to change?

For example: your attitude; changing negative thoughts into positive thoughts; your eating habits; your sleeping habits; thinking that you have to do everything for everybody; being perfect at all times.

Week 4, Day 6
» *DIRECTION* «

Slow Down

If you suffer from depression, melancholia or low mood, or if you already do everything slowly, skip this day and move on to the next.

This day applies to those of you who run around all day like a headless chicken at a hundred miles an hour, without a break, and then wonder where the day has gone. Today, try to do things more slowly. Eat more slowly, talk more slowly, walk more slowly, drive more slowly and as you do these things be aware of your body and try to relax it.

You may be one of those people who feel they need to be on the go all day long. You may feel that everything has to be done quickly because you have always felt like this and it has just become a habit. It may be a personality trait; some people just feel that it is normal to race to get everything done as quickly as possible. If this describes you, sit down and ask yourself the following questions:

- Is there a deadline to meet?
- Is there someone behind me actually telling me to go faster?
- Could I do this more slowly if I tried to?
- Do I really have to go on like this – full speed ahead?
- Am I sure that I couldn't stop and take a break?
- Will I get into trouble if I don't go at this like a sprinter?
- Have I always been like this?
- Where does it come from?
- What beliefs do I have that make me this way?
- Does my heart race? Is my breathing rapid and shallow? Do I perspire or tremble too much? What do these things tell me about myself?
- Is there a way I could think about how to do things differently?
- What has this full-speed-ahead mentality done to me?
- Is it harming me?
- Does it help at all in the long run?
- Where will I be in five years' time if I carry on like this?

OK, it's true that sometimes there is a good reason for going at breakneck speed, but all the time? No, I don't think so. If you are in a job where everything has to be done *now* and the pressure is catching up with you, perhaps it's time you thought about changing your job or your lifestyle. If this way of living is damaging your health or your relationships or your family, something needs to change, and I guess that you may already be aware of this.

So, if you can, if it's appropriate to do so and if your job allows you, for today, just slow down and see what happens. Reflect on this slowing down at the end of the day. Be aware of whether you feel any different and acknowledge the fact that nothing terrible happened just because you slowed down.

If you still find yourself hurrying about and you really are finding it difficult to implement this direction, sit down somewhere and practise some slow deep breathing. It will help. In fact, just focusing on your breathing will help. If you are at work and it's difficult to do this in your work area, go to the bathroom if this is the only place where you are able to have some privacy and quiet time.

Of course this is not just for today. This needs to be ongoing. You may be one of those hundred-miles-an-hour people who really do need to slow down on a more permanent basis. Chasing about all day can raise your blood pressure, increase your heart rate and breathing and cause your whole body to become tense. This in turn creates a vicious circle whereby your thoughts become tense too and tell you to do even more, putting extra pressure on you!

Week 4, Day 7
» *MEDITATION* «

Meditation On the Five Senses

Once you have settled into your meditation location and position, sitting comfortably somewhere where you will not be disturbed, close your eyes gently and take the usual three deep, abdominal breaths.

Follow this with normal breathing. Allow your body to breathe for you. Focus your attention completely on your breathing, watching the gentle rhythmic flow of simply breathing in and breathing out. If your mind should wander off, simply acknowledge this without judgement and bring your mind back to your breathing once again.

When you are ready to move on, and in your own time, go on to the next steps one at a time, spending as much time as you wish on each step:

Focus all of your attention on your sense of hearing: the internal sounds you can hear – the sound of your breathing; other sounds in your body or in your ears. Now the sounds in the room you are in, and beyond the room; the sounds coming from just outside; the sounds further in the distance. Be aware now of all the sounds you are hearing – all together.

Focus your attention next on your sense of sight: what you are seeing through your closed eyelids; the colours you see; the light; the darkness; the shapes; the patterns; the changes. Be aware of all you can see.

Now focus your complete attention on your sense of smell: the smells you are aware of; the smells in the room; the smells beyond the room; your own scent. Be aware of all the smells and scents mingling together.

Next focus your attention on your sense of taste: the taste in your mouth; any lingering taste from the food you have recently eaten; the liquid you drank; all the tastes inside your mouth.

Lastly bring your awareness to your sense of touch: feel your clothes against your skin; the hair on your head; the air on your skin; the temperature of the air in the room; the chair or floor supporting your body; any other items you can feel on your body; be aware of all the things you are physically feeling.

Return your attention back to your breathing; feel the air as it enters and leaves your nose; feel the temperature of the air as you breathe in and breathe out; feel your lungs expanding and relaxing with each breath you take; be aware of your ribcage opening and closing; your abdomen rising and falling; the whole of your respiratory system working in harmony; be aware of your heart beating; your heart pumping the blood round your body; your blood circulating round your whole body. Be fully aware of your whole body now.

Focus your complete attention now on your mind and body working together, as one. Still your mind. Be aware of the calmness you feel, how good it feels, how beneficial it is for you. Fully enjoy and embrace the moment, and each moment as it is presented to you. Simply watch your thoughts now as they gently come and gently go. No one making demands on you or on your time or your energy. Just being free. Completely free . . . and still ... and at peace .... Feeling better for this relaxation, this meditation.

Take your time, as slowly as you wish, to come back into the here and now and move and stretch slowly before you get up and move around.

Practise this each day this week and then whenever you choose to.

Week 4

» RECAP AND REFLECT «

Tick the box when understood, practised and achieved

 WHAT IS STRESS AND WHERE DOES IT COME FROM? Reread this until you fully understand it. Have you been able to recognize what causes your stress? Are you able to identify the connection between your causes of stress and your levels of stress? What have you done so far to reduce your stress levels? What helps the most?

 UNDERSTANDING THE STRESS RESPONSE: Do you now have an understanding of the stress or fight/flight response? Can you identify with this? Are you practising the four major antidotes? This is important for everyone – can you understand why it is important for you? What are you doing to manage your stress?

 THE THREE STAGES OF STRESS: What stage do you think you are at now? Can you understand how and when that happened? How does it affect you? What are you doing every day to help reduce your level of tension, pressure and stress?

 WHEN THE PRESSURE BECOMES TOO MUCH: What have you started to do from the list? What else can you do? Do you fully understand how important it is to manage your stress effectively? What do you think will happen if you don't do anything about your stress levels? How will you feel then?

 FROM STRESS TO ANXIETY: Can you understand why you become anxious? Can you understand the importance of reducing your stress and anxiety? How determined are you to reduce your stress and anxiety? What have you done so far?

 SLOW DOWN: Have you started to slow down now, if it is appropriate to you? If you find it difficult you need to be using more breathing exercises and more relaxation. Are you practising these enough?

MEDITATION ON THE FIVE SENSES: How did you like this form of meditation? How did you benefit from it? Remember to practise every day.

Now turn to your self-assessment rating scales and enter your scores for the end of Week 4.

Week 5

• • • • • • • • •

Week 5, Day 1
» *PHILOSOPHY* «
Be Kind to Yourself

ACCEPTING YOURSELF FOR WHO YOU ARE and what you are is enormously beneficial, but not always quite enough to gain lasting peace of mind. So today I would like you to think about being kind to yourself too. You may already be kind and compassionate to others but never, or rarely, to yourself. The chances are, especially if you are suffering from the negative effects of stress or anxiety, you're not going to be compassionate or considerate to yourself, even though this is precisely the time when you most need to be.

Being compassionate to other people, especially your loved ones, may come naturally to you. If you see someone suffering emotional turmoil you automatically turn to them and give them your full attention, trying your best to fulfil their needs. Sometimes it can be just a hug (if you're a hugger). To some, a hug is so powerful that they can physically feel the love and compassion coming through to them, without any words being spoken. We sometimes hug people when we see them just because it's a lovely thing to do. We know that to give a hug, and to receive a hug back, is a demonstration of love, support, friendship and compassion.

It's a great pity that you can't *physically* give yourself a hug, but instead, you can give yourself an *emotional* hug! Do you ever think to yourself, or even say out loud, "I just need a hug"? If there is no one around to administer this hug, another very effective way of self-hugging is to be kind to yourself. Instead of beating yourself up every day for feeling guilty or ashamed, angry, afraid or regretful for making mistakes, you can forgive yourself, be compassionate to yourself and offer yourself some kind and loving words, just as you would if a friend or family member was going through the same turmoil as you. You would probably find it easy to say some kind and loving words to them. You certainly would not tell them off or criticize them and tell them to pull themselves together! And yet isn't this exactly how you frequently treat yourself?

Negative emotions are something we all have in common. They are natural. We are expected to have them. Emotions are there to be experienced. Without negative emotions we wouldn't have the ability to recognize or enjoy positive emotions. It is perfectly normal to feel emotional in some way when things go badly wrong, or if you are threatened in some way. It is natural to be emotional when you lose someone you love, or when you are let down or betrayed.

So although we've discussed how to cope with or control emotions, and how relaxation or breathing can help control them, we have to recognize that it is a good thing to actually *feel* even the most uncomfortable of emotions. To suppress emotions is not good for us; in fact it can be quite harmful. If we push them down instead of feeling them or dealing with them, they will manifest somewhere in the body at a later date. The mind and body work together, as we have already seen; they are not separate entities but are *as one*, and if a negative emotion becomes lodged inside us, we become unwell.

When things fall apart it is often easy to blame or criticize yourself for not coping well, but the chances are, you would not criticize others in the same situation. So what's the difference between you and other people? Well, in this sense, there is no difference. Life is such that we all go through rough patches, we all suffer adversity, all of us go through difficult life changes, crises and traumas; they can't always be avoided. As they say, *life is a rollercoaster*. So we need kindness and compassion, just as the next person does. However, there may be occasions in times of stress, adversity and when you feel overwhelmed when there is no one around to give you what you need – in which case you need to be kind and compassionate towards yourself. You deserve it too!

Why *would* you be compassionate towards others, but not yourself? Think about it now for a few moments. It doesn't make any sense, does it? Who are you not to treat yourself in the same way as you treat others? It may be related to one of your beliefs that was formed early, perhaps when you were very young: "*I'm not important*" or "*I don't matter*", or "*I should consider other people – not myself.*"

Such beliefs need to be challenged: they are inappropriate, destructive and self-defeating. So next time you realize that you're giving yourself a hard time – stop! Think about who you are. Think about your own needs and whether these needs are being met. You are just as important as anyone else, and even if you haven't thought about that before, think about it now.

Here are some suggestions as to what you could do to be kind to yourself. But add your own too, as many as you can:

- Allow yourself to actually *feel* your feelings. It's OK. Don't push them down.
- Allow yourself to practise your relaxation and meditation without feeling guilty.
- Treat yourself to some new clothes (if you can afford it).
- Do whatever you want to do instead of what others want you to do (if appropriate).
- Have a full day off to enjoy doing what you like best.
- Treat yourself to a lovely meal (or just a cake!).
- Buy yourself some flowers.
- Go for a walk on a lovely day and relax in the sunshine.
- Have a warm relaxing bath with some aromatherapy oils to soothe you.
- Have a day or a night out with a friend.
- Stop giving yourself a hard time for being depressed or stressed and just allow yourself to do something about it.
- Forgive yourself.
- Care for yourself.
- Love yourself as others love you.
- Think of yourself as deserving compassion and kindness, just as others do.
- Allow yourself to make mistakes, just as others do.
- Don't give yourself a hard time for *anything*. After all, you are only human!

Week 5, Day 2

» *PRANAYAMA* «

Exercise for Anxiety and Panic

You must have mastered the breathing exercises learned previously before attempting to add this one on to the sequence. It is a little more advanced, needing slightly more control.

Pause the breath (neither in nor out).
Take the tummy all the way in.
Hold the tummy in and pause the breath for five seconds.
Breathe all the way in and out.
Hold for another five seconds (both the out-breath and the tummy).
Let the tummy out.
Breathe normally.

Only when you have mastered this, go on to the second stage:

> Pause the breath.
> Take the tummy in, in two equal steps.
> Hold for ten seconds.
> While holding the tummy in, breathe in and out.
> Hold the tummy and out-breath for another ten seconds.
> Let the tummy out in two steps.
> Breathe normally.

When you have completely mastered the second stage the tummy control can be increased to three steps and holding for fifteen seconds. This is quite advanced and may take some time to master.

> Pause the breath.
> Take the tummy in, in three equal steps.
> Hold for fifteen seconds.
> Breathe all the way in and out.
> Hold for another fifteen seconds.
> Let the tummy out in three equal steps.

There is no need to progress further. Use this exercise as soon as you become aware of any anxiety. Alternatively, use it as a preventative along with the whole sequence at least once a day.

Week 5, Day 3

» *DIRECTION* «

Does It Really Matter?

Depending on your perception of them, some pressures or major life changes have the potential to cause stress. For example: redundancy, serious illness, divorce or bereavement. As you would expect, these and other major life events can have a huge impact on our lives.

However, there are also the everyday stressors, decisions, dilemmas or minor predicaments that can easily accumulate, get out of proportion and eventually lead to stress and its unpleasant symptoms and effects. There are many examples of these but here are just a few:

Everyday Pressures

- Meeting deadlines and targets
- Unpleasant boss
- Noisy neighbours
- Being stuck in traffic
- Arguments with friends or family
- Not enough cash
- Being interrupted when trying to get something done
- Bad weather
- Car breaking down or in for repair
- Spilled cup of coffee

Identify those that cause you any stress, then make a list, including your own additions, in your workbook.

It is important to try to put things into perspective; these pressures are not life-threatening. If you have major stressors on top of these minor stressors, your anxiety levels are going to increase every time you encounter any of those niggling little nuisances. If you feel yourself getting stressed or wound up, or you feel a headache coming on, or you are feeling anxious, it means that your stress response has switched itself up a notch. Sometimes it is important to tell yourself to "*stop!*", take some deep breaths and tell yourself to let it go. In the scheme of things, such minor irritations are probably not that important and can probably be solved easily. They are not worth getting upset or angry about. They are not worth putting your blood pressure up, getting your muscles tense and causing yourself indigestion!

Make a large sign saying:

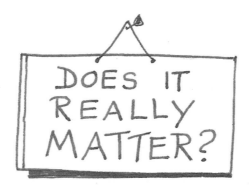

Place it where you can see it throughout the day.

Accumulative stress can be just as debilitating and as powerful as one major trauma. If you go through your whole day getting wound up about trivial things because you are not doing anything to alleviate the pressure, and the next day is the same, and the next, and the next, you are heading for a fall. If you are overworking and not doing anything to balance the work, before you know it, the stress will mount up and might overwhelm you without warning.

You can prevent this by simply adjusting your attitude to the trivial things that would normally upset you. So look out for when you are letting trivial things get to you. Laugh at yourself! Think how ridiculous you are being! Ask yourself how someone else would react. Would they tie themselves up in knots? No! Ask yourself if you are exaggerating, making mountains out of molehills and getting things totally out of proportion.

Other ways to deal with minor stressors:

- Remember to use your breathing exercises.
- Use the STOP Technique.
- Go for a quick walk.
- Run up and down the stairs.
- Ask yourself "*In the scale of things, is this* really *that bad?*"
- Find something to distract yourself from the issue.
- Think about something you are looking forward to.
- Write the problem down, then throw it away.
- Do a quick relaxation.
- Talk to someone else about it and ask what they think.

Week 5, Day 4
» ORGANIZATION «
Making Lists and Prioritizing

"The future starts today, not tomorrow."
— *Pope John Paul II*

Yoga philosophy teaches us to create peace of mind and harmony by living in the moment, doing one thing at a time and doing things in order of priority. This is quite easy to accomplish, unless of course you have had a scattered, butterfly mind for a very long time.

It is best to begin with writing a list of all the things you have to do for the coming day. Some people find it more useful to do this last thing at night so they can sleep peacefully and with a clear mind. If you make your list in the morning, do it right at the beginning of your day, or as soon as you arrive at work.

Once you have made your list, prioritize the tasks by numbering them or using the example below. Do not be tempted to do the trivial things that don't matter, or the easy things first! Many people make this mistake in order to get them out of the way; however, often as the day progresses there are interruptions and small jobs turn into much bigger jobs, with the result that you do not have enough time left to achieve the most important task on your list. This is where the stress comes in and you end up working longer hours or worrying about not having done what you set out to do. If this way of working continues, you are again setting yourself up for a fall and becoming anxious.

So, the answer is simple! All you have to do is tackle the most urgent or important task first, and then go on to the next most urgent task etc. At the end of the day you will only have the least important or most trivial things left to do, which should cause you less or no stress because you worry less about these and feel quite happy leaving them until another time.

Following the example below, make your first list now of everything you have to do for the rest of the day or for tomorrow. Even if you feel you don't need to make a list, do it anyway. It will help you to see just how useful this technique can be. It also means that you won't have to keep remembering to do something, or forget to do something important – this can cause stress. Besides, it's a great feeling completing things one at a time and crossing them off your list!

To Do List

Must do	Should do	Could do	Have done
1.	1.	1.	1.
2.	2.	2.	2.
3.	3.	3.	3.

Sometimes it will be necessary to move some items from your "Could do" list to the "Must do" list, otherwise they may never get done! You may want to use a separate notebook for making your lists. If you are already a master list-maker, simply continue doing what you're doing if you know it works well for you.

JUST A NOTE: If there is a job or chore that you really hate doing, so it never gets done because you always put it off until another time, you need to set a specific goal to complete it. With me, it's cleaning the oven! It always seems to end up on my "Could do" list and every time I open the oven door I think "Oh no! I still haven't done this." Of course when I do this I'm always in the middle of cooking, so it's completely the wrong time to start cleaning it – and, yet again, it doesn't get done. (Yes, I'm human too!). Eventually, when I have made a decision to clean it on a certain day at a certain time, I do get round to doing it. Of course I feel wonderful when it's shiny and clean. (Although the ideal solution would be to get my husband to clean it!)

To help with your time management the following may also be useful:

Make your list and write down the amount of time each task normally takes to complete. If you're not sure, then guess or estimate. Then put the items in the following chart:

Time Management List

10-min tasks	30-min tasks	1-hour tasks	2-hour tasks
1.	1.	1.	1.
2.	2.	2.	2.
3.	3.	3.	3.
4.	4.	4.	4.
5.	5.	5.	5.
6.	6.	6.	6.
7.	7.	7.	7.
8.	8.	8.	8.

Next, prioritize them and start work on the most urgent. If you complete a one-hour task in forty minutes, do some tasks out of your ten-minute list until it's time for a break.

Never do anything for longer than two hours; it is important to take breaks, even if it is just for ten minutes to stretch your body and have a glass of water. You can return to the task after your break, but *never, ever start another task before you have finished the one you are working on.*

Week 5, Day 5
» *CORRECT THINKING* «

Irrational Thoughts and Thinking Errors

"There is nothing either good or bad, but thinking makes it so."
— *WILLIAM SHAKESPEARE, Hamlet*

In Week 3, Day 5 you were asked to become aware of your negative thoughts and beliefs, and then change them to more realistic ones.

It is important to understand that many of the thoughts we have are very often automatic, especially the negative ones. If you have been conditioned or programmed, perhaps since childhood, to believe something, many of your thoughts related to that belief exist because of habit. You may never have stopped to question them, even though you realize that they are often irrational or don't make any sense.

We call these thoughts *automatic negative thoughts.* Today, we are going to look at these more closely in order to address the negative outcomes they create.

When something happens, whether it is positive or negative, our mind interprets the event and as a result we have a series of corresponding thoughts and feelings. Of course, if the event is interpreted as negative, our thoughts and feelings will also be negative, even though these thoughts may be irrational. For example: If two people are waiting for the same train, and the train is late, one person might think "Oh never mind, there's nothing I can do about it, I'll read the paper", but the other person might think "Oh no! That's terrible. I'm going to be late!" The first person has realized that the situation is out of their control and there is no sense in worrying about it. The second person has interpreted the situation as being stressful. The fight/flight response has fired up and their blood pressure, heart rate, breathing and muscle tension have all increased. They will feel anxious, angry and helpless, even though none of these reactions will make the train come any sooner!

You have learned that it is not the event itself that creates such feelings, but the views, ideas or beliefs you hold about that event or situation. It follows, therefore, that we need to question, challenge and change our views and beliefs in order to change how we feel and thus prevent ongoing stress and anxiety.

Remember that we are thinking all the time; the only time we stop thinking is when we go to sleep. Our negative thoughts are often unrealistic or distorted due to our distorted views of life or certain situations or circumstances. If a lot of our thoughts are negative and distorted, or unhelpful and irrational, then we are going to feel bad a lot of the time.

Cognitive Behavioural Therapy

In order for us to feel better we need to challenge and change those irrational thoughts and beliefs that cause us to feel bad. In order for that to happen, we must first become aware of our irrational or distorted thinking, so that is what we are going to do today.

Cognitive Behavioural Therapy teaches us that we all have what is generally known as thinking errors, distortions or cognitive distortions. These are common to all of us. Yes, even the most positive of people can have them too! However, people who are depressed suffer the most because for them, these distortions become more frequent and more exaggerated. Thinking errors keep us feeling bad because they convince us to believe that something is true, even though it actually isn't true at all. These thinking errors reinforce our negative feelings, telling us that we are right. It is only other people that recognize that we are being irrational; they will sometimes try to tell us this, but we are too entrenched in our beliefs to listen and to question.

It was Aaron Beck, an American psychiatrist, who introduced us to the theory behind cognitive distortions, and David Burns, also an American psychiatrist, who attributed the common names to the distortions.

Below are some typical examples of thinking errors or distorted thinking patterns:

1. JUMPING TO CONCLUSIONS · Automatically thinking that something bad will happen, even though there is no reason for anything going wrong; thinking that someone thinks badly of you without having any proof of this; believing that you know what someone is thinking even though you have nothing to base this on. Example: *I saw her looking at me, I know she hates me. She won't give me the job.*

2. ALL OR NOTHING THINKING · Or black and white thinking . There is no middle ground – it's either good or bad, or black or white, no in-between, no grey areas. You tend to judge yourself or other people on a single event because of one thing going wrong, completely discounting all the things that you, or they, have done right. Example: *Every time I do this, I get it wrong, I can't do anything right. I'm a complete failure.* Or *He made me a lasagne and I didn't like it – he's a terrible cook.*

3. CATASTROPHIZING · Making mountains out of molehills; grossly exaggerating outcomes; expecting that something terrible will happen, even when there is no just cause; totally overestimating the chances of disaster; viewing setbacks as normal and taking a defeatist attitude when things do go wrong. Example: *I would never go skiing, I know I would fall and break both my legs. I would never be able to walk again; I will lose my job and I won't be able to pay my bills. Where would I live without any money coming in?*

4. NEGATIVE MENTAL ATTITUDE · Focusing only on the things that go wrong, the things you and others fail at and the bad things in life; refusing to consider an alternative point of view or look on the bright side of life; you focus only on your and other people's weaknesses and faults, filtering out and disregarding any strengths and successes. Example: *People don't like me so I'll always be on my own, I never do anything right; Who needs other people anyway, they only get on my nerves; I wouldn't want a big fancy house, there'd be too much to clean; I don't bother with holidays, something always goes wrong.*

5. LIVING BY RIGID RULES · *Shoulds, Shouldn'ts, Musts* and *Oughts* tend to rule your life. You make these rigid statements and follow their instructions, creating unrealistic expectations of yourself and others. The outcome is often disappointment, anger, guilt, frustration and a feeling of being let down. Such rules for living are often adopted in childhood and may be inappropriate now, but they have never been challenged. Example: *I must do everything perfectly; They shouldn't be doing that; I ought to know this; I should be able to pull myself together; I must always do the right thing, if I don't I should be punished.*

6. BLAMING · You blame everyone else for anything that goes wrong or badly for you. You hold them responsible for your problems or your difficulties. You feel you are a victim; you feel persecuted; you blame your bad feelings on other people, organizations, the world. Example: *That man/woman ruined my whole life; they shouldn't have put their prices* *up, it's not my fault I didn't have enough money; the policeman booked me for speeding but I wasn't to blame, they ought to have more signs on the road.*

7. SELF-BLAME · You blame yourself for everything that goes wrong, even though you had no control over the event; you take responsibility for anything unpleasant that happens; you believe everything is your fault whether it is or it isn't! Example: *It's my fault he hit me, I should have known better; I made him late, I should have reminded him earlier; I blame myself for my daughter being horrible to me.*

8. COMPARING · You constantly compare yourself with other people in a negative way. You believe that other people can do things better than you; they are more attractive than you; they are nicer than you; they are faster, taller, slimmer, cleverer, younger, have more money, a bigger house, a faster car etc, etc, etc.

You may already be able to recognize some of these negative thinking patterns. Now try to think of an example you use often. It may help if you recruit someone close to you who doesn't mind pointing out whenever they are aware of your negative or distorted statements. Then, for the next week, work on increasing your awareness. Try to catch yourself thinking or speaking them out loud. Carry your workbook around with you and write them down. You may be surprised at just how negative you are being without realizing it! Once you become aware of your critical self it will be much easier to understand your negative feelings such as anxiety, anger, guilt and hopelessness.

It will help if you make a chart, something like the one below. It will draw your attention to how much you need to challenge and change your thoughts.

Remember, from today, you are just increasing awareness. You will find how to manage and challenge these thoughts in Week 7, Day 5.

Thought Chart

Date/Time	Situation	Thought	Thinking Error	Feeling

In the meantime, simply ask yourself these questions whenever you become aware of your thinking errors:

- How can I think about this in a different way?
- What would someone else say or think?
- How is this thought harming me?
- Is this always true?
- How would I feel if I didn't think like this again?

Week 5, Day 6
» *DIRECTION* «

A Trouble Shared...

One of the unpleasant symptoms or effects of stress, anxiety and depression is feeling alone and isolated. Often our thoughts whirl around our head making no sense at all. It becomes difficult to organize our thoughts as our problems and worries grow inside our head, getting bigger and bigger, crowding us until we feel that we are going to explode! They just go on and on, round and round, like a merry-go-round that you can't get off.

We discussed worrying thoughts earlier in Week 3, Day 1. It may be too soon for you to have already mastered the instructions for managing them. If you're still lying awake at night with a thousand and one thoughts whizzing around your mind and feeling that there is no end to the torment, remember to use your breathing exercises and try the Yoga Nidra relaxation to calm your mind and body.

Offloading your troubles will be of great benefit to you, and help can sometimes come from the least expected source, and not necessarily a health professional. It may be that you know someone who could help and who actually would like to be able to help. This may not be the person closest to you. It may not be a member of your family or your best friend or someone you know particularly well. Sometimes, it is easier to talk to a stranger.

- Find someone you can talk to easily.
- Find someone who will listen and not judge.
- Find someone with empathy, warmth and understanding.
- Someone who will not turn it into something that is troubling them.
- Someone you can trust.
- Someone who doesn't necessarily know all your life stories and everything there is to know about you.
- Someone who can point you in the right direction.

Once you have identified someone who can help, mutually decide on an appropriate time and place where and when you will not be disturbed.

Remember that we are all different. Others' opinions, values and beliefs may be different to our own. We lead separate lives, so someone else's advice may not always suit you or apply to your specific problem. If someone is offering advice and it doesn't feel right, then it probably isn't right for you. They probably mean well but it doesn't mean to say that you have to follow their advice.

If you prefer to seek professional help your doctor may be able to refer you to someone, or if you can afford it, there are many counsellors and other therapists out there these days who you can see privately.

Some of the benefits of offloading your troubles:

- You will feel a lot lighter.
- The burden will feel lifted.
- You won't feel quite so alone.
- Some of the helplessness may lessen.
- Your thoughts will become more organized.
- Your mind will become clearer.
- You will often find solutions to your problems by talking about them.
- You will hear another's point of view, which may be more realistic than your own.
- You will be able to put things into perspective.
- You may realize that things aren't as bad as they seem.
- You may feel comforted and supported in your plight.
- *Support* is a major coping strategy for managing stress.
- Your stress and pressure will lessen.

Let your helper know how grateful you are and what it means to be listened to. Tell them that you don't expect any answers; just being listened to makes all the difference. If it goes well perhaps you could do this on a regular basis.

If you really don't have anyone you can talk to, or prefer not to, don't forget that writing things down can also be a great help. If you haven't done this already and you are a great worrier, start a daily journal today. Write down your thoughts, feelings, your problems and whatever it is you are worrying about. You will find that you worry less when you write your inner thoughts down on paper.

Week 5, Day 7
» *RELAXATION* «
Progressive Muscle Relaxation

You may want someone else to read this out loud to you, or you could perhaps record it for yourself.

This *very* effective method of relaxation is very good for counteracting anxiety and involves deliberately tensing muscles, holding the tension on the in-breath for between five and seven seconds and then relaxing the muscles on the out-breath. It can be done sitting on a straight-backed chair or lying down flat on your back, with your feet apart and your arms by your side.

Begin by taking three slow deep breaths, relaxing on each out-breath.

Next, take your attention to your right foot. As you take a breath in, curl up your toes and tighten all the muscles in the foot, hold the tension for a few seconds and then, as you breathe out, release it, let go and relax.

Do exactly the same with your left foot.

Now the right calf: breathe in and tighten the muscle by pointing your toes away from you, hold, as you breathe out release and relax.

Now point your toes towards you, breathe in, tighten, hold and relax as you breathe out. Repeat for the left calf.

Next press your knees together, breathe in and tighten your thighs, buttocks and hips, both sides together this time; hold and then, as you breathe out, release and relax. Really *feel* all the muscles soften and relax now. Notice the difference. Relax more and more.

Now focus all your attention on your abdomen. Breathe in and draw the tummy in towards the spine, hold the tension, then release, soften and relax as you breathe out. Now return to relaxed breathing.

Next, the shoulders. Breathe in as you draw your shoulders up towards your ears, hold, release and relax on the out-breath. Let your shoulders drop now. Relax them more and more.

Now clench your right fist as you breathe in, tighten the muscles of your right hand, hold your arm out in front of you tightly, hold and on the out-breath, release and relax.

Allow your right arm, hands and fingers to become loose, soft, floppy and relaxed, just like a rag doll.

Do the same with your left fist as you breathe in, tighten, hold out your arm, hold and relax as you breathe out. Allow both of your arms to relax more and more. Feel them becoming soft and loose and heavy.

Now as you breathe in, stretch out the fingers of both hands, hold the stretch, then release and relax on the out-breath.

Next, lower your head slowly down towards your chest, feel the tightness in your neck muscles, breathe in and hold. As you breathe out release, relax and very, very slowly, raise your head again. Let your head sit comfortably on the top of your spine now.

Take a breath in and as you drop your head slowly backwards, open your mouth; hold for a moment. Breathe out, this time through your mouth, raising your head very, very slowly.

Take a breath in and tilt your head towards your right shoulder. You will feel a stretch on the opposite side of the neck - don't force it. Slowly raise your head back to centre as you breathe out. Repeat on the left side.

Next, as you breathe in, clench your teeth together; tighten your jaw and press your tongue onto the roof of your mouth. Hold the tightness, then breathe out, relaxing and letting your jaw drop down towards your chest.

Relax your jaw more and more, letting your mouth fall open and your chin sag downwards. Let your tongue lie shapelessly on the bottom of your mouth. Soften your whole face.

Breathe in and close your eyes tightly. Hold the tension all around your eyes, forehead and face and as you breathe out, relax and make your eyes and face soft and smooth. Be aware of the difference.

Breathe in, frown deeply and tense your scalp, hold, breathe out, release and relax. Relax more and more. Make your forehead wide, deep and soft. Let your chin sag downwards again, remove all expression from your face, let your lips separate.

Feel that all the muscles in your face are now soft and feeling much more relaxed than before. Be aware of the difference now. Try to keep it that way. Soft, loose, floppy and without expression.

Now take a long deep breath in and tense your whole body. Hold the tension and, as you let the breath go, let the tension go. Relax your whole body. Continue to let go of more and more tension.

Allow your whole body to sink into a state of relaxation. Let whatever you are sitting or lying on take the whole weight of your body. Allow yourself to sink down softly and deeply. Let your muscles soften more and more. Feel them warm and soft and loose.

Allow yourself to sink down deeper and deeper still now. More and more relaxed. Now imagine for a few moments that you are floating on a cloud, a soft, silky white cloud, just drifting across a clear, blue sky. Stay as long as you like but when you are ready, in your own time, drift slowly back into the reality of the moment. Stretch slowly. Breathe deeply and come slowly out of this relaxation.

Move slowly and lightly when you get up. If you feel dizzy stay seated for a little while until your breathing and heart rate return to their normal rate and flow.

Practise this daily and feel the difference.

Week 5

» RECAP AND REFLECT «

Tick the box when understood, practised and achieved

DAY 1

BE KIND TO YOURSELF: In what way are you being kind to yourself? Do something on a daily basis and try to get into the habit. Self-compassion is essential in balancing stress.

DAY 2

EXERCISE FOR ANXIETY AND PANIC: Are you practising enough? Have you mastered this exercise yet? Have you tried it out when you have felt anxious? If so, how did it help?

DAY 3

DOES IT REALLY MATTER?: Have you made your sign? Have you begun to question yourself a little more about certain things that you get upset about? Have you started putting things more into perspective?

DAY 4

MAKING LISTS AND PRIORITIZING: Are you prioritizing now? Have you made your lists? How can you benefit from this? How do you feel when you are able to cross the items off your list? How does list-making help you?

DAY 5

IRRATIONAL THOUGHTS AND THINKING ERRORS: Have you identified your thinking errors? Have you become more aware of when you are using them? Have you made a chart and entered the information? How do you benefit from stopping your negative thoughts? Are you able to challenge them and what difference has it made to you?

DAY 6

A TROUBLE SHARED...: Do you feel that you need to talk to someone? Have you thought about who that could be? Have you considered professional help?

DAY 7

PROGRESSIVE MUSCLE RELAXATION: Did you like this form of relaxation? How does it compare to the last method? If you haven't found anyone to read the script for you, record it yourself. How many times in a week will you practise this?

Now turn to your self-assessment rating scales and enter your scores for the end of Week 5.

Week 6

· · · · · · · · ·

Week 6, Day 1
» *AWARENESS* «

What is Anxiety?

"The only thing we have to fear is fear itself."
— *FRANKLIN D ROOSEVELT, American president*

ANXIETY IS A STATE THAT OCCURS as a result of being under too much stress and being unable to cope effectively with that stress. It can also be said that anxiety is actually a *symptom* of prolonged and continuous stress; because you are already not coping well, a major issue or a number of smaller issues can overwhelm you and manifest as anxiety. Other causes include too many major changes too close together, being physically tired or exhausted, or feeling run-down. If you are a worrier, and have worried too much for too long over just about everything, anxiety is the next likely stage. Chronic nervousness can also be a precursor to anxiety. When one too many traumas push you over the edge, anxiety is inevitable.

Anxiety can build up and worsen over a period of time; or, occasionally, a very first encounter with anxiety can be acute and come in the form of an anxiety attack or panic attack. It can come totally out of the blue and when least expected. It could occur while you are out enjoying yourself, or while you are at home or at work going about your business, but sometimes it can happen in the middle of the night and wake you up with a jolt. This can of course be very frightening – you don't know what's happening to you, you may think that you're having a heart attack as your heart races and you can't seem to catch your breath. Often it is an anxiety dream or nightmare that wakes you. Your unconscious mind activates the fight/flight response and your body responds. This is your body's way of telling you that you need to stop what you're doing, balance out the stress in your life and seek help.

It is important that we listen to what our body tells us. When we suffer pain it means that something is wrong. Without the pain we would carry on as usual and the problem would go unnoticed and untreated. Anxiety is also a powerful and important message, which we cannot afford to ignore. If we ignore the symptoms and effects of stress and just carry on regardless of how we feel, the body will need to show us in a different way that something needs to change. Similarly, if anxiety is ignored, our clever and intuitive body has to find a more powerful way of stopping us doing any further damage to ourselves. This is often when a panic attack occurs. The attack frightens us enough to find help and make the very necessary changes to our lifestyle.

In today's world anxiety is extremely common. One in five people visit their doctor because they are feeling tense and anxious. Their symptoms may include breathing problems, digestive upsets, skin rashes, sweating and palpitations. But unfortunately the patient is very often only treated for their symptoms and not the root cause. Even if stress and anxiety are recognized, treatment has traditionally been with medication.

The good news is that many doctors now recognize that there are other more effective ways to treat anxiety and refer their patients to an expert who can help them with various kinds of therapies. Unfortunately, not all patients are able to access these services and many are too anxious to attend.

On one occasion a lady was referred to me who had been diagnosed with several severe anxiety disorders. She wasn't able to come to the clinic due to her panic disorder and agoraphobia, so I visited her at home, which is common in cases like this. After I had waited at the door for a few minutes, she eventually opened it to let me in. Once I was inside, she closed the door very quickly and immediately started to have a panic attack. It took a few minutes, but I was able to calm her down with a quick and easy breathing exercise, a calm and reassuring voice and the promise that her panic was harmless and quite normal under the circumstances.

She was very surprised that she was able to regain control so quickly. She said her panic attacks normally lasted for at least half an hour and she often thought that she was going to die. It was her husband who had called the doctor out to see her when he too thought she was going to die. She couldn't understand why she was still alive!

Once she was able to talk to me it transpired that she hadn't left the house for three years; even the thought of going out would bring on a panic attack. She also suffered with generalized anxiety (which caused her to feel anxious most of the time), depression and insomnia. I had to visit her at home twice a week for a month to teach her some of the skills described in this book. Subsequently, I visited her weekly and within six weeks, following a gradual exposure system (see Week 6, Day 5) we were able to walk round the block together, go into a small local shop (where she was able to buy a newspaper), and walk round the park. She returned home with a huge smile on her face. With more work over the following few weeks she was able to come to the clinic, unaided, where she attended my eight-week stress and anxiety management course. By the end of the course she had made such good progress that there was no need for me to see her again. However, some time later she telephoned me to say that she had been on holiday, been to her cousin's wedding and now did the weekly shopping in a large supermarket in the centre of town!

Anxiety can sometimes be related to the kind of person you are or the personality traits you have developed throughout your life. For example, if you are a very sensitive person and you easily become emotional, or you have a habit of getting things out of perspective, anxiety may be a problem for you.

Other people actually *learn* to become anxious! This is usually the result of being in an environment where one or both parents display anxiety in their behaviour and the things they say. You begin to mimic your parents' anxious behaviour (just as children do with other parental behaviours) and adopt their beliefs when you are very young. For example: if your mother was afraid of spiders or of crowded spaces, and she showed her fear, it could result in you assuming the same fear. However, it is also possible that when you were a little older you could make a conscious decision that you were not going to follow in your parents' footsteps. So it doesn't always follow that if both of your parents are anxious you too will become anxious.

So, as you can see, anxiety is a complex issue and can be difficult to overcome without the necessary coping strategies and techniques. From the large selection and diversity of strategies, skills and techniques described in this book, you will find something, or many things, that will help you to control and overcome the anxiety that invades or ruins your life. However, you need to recognize that what helps one person may not be as effective for another. My advice to you is to practise all of the skills, not only to establish which ones suit you best but also because you will be building up your resource bank, and the more skills you acquire, the less stress and anxiety you will experience. Remember, stress is an imbalance between demands and your coping strategies or resources. Resources are ways and means of managing and overcoming your stress and stress-related disorders. Once your resources outweigh your stress you will be on a winning streak!

A young man was referred to my stress and anxiety management course. He told me that he had tried everything to conquer his stress and that nothing worked. I asked him what he had tried. He replied "Hundreds of things." The subsequent conversation went on something like this: (We'll call him John)

ME: Hundreds of things?
JOHN: Yes, hundreds.
ME: Oh, well I may not be able to help you then, because this course doesn't actually cover hundreds of things. Have you really tried so many things?
JOHN: Well, maybe not hundreds.
ME: How many things then, fifty?
JOHN: Well, maybe not fifty.
ME: Twenty?
JOHN: I don't really know.
ME: Tell me what you have tried then.

> JOHN: Tablets that the doctor gave me, and they didn't work.
>
> ME: What else?
>
> JOHN: I tried some relaxation but that didn't work either. I had to stop after about five minutes because I became so agitated.
>
> ME: Anything else?
>
> JOHN: I can't really remember, but I know this course won't help me because nothing does!

He did join the course, and eight weeks later he was discharged with no further help required.

My point is that many people, apart from exaggerating, don't really know what's out there to help because no one ever talks to them about how to cope with stress, anxiety and depression. This is your opportunity to arm yourself with not just two or three coping strategies, but many. The more you have, the more confident you will feel, and the sooner you will *Get Your Life Back*.

Of course, as we have previously seen, some anxiety is a natural state for human beings. It is acceptable that we become anxious in certain situations, like speaking in public or taking an examination, crossing a very busy road or being threatened in some way, because we (often rightly) perceive these situations as confrontational or challenging. The adrenalin flow actually helps us to perform more effectively and more efficiently; it is only when anxiety gets out of control or is inappropriate that it becomes a real problem. It is this understanding of anxiety that will help you. Once you begin to realize that it is normal in certain circumstances, that it won't kill you or even harm you in any way, and that it can be controlled with easily acquired skills, you will begin to feel more confident. This subsequent confidence will actually help redress the balance and prevent the anxiety from developing in non-threatening situations.

You have already learned a variety of skills that you can use to control, reduce or even eliminate the symptoms and effects of stress, including for example, breathing exercises, relaxations, meditations and positive thinking. Now that you realize that anxiety occurs as the result of stress, you can see that you now have skills that control both stress and anxiety. However, there are additional skills to learn that can help specifically with anxiety issues and disorders.

Anxiety can affect us in five different ways

Many people think that anxiety is just one single condition and that it only affects us physically. However, this is not the case; as you have discovered already, the mind, body and spirit work as one. They are not separate. If you have a *thought* your body will react and you will have an emotion. If you have a *physical symptom* you will have a thought and a corresponding emotion. If you have an *emotion* both your body and your mind will respond to that emotion.

However, it doesn't end there. There is a fourth and even a fifth dimension. Your behaviour will be the consequence of your thought, physical symptom and emotion. This behaviour normally manifests itself in running away from the scary situation you are in, or avoiding that situation in the future – or *both*! The fifth dimension is a psychological one. This means that everything you experience, whether good or bad, is registered in your psyche or subconscious. You may not remember all of it, or any of it, but it is still there and affects the way you are today. If a bad experience or trauma from the past is triggered by something today, perhaps by something you see, hear, smell or taste, or even a thought, the feelings you had back then can rise from your subconscious and come hurtling to the surface. Anxiety or panic will not be far behind – unless, of course, you are able to control them with a coping strategy from your resource bank. If this effect is frequent or constant and unending, it can result in a more serious anxiety disorder. Depression is the most common psychological effect of stress and anxiety.

The most common symptoms of anxiety are rapid heart rate, shallow rapid breathing, sweating, nausea and trembling, but there are many more. From the lists below, tick or highlight all the symptoms you are experiencing at the present time and write them in your workbook with today's date. As anxiety is in itself a symptom of stress, all the symptoms and effects below are the result of both anxiety and stress.

If you are experiencing any of the symptoms below, you may be feeling anxious about the symptoms themselves, too. Anxiety breeds anxiety.

Physical Symptoms & Worry

1. Mentally

Believing the worst will happen	Negative thinking
Getting things out of proportion	Poor judgement
Heightened alertness	Self-criticism
Inability to concentrate	Thinking there is something wrong with you
Memory lapses	Worrying

2. Physically

Aches and pains	Headaches and migraines
Asthma and other breathing problems	High blood pressure
Blurred vision	Muscle tension and stiffness
Chest pains	Nausea
Digestive problems such as indigestion, constipation, diarrhoea	Palpitations or racing heart
Dizziness	Poor sleep
Dry mouth and difficulty swallowing	Sweating
Excess blushing	Tingling
Excess sugar in blood	Trembling
Frequent need to visit the toilet	Ulcers

NB. Please check with your doctor that your symptoms have no physical cause. For example, thyroid problems sometimes have similar symptoms to those of stress.

3. Emotionally

Anger, hostility and rage	Low self-esteem
Being inflexible	Mood swings
Demotivated	More fussy or fastidious
Fear	Sadness and tearfulness
Irritability	Unable to make decisions
Loneliness	Unable to solve problems
Loss of confidence	Worrying

4. Behaviourally	
Apathy	Inability to sit still
Avoiding certain places, events or people that trigger the anxiety	Nail-biting
Carelessness	Needing to sit near a door or an exit as an easy means of escape
Excessive smoking, drinking, self-medicating, eating too much or too little	Pacing
Feeling of wanting to or actually running away from certain situations or places	Perfectionism
Fidgeting	Self-neglect
Foot-tapping	Sleeping too much or too little
Hair-twiddling	Stopping socializing

5. Psychologically	
Depression	Post-Traumatic Stress Disorder (PTSD)
Hopelessness	Self-harming
Obsessive Compulsive Disorder (OCD)	Withdrawal
Phobias	Yearning for a better life

This long and wide-ranging list is not meant to worry or alarm you! Just because I've recorded all these symptoms here doesn't mean to say you will get all of them – you may only recognize a few, or even not any of them. They are just here to help you understand your symptoms as being those associated with stress and anxiety. We are all unique individuals and will all therefore have different symptoms.

Some, however, are common, such as a racing heart and shallow breathing, avoidance and needing to sit near the exit door. You can watch all your symptoms reduce as you journey towards *getting your life back*. Remember to identify them now and check again when you have completed Week 12.

> **To sum up:**
> - Anxiety is extremely common.
> - Anxiety is a normal human emotion and sometimes keeps us safe from harm.
> - Anxiety can be a symptom of too much stress or pressure and the inability to cope with it.

- Anxiety is not always recognized or diagnosed, particularly if your symptoms are more uncommon.
- Anxiety occurs depending on what kind of person you are.
- Anxiety can be the result of your past experiences.
- Anxiety can affect us in five different ways: mentally, physically, emotionally, behaviourally, psychologically.

Week 6, Day 2
» *UNDERSTANDING* «
Understanding Anxiety

"Nothing in life is to be feared, it is only to be understood."
— *MARIE CURIE*

Unfortunately, once anxiety has settled into your system, if you have no coping strategies or skills to deal with it, the more anxious you will become. You will then become more anxious about your anxiety. It may seem as though there is no way out; because of this, your anxiety stays put and over a period of time there is a danger that it will increase even further, become more severe and spiral out of control.

If you have started to avoid certain situations or places because of your anxiety, it will have knocked your confidence, and if you have less confidence you are more likely to avoid more and more situations. This reduction in confidence and increase in anxiety triggers even more anxiety, which in turn causes more unpleasant forms of anxiety such as panic attacks, phobias and Obsessive Compulsive Disorder (OCD). Remember, anxiety occurs when you have too much stress and you are unable to cope with it effectively. Once stress is perceived, whether it is real or imagined, the fight/flight response kicks in, resulting in a series of biological changes in your body in order to prepare you to fight or escape the perceived danger.

Below is a list of symptoms and effects of the fight/flight response along with their corresponding physiological explanations. This detailed list will help you to understand and gain knowledge of why you are affected in these ways. Once you are able to recognize these symptoms and understand why you have them, you will be able to stop feeling so anxious about what is happening in your body and realize that these symptoms are perfectly normal under your current set of circumstances. This understanding will help you to avoid the vicious circle discussed above.

Symptoms and Effects of Fight/Flight	Physiological Explanations
Tension in back, neck and shoulders	Upper-body muscles contract ready for a fight
Headache and dizziness	Biochemical messages are sent from the brain to adrenal glands to release adrenalin
Blurred vision	Pupils dilate in order to see more clearly
Dry mouth	Saliva dries up owing to digestive system closing down as blood is diverted to where it is most needed
Indigestion, nausea, heartburn and ulcers	Digestive system slows or stops as energy is transferred to the brain and the muscles in arms and legs
Frequent urination and diarrhoea	Sphincter muscles relax, preparing the body to become as light as possible ready to flee the danger
Excess sweating	Perspiration cools the body as it is absorbed back into the skin through the pores
Blushing	Adrenalin causes the small blood vessels to widen and move to the surface of the skin
High blood pressure and racing heart	The heart beats faster, causing blood pressure to rise, enabling more oxygen to flow to the limbs and brain
Excess sugar in the blood	The liver releases sugars and fats to provide fuel for quick energy
Rapid, shallow breathing, gasping, asthma	Breathing becomes rapid and shallow to increase oxygen in the muscles
Chest pain, tightness in chest, palpitations	As above
Tense, aching jaw and clenching of teeth	Primitive man showed his teeth in order to look more fierce
Hair standing on end	Stone Age man was hairy; this helped him to look bigger and more fierce
Senses heightened	Enables quick decisions and responses to take action

When we are in real danger the processes described above help to save our life as the body prepares us to fight or take flight. But when we are under continuous and prolonged stress and not coping well, the fight/flight response is triggered in normal everyday situations. This can be frightening, as it appears to come from nowhere and not to make any sense. Many people think they may be having a heart attack and are taken to hospital, only to be sent home after tests show that they have a healthy heart. What they sometimes realize, though, is that because they have not balanced out their stress with rest and exercise or other coping mechanisms, they have pushed themselves beyond their limitations, causing these severe and worrying symptoms to appear out of nowhere while out shopping, in the middle of a meeting or during other everyday activities. It is our body's way of attracting our attention, telling us in no uncertain terms to stop, take stock of exactly what is happening and seek help. It is often only at this point that people do get the help they need.

Many of my patients and clients have said they were glad they had reached breakdown point or burnout, as it forced them into doing something about the unreasonable amount of stress in their lives and the way they were dealing with it. They would frequently tell me that they just wanted to get their life back!

Two factors that may contribute to and prolong anxiety

1. YOUR BEHAVIOUR · When you are anxious about going to certain places it is understandable that you will avoid going there if you think you will become anxious or have a panic attack. You will want to stay away. But by avoiding these places you are only setting yourself up for failure and remaining on that vicious circle. The more you put it off, the worse your anxiety becomes. You begin to see yourself as being limited, believing you are weak and lacking in confidence. You then begin to think that if you will become anxious there, you will be anxious in other places too. The specific then – dangerously – becomes the general, and before you know it you are afraid of going anywhere. You are therefore never able to give yourself an opportunity to overcome your anxiety; you are unlikely to discover that you can actually control it by using simple techniques such as breathing exercises, positive thinking and making small improvements one step at a time.

2. YOUR BELIEFS · If you *believe* you will get anxious or have a panic attack, the chances are you will. Remember the quote "Whether you think you can or think you can't, you're probably right." The fact is that your thoughts and beliefs (cognitions) directly affect your feelings and thus your behaviour and outcomes. Put simply: if you *believe* you will be anxious, you *think* you will be anxious; you therefore *become* anxious and run away and the outcome is that you *fail* to overcome your anxiety. The next time you are in the same situation, exactly the same will happen. If you carry on doing what you're doing – you'll carry on getting what you're getting!

Remember the example in Week 4, Day 1 of someone, as a child, going shopping with their mother and losing sight of her for a minute or two? Here's what might happen to make this anxiety become a habit:

> The next time you were going to go shopping with your mother you remembered the frightening event from your last trip. You started to get worried that you would lose her again and the very thought of going to the shops caused you to get anxious. Or, maybe you went without worry but when you got to the point where you had lost sight of your mother it triggered the thought that you would lose her again. That negative thought or trigger would then have fired up the fight/flight response, causing stress hormones to flood into your bloodstream in a flash. Within a moment your body would have thrown you into a state of panic, even though this time there was no danger and the panic was unnecessary and inappropriate.

So, the irrational belief was formed that when you go shopping you panic. It would also set up a long-term and self-fulfilling prophecy. I have worked with many people who have suffered for much of their lives with this kind of anxiety, but it usually only takes a few sessions to help them overcome it. With a belief formed in early childhood by one frightening incident, it doesn't make logical sense to base your current belief on that single incident that happened long ago when you were a young chid. If you can attach logic to your present fear in this way, that fear will often quickly disappear back into the past where it belongs.

It goes without saying that not everyone will react to being lost for a few moments in the same way as the person in the example above. Remember, we are all different, unique individuals and it very much depends on our previous experiences and what kind of person we are.

Take some time now to think about your own reality and how, where and when your anxiety started. It doesn't necessarily have to have started when you were a child; it could have been a more recent crisis or trauma, or simply an upsetting event. Is there a moment in your life that might have triggered your initial fear and resulted in you believing something that makes you anxious today? Think about it and try to rationalize it. Ask yourself how things are today compared with how they were at the time of the event. Could your behaviour today be based on something that happened years ago? If so, ask yourself if it is still true today and whether there is another way of thinking and behaving in this present time.

In conclusion, what we believe about ourselves, the situation we are in, or about the world in general, has a direct impact on what we do and how we live our lives day by day. If we have a belief that is irrational or unrealistic and that limits us, it can cause anxiety, panic and other stress-related conditions.

What unrealistic or irrational beliefs do you have that cause and maintain your anxiety? Do you believe for example that:

- Shops are scary places.
- Leaving your home will cause you to panic.
- If you have a panic attack you will embarrass yourself.
- If you fly in an aeroplane it will crash and you will die.
- If someone criticizes you, you won't be able to bear it.
- If you don't check the locks on the doors and windows ten times, someone will break into your house.
- If you make someone angry they will get aggressive and hit you, so you are never able to go out and socialize.
- If you get ill it will be the end of the world, it will be catastrophic; you will never get better, or you will die.
- If you speak your mind people won't like you or respect you.

- If you get too close to someone they will leave you
- If you don't have any qualifications you will never get a job and people will think you are stupid.

If you can identify with any of the above examples, or if you are aware of a similar irrational and limiting belief, you may have certain behaviours that will keep your anxiety going:

- **Your social life is non-existent or limited/You don't go on holiday**
  You stay at home because it's safe. You therefore never give yourself the opportunity to learn that you can be safe even if you do leave your home.
- **You develop certain rituals**
  Checking or touching something or counting things. These obsessive rituals attempt to satisfy your mind that you will be safe and nothing bad will happen, either to you or your loved ones. This behaviour prevents you from learning that nothing bad will happen even if you don't go through the motions of your ritual.
- **You adopt a Just In Case (JIC) attitude**
  For example: you take a plastic bag with you wherever you go – just in case (JIC) you're sick from anxiety; you carry something with you that will keep you calm, like a crystal, or worry beads or your medication – JIC; you always have your doctor's phone number on you – JIC. Such safety activities just prevent you from discovering that everything will be fine even if you don't take your precautions.
- **You don't put yourself up for promotion or apply for a better job**
  You make the decision to stay as you are because it's easier that way. You convince yourself that if you did attend an interview you would be so anxious that it would result in a panic attack and you would lose control. You wouldn't get the job anyway. This prevents you from moving forward, making progress and realizing your full potential, which may cause you to have regrets in the future.
- **You neglect yourself and don't bother to take a pride in your appearance**
  You have the negative attitude of *what's the point*? You believe that if anybody gets too close to you they will eventually hurt you and leave you. You ostensibly keep any potential admirers away by not making yourself look attractive. You believe that by doing this you are keeping yourself safe from any further abandonment or rejection. The result of this type of behaviour is often loneliness and even depression.

To sum up:
- Anxiety occurs when your stress outweighs your ability to cope with it
- The fight/flight response switches on whether the threat is real or imagined
- Anxiety continues if you do not have any coping strategies in place
- Anxiety is maintained both by your beliefs and your behaviour
- Your irrational beliefs and behaviours prevent you from learning that there are other ways of overcoming stress and anxiety
- Your irrational beliefs prevent you from living life to the full, living in peace and happiness and realizing your full potential

Week 6, Day 3
» *PHYSICAL HEALTH* «
Activity Activity Activity

Hopefully you are continuing to exercise for a minimum of twenty minutes at least four days a week. You may remember learning earlier that exercise is one way we can switch off the fight/flight mechanism; the energy we use when exercising mimics the energy primitive man would have used to escape from real danger. After either running away or fighting, once he was safe and out of harm's way he would rest and his body would return to normal. Of course, in modern times we have no need to flee or fight because our fight/flight response (or stress response) is activated by things that we perceive to be stressful that probably aren't, rather than by a dinosaur or an unfriendly tribe. However, because we don't burn up the energy our body makes when we are stressed, the stress hormones continue circulating around our body and the stress will remain in the system until something is done to counteract it. In other words, if you exercise regularly your stress levels will reduce, and if you supplement exercise with rest and relaxation you are going a long way to overcoming stress, anxiety and depression.

You may have chosen several different ways to exercise, or maybe you are just sticking to one, such as walking. It doesn't matter as long as you are doing something – but make sure that it is a low-impact exercise, not something too strenuous or aggressive like squash or weightlifting. Don't forget that exercise is not only a major way to combat stress, anxiety and depression; it also keeps you healthy and fit. If you are overweight, it will help with that too.

After you have been exercising for some time, there is a danger that you may begin to lose motivation. This often happens with exercise regimes: you start off with good intentions but somewhere along the line, for some reason, those good intentions tend to fade away. Don't worry though; this happens to most of us and if it has happened to you, start again from today. Set your goal, make your commitment, find your incentive and imagine what the outcome would be if you discontinued your exercise regime. Go back and reread the section on the benefits of exercise. Continuing to exercise is vital if you are determined to *Get Your Life Back*. Remember, peace of mind is not only about being still in relaxation and meditation.

You can of course exercise without even leaving the house

- When you are doing your chores try to move around a little more, and move more quickly.
- If you have stairs in your home run up and down them as many times as you can – but stop when you become too tired.
- If you are unable to leave your home, walk around the house instead. Walk around your furniture, up and down the stairs etc. Go into every room several times and keep going until you feel tired or until the twenty minutes are up. You may find this quite enjoyable and you will feel good about yourself because you've been for a walk and didn't even have to go outside.
- If you have a garden, tend to it (weather permitting). Make gardening your new hobby or interest. It is particularly good for you if you are depressed. Not only are you exercising and releasing endorphins (the feel-good hormones), but you also have something lovely to admire, which will instil a feeling of peace and tranquillity. You will also have a feeling of achievement and satisfaction when everything is looking lovely.
- If your ceilings are high enough, do some skipping.
- If you have the means and you have the room for one, buy a small trampoline or trampette to bounce on. They are not very expensive and don't take up much room when stored. Rebounding exercise has numerous benefits for both body and mind. It is said to be one of the most beneficial forms of exercise ever developed – and I can personally recommend it!

- Use exercise DVDs. There are plenty of these around but make sure they are suitable for your level of fitness. If you have not been exercising for a long time, start with just a few minutes and increase the time gradually week by week until the whole session is comfortable for you.
- If you know any keep-fit exercises, clear a space and do them there, but be careful you don't overdo it and be sure they are suitable for you.
- Put some lively music on and dance to it. This is a wonderful way to exercise; as well as increasing your fitness it will increase your enjoyment too. Upbeat music is an ideal therapy if you're feeling low or depressed, so dancing to it will double the benefit.
- Try exercising while you're watching TV, even if it's only doing simple and safe stretching exercises on the floor. If you have an exercise bicycle you can catch up on the soaps or watch a football match while exercising. I know my advice to you on Week 2 Day 4 was to do one thing at a time, but I will forgive you in this case!
- If you do yoga, t'ai chi or Pilates you will probably be expected to practise at home anyway. Just don't forget to do it, and ideally practise every day.

Build some of these suggestions into your daily routine, or write them down as goals. But if you suddenly feel spontaneous – just do them!

Week 6, Day 4
» *MANAGING STRESS* «

Take a Break and Balance Your Stress

"Rest and be thankful."
— *WILLIAM WORDSWORTH*

You will have been very busy since starting this journey, learning about stress and anxiety and how it affects you. You will also have been busy thinking about and writing down your goals in order to reduce the stress in your life and increase your ability to manage and overcome it. If you have been achieving your goals, today is the day you can reward yourself. There has certainly been a lot to think about and digest, and there's still plenty more to come.

So today you can take a break. As you will learn in any stress management programme, you must take breaks; they are vital in order to balance out the stress you are under. All work and no play not only makes Jack or Jill a dull boy or girl but it also makes you tired and sometimes exhausted, thereby increasing the pressure, which in turn creates more stress. Work needs to be balanced with rest and breaks.

If you are guilty of not taking a lunch break or you are eating lunch at your desk or place of work it is important that you change this pattern and start to take all the breaks you are entitled to. Also, make sure you eat healthily at lunchtime, thereby increasing your blood sugar levels, which will have dropped during the morning. The food will supply you with an increase in energy. A sandwich containing protein is ideal.

If you are committed to *getting your life back* you must take adequate breaks. You will know now that the more pressure you are under, the less productive and efficient you are. This is a proven fact, although one that you may never have considered before. You may think that if you carry on working through your lunch break you'll get more done, but this is simply not the case: if you take a break, preferably away from your desk or place of work, and if you also include some exercise, such as walking, you will function much more effectively when you return to work. The same is true about holidays: a holiday from work for one or two weeks will recharge your batteries. You will work more effectively and your productivity will increase. If you are an employer I recommend that you ensure that your workforce takes all the breaks and holidays to which they are entitled. Watch productivity, efficiency and staff morale rise!

So, what would you like to do today? It's your choice: you decide. There is no pressure today. Take the weight off your feet and the pressure off your shoulders. Today is a holiday. Find some freedom, some relaxation, some rest, peace, space and something to enjoy. All of these will help to balance out your stress.

Think about what you could do. It mustn't be a task or a chore. You can even have the day off from achieving your goals (unless of course your goal for today was to relax or meditate or do something you really enjoy).

Perhaps there is something nice you've been meaning to do for a while, but haven't got around to yet? Maybe you've been intending to go to see that new movie at the local cinema. If you have children, spend some quality time playing with them, having fun, taking them to a park or finding something to laugh about. What about going out for a meal with someone you love? Maybe you haven't seen a particular friend for some time. Why not call them to find out if they would like to meet up?

I know some of you might just like to do nothing at all because for the past few days/weeks/months you have been so busy you haven't had time to just sit and rest and relax. Maybe you would just like to stay at home and watch TV or read a book or a magazine. Or invite someone round. You don't always have to go out somewhere to have an enjoyable time.

Why not think about pampering yourself? It doesn't have to cost too much. You could start with a nice long lie-in. Perhaps you've got someone who could bring you breakfast in bed? If not, spoil yourself and have something really luxurious for breakfast (you may have to plan in advance for that). You could then have a lovely long soak in a warm bath with some fragrant aromatherapy oils to help you relax. If you can afford it, why not treat yourself to a spa day and have a whole day of bliss.

You may have a hobby that you haven't pursued for a while. Today is the day for you to return to it. If you enjoyed it before, you could enjoy it again. If you haven't got a hobby or an interest, maybe today is the day to discover one.

If today isn't a good day for you to rest and enjoy yourself, you can postpone it until another day, but do it soon. If you are in employment think about booking an annual leave day and, if you have enough days left, make it a regular thing – for no other reason than simply to take a break.

Week 6, Day 5
» ANXIETY SOLUTIONS «
The Gradual Exposure System

We have addressed various ways of managing generalized anxiety and panic attacks, including breath control exercises, the STOP Technique, challenging negative thoughts and relaxation techniques. By now, therefore, I would expect your anxiety to have reduced or even been eliminated completely, but for those of you who are still living in the clutches of anxiety there is another very helpful technique, which I call *the gradual exposure system*. This simply means gradually confronting your fears, one step at a time. It is frequently used to help overcome anxiety in all its forms, including panic attacks, phobias, OCD (Obsessive Compulsive Disorder) and other behaviour issues. I also often used it for patients suffering with agoraphobia.

This goal-setting and achievement technique is extremely effective if you follow it correctly, practise every single day and give it your total commitment. As I am not there personally to help and encourage you, you will also need someone who understands your condition and is willing to support and encourage you as you work your way through the steps. They need to congratulate you and praise you when you achieve your goals; and they need to know that it is vitally important that they do not allow you to back down, or give in to your pleas to stop when the going gets tough! They must be strong enough to see you work through your anxiety and to remind you constantly to use your breathing exercises and positive affirmations.

That being said, it is possible to achieve success on your own providing that your steps are small ones, you are brave enough and you have a strong determination and will to succeed.

The system involves setting and following a step-by-step plan in order to overcome the anxiety and panic attacks that have been created by fear. It further involves repeating and practising the steps one by one, starting with the easiest step first. Once you are able to perform the first step without any fear, you then – and only then – go on to the next step, and so on until the fear is completely eliminated. Let me give you an example of how this works.

> When you first learn to drive a car you might be terrified. You think that it is impossible to look where you're going as well as steer round a corner, change gears, use the indicators and switch the wipers on if it's raining. However, after several lessons it all starts to fit into place and you feel a bit more at ease – but you might still be nervous. As you progress you begin to drive along busier roads that are full of traffic and littered with traffic lights and pedestrian crossings. This probably causes you to become nervous again. However, once again with practice you become more accustomed to it, and after a little while it doesn't feel so bad at all.
>
> When you take your driving test your anxiety level might rise sky-high, but once it's over, your confidence grows, you feel much more at ease and think of yourself as being a competent and accomplished driver. As more time passes your confidence grows even more and before very long you are driving "unconsciously". That's not what it sounds like! It means that you can steer the car round a corner, change gears, turn on your indicator light and listen to the radio all at the same time without really thinking about what you're doing. You've certainly come a long way since you first sat in the driving seat for your very first lesson, feeling terrified. You have successfully confronted and overcome your fears.

As you progress through the gradual exposure system it is important that you incorporate the breathing exercises that you have already learned. I would particularly recommend the 7/11 exercise as described in Week 1, Day 2, and the exercise for anxiety and panic in Week 5, Day 2. Both these exercises are especially helpful for anxiety and phobias. However, I would recommend that you do the whole sequence of all the breath-control exercises you have learned so far before beginning each step. By now you will have discovered which of the exercises work best for you and I recommend that you deploy these while you carry out the exercise. You should also rate your anxiety on a scale of zero to 10, where zero is having no anxiety at all and 10 is full-blown panic. It is natural to expect some anxiety but it is very important to remember that anxiety will not stay with you forever. It will always reduce and, if you focus only on your breathing exercises and positive affirmations, it will come down more quickly, as shown in the diagram below. It is important to continue to practise each step until there is no anxiety at all. Only move on to your next step when you have achieved this.

How anxiety reduces each time the step is practised

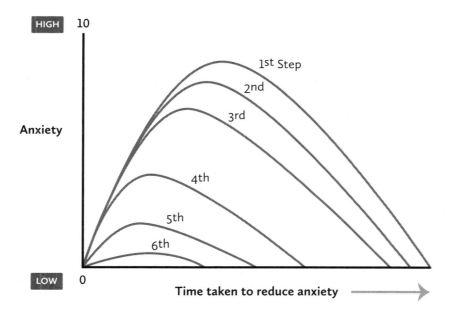

Here is an example plan for someone who suffers from agoraphobia. This is an irrational fear of open spaces and/or public places that can become so severe that sufferers are often reduced to becoming prisoners in their own homes. The plan can be adapted to suit an individual's specific needs, and when you are formulating your own plan it is important to remember that this *is your* plan and *you* are in control. Make the steps easy for yourself. You don't have to conquer your greatest fear in one go. The idea of this process is to take tiny steps, one at a time, that you can achieve – although preferably with a little help and support. Feeling good about your achievements will motivate you to do more. As you accomplish more and more you may find that you are able to skip a step or two because you are doing so well and feel eager to reach your ultimate goal. However, it is more advisable to go through all the steps just to make sure you have actually conquered each one.

Don't be concerned about setbacks; these are perfectly normal and extremely common in people attempting to overcome the fear they've had for a very long time. Just go back to the last step or start again. Always focus on your achievements so far and *know that you can do it.* It is a tried and tested remedy and I have seen it successfully applied many times, even with the most severe phobias and obsessional behaviours. This process *will* help you to *Get Your Life Back.*

Example Step-by-Step System

STEP 1 · After practising the full range of breathing exercises and using any relaxation techniques you feel you need, stand at your open door with your friend/supporter. Rate your anxiety on a scale of zero to 10 and continue to rate it throughout the whole exercise. Using the breath-control exercise of your choice and positive statements such as *I am calm, I am safe and I am in control now,* stay there. Do not move away until the anxiety goes completely, down to zero. Repeat this step several times a day, until there is no anxiety at all and you are able to stand at the open door without using your breathing exercise. Then do the same again, this time on your own. It may take a few attempts or, in some cases, a few days. Remember – your anxiety will always reduce, and the more you practise this, the sooner you will be free.

STEP 2 · Next step. After your sequence of breathing exercises, with a friend/supporter, walk to the garden gate (or a few yards/metres away from your door) and again follow the same procedure as in Step 1. Do not attempt the next step until you can do it on your own and without any anxiety at all. This, and all the steps, may take several days.

STEP 3 · As above, start with your friend/supporter and walk several more metres away from the house. Perhaps to the next lamp post or tree, or any other object you can use as a target. When you are able, do it on your own. Reward yourself in some way for doing so well. Always praise yourself after achieving your goals.

STEP 4 · Now walk further away from your home, first with your friend/supporter and then alone as soon as you are able. Again this needs to be to a specific goal or target, such as the corner shop or to a bus stop. You must not return home until you have full control and there is no anxiety at all. You need to learn that you can do this; you can control your emotions and bring your anxiety down to zero and nothing terrible will happen to you.

STEP 5 · Now with your friend/supporter, walk to the next target. Remember to do your breathing exercises and tell yourself that you are safe and in control. Return only when your anxiety has come down. When you feel ready, do the same on your own without any support. Practise as many times as it takes for your anxiety to have disappeared completely.

STEP 6 · Next, again with a friend/supporter, walk to your next agreed target, which needs to be much further this time. Do not go beyond your target even if you think you can. By this time you are doing really well, but don't try to run before you can walk (if you'll pardon the expression!). Just give yourself lots of praise and a pat on the back. Remember you are in control. Continue with this process until you are able to reach the target without any anxiety. Allow yourself to practise this as many times as it takes. Gradually reduce the time spent with your friend/supporter at your side until you can do it alone.

STEP 7 · This last step of your plan is of course to go as far as you wish. Start with your supporter if you feel a need to, but make sure you get to the point where you can do it alone. It may be several weeks before you completely overcome your fear, but it all depends on how much practise you put into it. Always remember: IT CAN BE DONE AND YOU CAN DO IT!

This process isn't as complicated as it seems. I have gone into a lot of detail, so that it leaves you with no doubt about what it is needed, but it can be simplified: see the chart below.

Simplified Plan

	Breathing exercises and relaxation first
	Begin with support, end without support
Step 1	Stand at the door
Step 2	Walk to the garden gate
Step 3	Walk to the first lamp post
Step 4	Walk to the next lamp post
Step 5	Walk to the shop on the corner
Step 6	Walk round the block and back home
Step 7 Ultimate Goal	Walk to the park, round the park, call in at the café in the park for a cup of tea and return home
Next	**Plan next programme, which will result in being able to go shopping in town**

If you also have a fear of being in a public place you will need to create a new programme for this fear. However, once you have overcome your fear of leaving home and walking around on your own, the next one probably won't take as long; your confidence will have increased significantly and you will be accustomed to using your coping strategies and discovering what works best for you.

Tips for overcoming your fear

- Remember that your panicky feelings are perfectly normal reactions to something you are afraid of, even if it is an irrational fear. It is your *thoughts* that are causing an over-exaggerated response, *not the reality* of the situation.
- Stay focused on what is happening. Stay in the present moment. Do not allow yourself to think about what *might* happen.

- Your feelings of anxiety or panic are not harming you. Don't be afraid of them. They are not dangerous or life-threatening. Even though your heart is racing and your breath is out of control, it is just your body going into overdrive because of what you think and believe.
- Accept your feelings and your physical reactions. Do not fight them. Just let them happen. You don't need to fight. Your body will return to normal very soon.
- *Do not run away!* Running back to safety will make it worse for you in the long run. Stay where you are and use your breathing exercises and positive affirmations to help you to control anxiety and panic.
- Try to relax your muscles, especially in your face, shoulders and back.
- When the anxiety has passed, continue with your plan.

This system is also very effective for reducing or overcoming OCD. Work out a similar step-by-step plan that involves very small changes for each individual behaviour. For example: if you are washing your hands fifty times a day, miss out just one hand-wash, using your coping strategies until the anxiety dies down. Alternatively, reduce the amount of time you spend washing your hands. If your problem is needing to have the cutlery in the drawer all facing the same way, just place one knife the other way until your anxiety is under control, then work on two knives being the other way round. Continue with the plan until you are able to fully accept the cutlery being placed any way round they happen to fall into the drawer. Then move on to the next compulsion. Just work on one at a time.

Week 6, Day 6
» DIRECTION «
Be Mindful of Your Anxiety

Whether you have been anxious for a long time or it has just begun, there are many ways in which you can overcome it. Below I have outlined a different approach that you might like to try.

Observe and accept your anxiety for what it is

This approach in one way conflicts with the advice "*accept what you cannot change*", but only inasmuch as we know that you *can* actually change your anxiety state. It is perfectly possible, and over many years I have worked with many hundreds of people who have done exactly that, even those who were in extremely high states of anxiety. However, for the purpose of this approach, we will assume that the advice "*accept what you cannot change*" is valid. Give it a try – you have nothing to lose.

People who suffer with anxiety can spend their whole day fighting it. They hate it and just want it to go away. This hatred of anxiety causes more anxiety, which results in their fight/flight response being switched on twenty-four hours a day.

Because of this they are never going to be able to overcome this anxiety; they spend all day simply going round the vicious circle, and become angry and anxious about that too. You can imagine the scenario of someone telling their anxiety to stop, shouting at it to go away and leave them alone. Eventually it becomes a monster that bullies and torments them. They end up hating themselves because nothing appears to help. They despair of themselves for getting into such a dreadful state of helplessness and powerlessness, but powerlessness is itself a major cause of stress and so the situation just gets worse and worse.

The alternative approach is to accept your anxiety for what it is. You can conclude that, owing to the circumstances in which you live, it's no wonder that you are anxious. Anybody would be! You may be in a situation that would make even the calmest person anxious. So, be mindful of this. The acceptance will actually switch one level of the anxiety off, so at least you will stop being anxious about being anxious. Acceptance is a positive state that balances out the negative states of worry and anxiety. You cannot be anxious and accepting at the same time. It may take a little time and some practice but, maybe surprisingly, it really can work. Start now, just being mindful of your anxiety, and take the following steps:

1 · **Be aware of your anxiety and watch it as it changes patterns**
Try to become aware of your anxiety happening within you. Many people describe their anxiety as something rising up through their body. Feel it, know where it is, score it on a rating scale from zero to 10, zero meaning no anxiety at all and 10 being the worst it can be. Watch your scores fluctuating for a little while, but gradually reducing. Be aware of which specific symptoms you are having and where in your body they are. Is your heart beating fast, is your breathing rapid and is your chest tight? Watch your anxiety as it rises and falls within your body. Give your anxiety a colour, a shape or even a name! Be mindful of how your anxiety is making you *feel*. What other *emotions* are rising within you as a consequence of your anxiety? Perhaps you are angry or impatient or fed up with it. What exactly are you doing as a consequence of your anxiety? Are you at all curious about how your body is changing so quickly? Do you marvel at the fact that your body is attempting to keep you safe from harm even though it is actually only your imaginings that cause this reaction, not reality? (Your fight/flight response believes that the threat is real; it doesn't know the difference between reality and your imaginings. It just recognizes that you are afraid and that it needs to get you to escape from it!)

2 · **Give yourself a running commentary using only positive language**
For example: "The anxiety is like a big red balloon in my stomach. My heart is pounding and I can hear it crashing against my ribcage. My breathing is fast and high up in my chest, but the book says that this is perfectly normal when I think that something is frightening. My breath is dark and cloudy and I'm now beginning to feel a little queasy, and my palms are sweating but I know that that is normal too and not harmful in any way. Now my

heart is slowing down a little and I'm able to slow my breathing down just by concentrating on what is happening. My anxiety has now turned from red to pink and my breath is white and smooth. My score was seven when I started to pay attention but now it's down to five. I'm feeling as though I have some control over my anxiety... and now it's only a four... I'm trying my best to get it under control and I am succeeding. I know I can do it."

3 · Stay positive

Put it into perspective. It's not the end of the world if you are anxious. You are not going to die and nothing terrible is going to happen. You've had anxiety before and it can get very high, but it always plateaus out and then comes down again all by itself. You also know that you have always survived it. If other people can get over it, so can you. So start to look forward to the day when you finally conquer it, just like they did.

As you can see from the graph below, your anxiety level may rise very high but in time it will always come down again. The human body is not capable of maintaining very high levels of anxiety for very long periods of time. If you suffer from Generalized Anxiety Disorder (GAD), where you feel anxious all the time, as well as having fluctuating anxiety levels in certain circumstances, the high level of anxiety may only come down to its usual level, as shown by the dotted line in the diagram. Your GAD obviously needs to be addressed too. All the stress and anxiety coping strategies described in this book are designed to remove all levels of anxiety.

Anxiety Reduces with Time

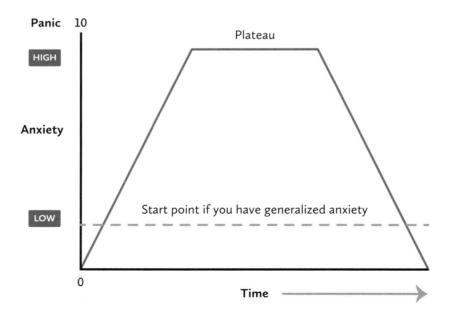

Remember that the thing you are afraid of is not always the cause of your anxiety. It is more likely to be your own thoughts and beliefs (cognitions) that cause you to be anxious. Of course sometimes a threat could be real (such as someone attacking or threatening to attack you), but more often than not it is an irrational thought or belief. For example, the majority of people do not find travelling on a bus frightening. If you are afraid to get on a bus it is because of your fear of fear, or fear of having a panic attack. Attending a social function, going out on your own, being in enclosed or open spaces, travelling in an aeroplane etc. are all things that most people do without feeling afraid. Your fear may be based on something that happened or something that you were told a long time ago and which is not relevant or appropriate today. Many people love to experience the very things that cause you to feel afraid. The realization of this is the first step to recovery. Try to think of this in a positive way. Have a think about why the majority of people don't consider these things to be frightening. Think about why they don't have panic attacks. What is different about them? How do they cope under stress? Try to observe other people in the situations that cause you to feel threatened. How do they act, or react? How do they walk? Look at their posture. Be mindful of how they talk. What is it about their personality that differs from yours?

The point is that although we are all different, with different backgrounds, different values, beliefs and opinions, we can all learn from one another. It is possible therefore to pick out certain qualities or strengths that you admire in others and make a conscious decision to adopt them for yourself.

Week 6, Day 7
» MEDITATION «
A Powerful Encounter

Sit or lie comfortably, close your eyes and take three slow deep abdominal breaths. Allow your body to relax completely. Allow it to sink down and let go of all the tensions of the day. With each breath you breathe out, allow yourself to become more and more relaxed and come into the present moment, harmonizing mind and body.

When you are ready, visualize yourself at the top of a flight of ten steps. Now slowly start to count down from 10 to zero as you descend down the steps, and with each slow count allow yourself to sink deeper, and deeper still, into a perfect state of relaxation. When you reach zero you find yourself at the bottom of the steps and in a beautiful garden on a lovely summer's day with a clear blue sky and a beautiful bright golden sun. The sun is warm on your face and the soft gentle breeze refreshes you as you walk along a path bordered by beautiful and fragrant flowers. You can smell their perfume. The only sound you can hear is the melody of sweet birdsong. You can feel the ground beneath your feet with each step you take. You can taste the salty sea air drifting up from the secluded and beautiful beach at the bottom of the garden. The garden is yours, and you can have anything you want to have in it. The trees and shrubs and flowerbeds are of your making, as is the house you are now walking towards. Everything belongs to you. It is part of you and your imagination. You can create and change anything you wish, whenever you choose to visit. You can even bring it to your mind whenever you want to feel calm and peaceful or safe and happy. Your visits can last for however long you want, and can be for whatever reason you need. This place is your sanctuary. It is a place where everything is positive, perfect and peaceful.

You now approach an open door that leads into a large and beautiful garden room. The décor and furniture is of your creation. It is just as you would want it to be. There is a table in the room with people seated round it. They are your personal assistants, advisors, confidants, mentors and guides. They can be anybody you want them to be – perhaps people who have been an inspiration to you at some time in your life: a best friend, a member of your family who you look up to, a famous person from history or literature who you have admired, or anyone you think may be able to help or counsel and guide you. Now take a seat at the head of the table.

You may now ask a question to each of the people present. You can ask for advice or guidance, or an answer to an issue you are dealing with at this moment in time. When you have posed your question listen to each of them in turn.

Once they have each given their advice or guidance, thank each one of them and show your gratitude. One of the group now tells you that you can return at any time and that they are always there for you.

Now walk slowly through the door to the garden and along the path to where you began your walk. Once again, feel the sun and the warm breeze on your face. Smell the scent of the flowers and the fresh sea air. Hear the sound of the birds singing and feel the ground beneath your feet.

You now reach the bottom of the ten steps you came down earlier. Begin to climb slowly up the steps and, with each slow and deliberate step you take upwards, count the steps from zero to 10, each step bringing you slowly out of your deep relaxation, each count bringing you back to reality, becoming more and more aware and alert and taking you further and further back to your room. When you reach the tenth step you find yourself back in the present moment, back in reality. Fully back in your room now, take a deep breath and allow your awareness to return.

When you are ready, open your eyes and allow your breathing to return to its normal rate and flow. Get up only when you feel fully alert and ready to continue with your day. You may want to make some notes about your meditation and all the advice you received.

NOTE: This meditation is extremely useful and very powerful if you have something on your mind or if you are seeking a solution to a problem. Whenever you feel anxious, worried or stressed about something, you can choose to just slip into part of the meditation to ask for guidance. You can change the people present in your room whenever you want. You may just invite one person to the table, or an expert in the field that is causing you the problem.

It goes without saying that the answers you receive are coming from yourself, your higher self, your subconscious, but the answers or messages you get are valid and true. Trust in your intuition, your insight and your true, inner self. All your answers lie within.

Week 6

» RECAP AND REFLECT «

Tick the box when understood, practised and achieved

 WHAT IS ANXIETY?: Are you now aware of what anxiety is and how it affects you? Did you recognize your symptoms from the long list? Do you now realize that anxiety is normal and does not harm you?

 UNDERSTANDING ANXIETY: Why do you become anxious? What are your symptoms and effects, and what maintains your anxiety? Do you have any beliefs that you can challenge, or behaviours you can change?

 ACTIVITY ACTIVITY ACTIVITY: What activities have you taken up since reading this page? How do you think they will help?

 TAKE A BREAK AND BALANCE YOUR STRESS: Did you take a break? What was the effect? Are you committed to keeping this up? Do you realize the importance of having breaks?

 THE GRADUAL EXPOSURE SYSTEM: If this applies to you, have you thought about how this method could help to enhance the quality of your life? Are you able to make a plan yourself or will you need help? Who can help and support you in achieving your goals? Don't put this off; try to start your plan as soon as possible.

 BE MINDFUL OF YOUR ANXIETY: Have you tried this technique? How did you find it? How does it help?

 A POWERFUL ENCOUNTER: Did you like this? Were you able to visualize and follow the instructions? How did it help?

Now turn to your self-assessment rating scales and enter your scores for the end of Week 6.

Halfway There

Remember Reflect Review

TICK THE BOXES if you are following the advice or using the exercises. Put a cross if you are not. Then identify which items you are not using that you need to be using. Reflect on why you aren't using them. If you then feel it is necessary to add them to your practice or routine, make a note in your workbook, make a commitment and a plan to add them when the time is right for you.

- ☐ Taking one day at a time and living in the moment
- ☐ Practising all the breathing exercises at least once a day
- ☐ Applying the breathing exercises whenever you feel stressed or anxious
- ☐ Accepting those things which are out of your control and cannot change
- ☐ Thinking positively
- ☐ Practising a method of relaxation at least four times a week
- ☐ Practising meditation every day if possible
- ☐ Exercising at least four times a week for twenty minutes or longer
- ☐ Making lists and doing one thing at a time in order of priority
- ☐ Eliminating worry or striving not to worry so much
- ☐ Remembering and feeling proud of all the things you have achieved
- ☐ Remembering and realizing that your thoughts affect your feelings
- ☐ Using the STOP Technique when you have a negative thought or feeling

- [ ] Understanding the fight/flight response and the associated effects

- [ ] Slowing down when or if you recognize the need

- [ ] Being kind and compassionate towards yourself

- [ ] Asking yourself *"Does it really matter?"*

- [ ] Recognizing when you are making thinking errors and stopping them

- [ ] Talking to someone you trust about your problems

- [ ] Understanding what anxiety really is and applying your coping strategies

- [ ] Taking regular breaks and recognizing when you need to

- [ ] Being mindful of your anxiety

- [ ] Re-evaluating your goals

- [ ] Scoring your ability to cope and level of stress at the end of each week

Week 7

· · · · · · · · ·

Week 7, Day 1
» *PHILOSOPHY* «

There's No Such Thing as a Mistake

"The successful man will profit from his mistakes
and try again in a different way."
— DALE CARNEGIE, *writer and lecturer*

I KNOW IT SOUNDS RIDICULOUS to say there is no such thing as a mistake. You are probably already thinking that I've lost the plot because I don't know you, nor that you've made plenty mistakes in your life, and so has everybody else. Well, I'm just being philosophical: I remember learning this many years ago and thinking that this would really help me, not only to let go of the past, but also to learn that there is always more than one way of looking at things. It really did help me to understand how and why we do certain things in our life that we later regret. I have passed this philosophy on to many of my clients when they felt in the depths of despair because of something they had done or not done. It helped them to let go of some of the misery and anguish that caused a lot of their stress and played a big part in many other areas of their lives.

Read the advice below and take it to heart. Let it sink in. Mull it over in your mind. Contemplate the wisdom of it. Consider the outcome if you are able to apply it to your own life. It makes a lot of sense and it will help you to move on, cast off any annoying, exasperating regrets and bring you a little closer to the elusive peace of mind you so fervently seek.

If you are constantly dwelling on the past and wishing you'd done things differently, just think how negative that is and what those negative thoughts will be doing to you, or have already done to you. Remember: *"As you think, so you become."*

Think about this instead: If you could go back into the past, with the knowledge you have now, with the feelings you have now, with the skills and abilities you have acquired and with the circumstances you find yourself in now, then of course you might make different choices, do things differently and go about things in an entirely different way. However, at the time of making what you now believe was a *mistake* your circumstances were very different to what they are now. You did not have the benefit of hindsight, and your situation was very unlike your present situation. When you made that *mistake* you made it based on the facts you had at that time and how you felt at that time. You acted or reacted with none of the knowledge and wisdom you have today. You responded to the reality of that moment in time, not today's reality. You certainly did not wake up that morning and decide that you were going to make a mistake that day, a mistake that you would regret for the rest of your life!

Another consideration is that people will always try to do their best. No one deliberately chooses not to do their best. No one makes a mess of their lives on purpose. No one ever sets out to make a blunder that will affect their life in a negative or destructive way.

When choosing to do something, we don't automatically think how we will feel about our actions and decisions in ten or twenty years' time, or the next day or even the next minute. We probably often don't even think at all before we act. How many times have you said to yourself, "Oh, I wish I hadn't done that or said that!"? We often have such thoughts after having said or done something we then regret. So as time passes and much water flows under the bridge, it stands to reason that we may have regrets, because we have learned so much more and we can now perceive our actions from a totally different and new perspective.

If you can recall the reasons why you made that so-called *mistake* and what circumstances led up to it, it may help you to see it from a philosophical perspective. Many people believe that everything is meant to be and that all experiences are worth having, good or bad. We can rejoice in the good experiences and learn from the bad ones. The fact is that we *can learn something from our mistakes*, even if it's simply not to make the same mistake again! We can certainly learn to do things in a different way and recognize that there are different ways of doing things. We can observe how others go about their lives. We can realize that we have choices; that we can change the way we think and feel and behave. We can even learn to stop and think before we act. We can learn to relax, put things into perspective and let go of the past.

Some people believe that our lives are predestined and that fate rules our lives, in which case they believe that we were meant to make that *mistake* in order to fulfil our destiny.

Another school of thought is that we can grow stronger with adversity. I am a great believer in this opinion. I'm sure that once you have got your life back on track and you are coping well, you too will adopt this belief. If we can learn from our so-called mistakes, surely that has to be a useful lesson that we would not have learned if we had not had that experience in the first place!

Again, a reminder that we need to keep focused on the present and not dwell on the past. This is true even if you are now able to adopt a more realistic belief about your mistakes. Always keep focused on the present and don't forget the STOP Technique if you find yourself dwelling on your past mistakes again.

Now recall an experience that you once referred to as a mistake and reframe it – in other words, think about it in a different way. Focus on what you really did learn and how you can use that information, now and in the future.

Finally, remember that it may even be possible to be grateful for the mistake you made! You may even be glad you made it because of the circumstances it eventually led you to. We often find that something good comes out of something bad. For example: I sometimes think that if I hadn't made certain mistakes and lived through some adversity, I would not be doing what I'm doing now, and therefore I wouldn't have written this book. And you wouldn't be reading it! It's amazing how life can pan out due to one particular event opening new doors and presenting new opportunities. Start to think that good things *can* happen in the future, that you can turn things around, despite all the wrong turns you've previously made in your life.

Week 7, Day 2
» *PRANAYAMA* «
Alternate-Nostril Exercise

This exercise is also known as the Tranquillizer. Many different forms of yoga use this technique to calm the mind and induce a feeling of peace and stillness. The exercise is also helpful for overcoming phobias and relieving sinusitis, asthma and bronchitis.

It involves breathing through one nostril at a time, as slowly and as deeply as possible. As always, use abdominal breathing.

When you try this breathing exercise for the first time, you may want to disregard the hand position described below and just use your thumb and first finger to close the nostrils. Press lightly but just enough to stop the flow of air.

Place the tips of the first and middle fingers of your right hand together on your forehead. As you work your way through the exercise use your ring finger to close your left nostril and your thumb to close the right nostril. Before you begin, breathe out normally.

Now close the left nostril and breathe in as slowly and as comfortably as you can through the right nostril. When your lungs are full, close the right nostril and hold for a moment.

Release the left nostril and breathe all the way out just as slowly.

Leaving your right nostril closed, breathe all the way in through the left and hold for a moment.

Close the left, release the right and breathe out through the right.

This completes the cycle. Repeat two or three or more times if you wish; there is no limit.

If you have any difficulty following the instructions above just remember: all you are doing is breathing in through one nostril and out through the other.

As you will feel very calm after carrying out this exercise, be careful to stand up slowly when you are ready to do so. If you feel a little light-headed, it is simply because you have been taking in more oxygen than you are used to. Just sit down for a little longer until you feel all right again.

Add this exercise on to the sequence you have previously learned.

Week 7, Day 3
» *DIRECTION* «
Relax Your Face

If you suddenly become aware that you are very tense, wearing a frown or clenching your teeth, but you haven't enough time to do a full relaxation session, try the following quick and easy method. It only takes a few minutes but it does make a difference. You can do this quick relaxation at any time as long as it is safe to do so: for example waiting in a queue, before an interview, or even, if you are stationary, while you are stuck in a traffic jam.

- Begin by taking three slow deep abdominal breaths in and out through the nose.
- With each breath you breathe out, allow yourself to relax.
- Allow a feeling of relaxation to come over you – give yourself permission to relax.
- Now slowly lower your head, allowing your chin to come down towards your chest.
- Take a few more seconds to let your head drop more... and more... and even more.

- Now let your face become soft, and feel gravity pulling the muscles in your face downwards.
- Be aware of your cheeks loosening and sinking downwards.
- Let your mouth fall open naturally and let your lips feel as if they are becoming bigger as they loosen and begin to droop. Loosen your jaw and let it drop down as far as possible. Let it get more and more relaxed.
- Allow your eyes to close gently and allow your eyelids to fall into their most comfortable position – either open or closed, whichever way feels more relaxed.
- Let them relax more... and more... and even more.... With each breath that you breathe out, allow your eyes to become softer and softer.
- Now allow your forehead to become wider and deeper. Feel it softening and smoothing, becoming softer and softer, smooth and relaxed.
- Let your whole face feel soft and loose and very relaxed, dropping and drooping down . . . and down . . . towards your feet.
- Let your shoulders drop and your arms feel heavy and loose and floppy.
- Let your hands and fingers go loose and soft and floppy.
- Finally allow a feeling of peace and relaxation to spread through your whole body. Remain like this as long as you wish or for as long as you are able. Know what it feels like, remember what it feels like, so you can return to this feeling whenever you need to, whenever you choose to.
- When you are ready to return to what you were doing, raise your head very, very slowly until it sits comfortably on the top of your spine and open your eyes very slowly.
- Try to keep this feeling with you for as long as possible. Be aware if your jaw begins to tighten again or your forehead returns to a frown. Replace it with the softness just by thinking about it.

When you have used this relaxation several times it will become very much easier to do. You will be able to accomplish the soft-face feeling more quickly, and sometimes at will. Just think "*soft*".

It is worth remembering that as your mind affects your body, so too does your body affect your mind. So when you relax your facial muscles it will have a direct and beneficial effect on your mental and emotional well-being too.

Week 7, Day 4

» *SELF-ESTEEM* «

The Confidence Trick

"With confidence, you have won before you have started."
— *MARCUS GARVEY, journalist and publisher*

Our self-esteem often takes a knock when we find ourselves losing or lacking confidence. We sometimes envy those around us who are full of confidence, and find ourselves wishing we could be more like them. For some, it could also be a matter of wishing we were how we used to be. But anxiety and depression can easily and very quickly strip us of confidence and self-esteem. Of course, when we lose confidence our anxiety rises even higher, especially when confronted with something that we are expected to do but don't particularly want to. Speaking in public, attending a social function or even just going shopping are typical examples for those who endure the symptoms and effects of anxiety.

Unfortunately, the longer we stay anxious, the more our confidence and self-esteem plummet. It is possible to reach a point where our intrusive and automatic negative thoughts and beliefs convey to us that we're just not good enough, that we can't do things that others do easily, or that we are a complete failure. This in turn leads to hopelessness and helplessness, which causes us to focus even more on the negatives. We easily forget or dismiss the fact that we do still have strengths, skills and abilities; at this moment in time we are just not able to apply them. In essence, we become trapped in a vicious circle of anxiety, lack of confidence, low self-esteem and helplessness. The helplessness leads to further anxiety; and round and round you go until you are able to summon up some courage and fortitude from somewhere and change something into a positive. Of course, it isn't always easy to revive your strengths, but if you have been following the advice in this book you should, by now, be well on your way and in a good place to start making those necessary changes.

Below is an exercise to help increase your confidence and raise your self-esteem. With practice, not only will you be able to master it, but also apply it often and in lots of different circumstances:

Try to remember a time when you *were* confident, a time when you felt good about yourself, happy and proud to have achieved something, or perhaps a time when you were applauded, praised or complimented for doing such a great job. Remember a time before you became stressed and anxious or depressed. It doesn't matter how far back you need to go. It could even be a memory from your childhood. It could be as simple as winning a race and feeling very proud of yourself; or a time when you achieved something you had never thought possible. If you can't recall such an occasion, use your imagination and make one up! The exercise will still work. It can be anything you want it to be. The exercise is best done standing up, if possible.

Stand very tall and stretch your spine. Stand with your feet shoulder width apart and firmly planted on the floor. Stand with your head held high, shoulders back, chin up with a confident look on your face (you can just pretend). This is the *confidence stance*, which you will use at times in the future when you need to feel confident and strong. Changing your posture changes the way you feel.

Close your eyes, take three slow deep abdominal breaths and mentally *be there* at the time you remember being confident. Be there when you were stress-free, confident and felt happy with yourself. Try, if you can, to mentally step inside yourself, become the person you were at that time and in that place, *feeling* what you felt then.

Try to remember everything you can about the situation you were in. How were you standing or sitting? Where were you at the time? Have a good look around, seeing everything and everyone else that was there with you.

Remember, you are not watching yourself there, you are *seeing* and *hearing* and *feeling* everything from the perspective of yourself *as you were then*. You have become that you from your past.

What were you saying and what did you sound like? How were you saying it? What tone of voice were you using? Who was listening or watching? How did they respond? What were they doing or thinking?

Now take a deep breath and breathe in the confidence you felt at that time, seeing what you saw, hearing what you heard and feeling what you felt.

Continue breathing in the confidence. Breathe it all the way into your *very being*, your heart and soul. Feel that confidence inside you now, and give the confidence a colour.

Focus your mind on the colour now. Feel it flowing now all the way through your body; up to the top of your head; down into your hands and fingertips; down through your legs and into the tips of your toes. Your confidence colour now becomes brighter... and brighter still... and yet still brighter, and more vivid. Your whole body shines with confidence. Your mind now becomes infused with confidence. You can feel it circulating through your mind. Your whole being is now one of power and strength and super-confidence. Now imagine your aura shining bright as it encompasses you in self-assurance, self-belief and fortitude. Feel yourself enveloped in strength and love and power. Visualize the beautiful bright shining colour of power and strength all around you, above you and below you, flowing all the way through you.

When the new feeling is at its maximum and the colour at its brightest, feel that confidence colour settling into one specific point in your body.

When you have done this, place your hand there so that the confidence now flows directly into your hand. Feel and imagine the colour in the palm of your hand.

What does it feel like? What temperature is it? What is the texture? Remember these imaginings because you are going to use them again in the future.

Your hand is still connecting with your body and the colour of confidence is still flowing into it.

Remain in this position for a few moments while saying *"I am strong and confident now. Confidence fills my whole being."* Repeat this *positive affirmation* several times and when you feel satisfied that you have done enough, let it all fade away slowly and come back into the present moment, returning to the here and now.

After a few minutes, go through the whole exercise again. Practise it several times until you feel that you can do it more quickly and more effectively. Practise it again every day and notice how it affects you. You can make any changes you feel you need to, or you may wish to add something to enhance the exercise or make it feel more comfortable for you, or more personal to you.

When you feel you are accomplished in the exercise, the next part involves you adopting the confidence stance and simply placing your hand on that part of your body where you lodged the confidence colour. Feel the colour and the confidence flowing from your hand into your body, into your mind. Bring back all the feelings and senses you have been practising, take a deep breath and allow the colour to spread through your whole body. This will anchor the confidence in you so that whenever you are in a situation where you need to be confident, by placing your hand on that special point of confidence, breathing deeply and mentally repeating your affirmation, you will have all the confidence you will need.

In a life coaching session some years ago, my client told me that she was very nervous about an interview she was attending the following week. I suggested that we rehearse the interview, with me being the interviewer. I asked her to stand outside the room and when she was ready, she was to knock on the door and then enter the room. She agreed but told me that it would be a waste of time because she wouldn't get the job. I certainly had my work cut out! The rehearsal went something like this:

A quiet little knock on the door. I asked her to come in. She came in looking like a timid little child with her head held down, her shoulders hunched up and a terrified look on her face. I stood and reached out to shake her hand.

Her handshake was extremely limp but she did introduce herself, albeit very quietly. We both sat down. She sat with her feet tucked underneath the chair, looked down at her white-knuckled hands clenched together and looked up at me through a furrowed brow.

I'm afraid that's as far as we got before I could not let it go any further. I demonstrated to her exactly what had just taken place, using her mannerisms and her body language. I asked her if she thought I would get the job if it were me being interviewed, based on how I looked, even before any questions had been asked. She said no, I wouldn't because I didn't look as though I was confident enough, or had any ability to do the job.

I then became the interviewee and she took my place as the interviewer. I stepped out of the room, took a deep breath, put a confident smile on my face and knocked firmly on the door. I adopted the confidence stance, looked her straight in the eye with a smile, shook her hand firmly and introduced myself with an assured tone to my voice. I then asked her if I had the job and she replied "Yes, certainly, I wouldn't have needed to ask you any questions!"

I spent some time teaching her the exercise as outlined above. She practised it several times and then we went through the practice interview again. The exercise worked well for her, and it made such a difference she was like a different person. Needless to say, I definitely would have given her the job!

Week 7, Day 5
» *CORRECT THINKING* «

Take Charge of Your Thoughts

"Keep your face to the sunshine and you cannot see a shadow."
— *HELEN KELLER, author*

Do you ever stop to think about what you're thinking about? You may be surprised at what you find! It is estimated that we have between 50,000 and 70,000 thoughts every day – and that if you are depressed 70 per cent of those thoughts could be negative!

Just think how anxious you are going to feel if you are having all those negative thoughts each and every day.

- Are you allowing your negative thoughts to control your life?
- Is this what you really want for yourself?
- How long are you willing to continue to allow your anxiety and negativity to rule your life?
- Surely there is a better way, a healthier way.
- Surely your life is worth finding a way to help you *Get Your Life Back*.

Well, I'm here to tell you that there is a better way. There is a much better way! There is a way you can live your life to the full without anxiety and depression controlling it. You have already made a good start; if you have been following the book over the past six weeks you have already come a long way. Today's exercise will set you on your next step to a new life – a better life.

From now on you will try your best to become more aware of what you are thinking about or focusing on. Just stop occasionally and think:

- Am I being negative?
- What harm is this thought doing?
- How does this thought make me feel?
- Do I feel anxious because of this thought?
- Am I behaving in a negative way because of this negative thought?
- How long have I been having this negative thought?
- Is this negative thought always true?
- Is this thought appropriate or relevant for me in my present circumstances?
- Do I need to stop having this thought now?
- Which thought could I choose to have instead?
- Is this new thought more positive?
- How am I likely to feel and act if I adopt this new positive thought?
- How do I feel now?
- How will my life improve by having this new positive thought?

Do not let your anxiety control you and your life. Ask yourself:

> - How long have I allowed my anxiety to control my life?
> - Is it time now for me to control my anxiety?
> - Am I still willing to allow my anxiety to control my life?
> - How important is it to me to stop the negative thoughts and start to control my anxiety by having positive thoughts?
> - How would I be different?
> - How much would my life change?
> - When am I going to start? (If you haven't started already!)

If your anxiety levels are very high, your anxiety will increase if you fail to stop it. You need to be proactive in managing your anxiety – no one else can do it for you. No one else can get inside your head and brush away the negative thoughts and beliefs. However, *you can take control now* instead of allowing your thought processes to control you. So take charge *now* by monitoring, catching and changing the thoughts that are causing your anxiety and controlling your life!

You could start with one particular area. For example, you could simply decide that for today you are going to try only to have positive thoughts about yourself, or perhaps another person, the television, the garden or anything that causes your negative thinking.

If you suddenly catch yourself being negative:

> - Just say "Stop" to yourself, take a deep breath and change the thought to a positive or at least a more realistic one.
> - Reassure yourself that you are now calm and in control.
> - Remind yourself that you have your breathing exercises and other coping strategies to help you.

REMEMBER: Your mind is your own. They are *your* thoughts. Take charge!

Week 7, Day 6

» *DIRECTION* «

The Wheel of Life

I was first introduced to the *Wheel of Life* in 1997 by Jack Black, who was then one of the UK's top motivational speakers. I attended his outstanding two-day course in London, and it changed my life. Not simply because it helped me a great deal, but because I have passed on his teachings to the great majority of my patients and clients. Without exception, they would say how helpful the *Wheel of Life* was to them. The *Wheel of Life* is used not only in mental health services but in life coaching, stress management, personal development, learning, employment, business and management establishments throughout the world. I hope you find it helpful too.

The *Wheel of Life* helps you to compartmentalize key areas of your life to help you identify exactly where you are struggling, and where you need to focus your energy and set goals in order to create a balanced life.

It is a useful tool for everyone, not just for those with a stressful life. Here are just some of the many ways it can help:

- It helps you to identify how you are journeying along life's path.
- It improves your awareness of your life with all its many different aspects.
- It points out how your life can change from week to week.
- It identifies how well you are coping with life's twists and turns.
- It identifies areas in your life that you need to improve in order to create balance and harmony.
- It identifies the positive areas in your life where things are going well and no changes or improvements are necessary; it helps you realize that life isn't all that bad.
- It assists you in achieving your goals and aspirations and the life you want for yourself.
- It helps you to *Get Your Life Back*.

The *Wheel of Life* is divided into key areas, or departments. You give each department a score from zero to 10, based on their condition, your attitude towards them and how you feel about them.

The wheel shown below is a perfectly rounded and perfectly balanced wheel with a score of 10 in every department. This is not a very realistic wheel and I would not expect to find anyone with such a perfect life! However, many will come close and this exercise will assist you in your endeavours as you work to make your life healthier and happier and come closer to finding that elusive peace of mind and serenity.

The Wheel of Life

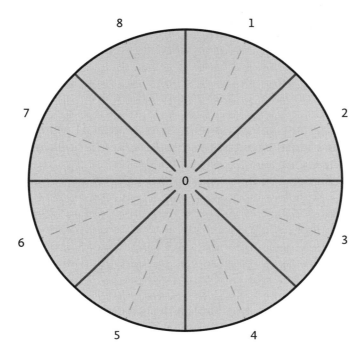

To create your *Wheel of Life* you first divide it up into the eight key areas, or departments. You can choose different departments from the ones given below if you wish.

Your Life Departments

Department	Score	Department	Score
1. Mental Health		5. Home Environment	
2. Physical Health		6. Finances	
3. Attitude of Mind		7. Family Life/Relationships	
4. Work/Career		8. Social Life/Interests/Hobbies	

Then give yourself a score in each department on the rating scale below of 0 to 10 where 0 = the worst it can be and 10 = the best it can be – everything is as it should be.

Your Department Scores

Worst Case				Average					Best Case
1	2	3	4	5	6	7	8	9	10

Once you have entered your scores, place them on the dotted line in the wheel that corresponds to that department by putting a cross there. Zero is in the middle of the wheel and 10 on the circumference (outside edge).

If for example you score a 4 in *Physical Health*, count the divisions from the centre start of the line (0) (marked 2 for physical health) and mark an X at that point as demonstrated below:

Enter your scores as below on the dotted lines in the wheel.

$$0 - - - X - - - - - - 10$$

Once you have marked all your crosses for all the departments, join up the Xs. You may end up with a wheel looking something like the one below:

Example Wheel of Life

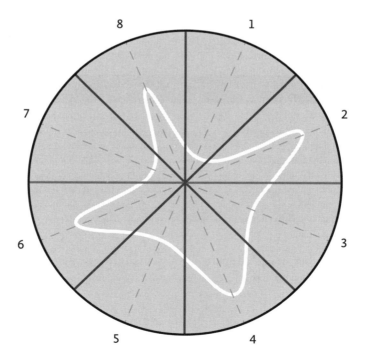

Remember not to be too negative in your thinking when you are assessing your scores. I have met people who say they are zero in every department, but on questioning and helping to increase their awareness, they are usually able to agree that there is in fact something good and positive going on in their lives. They just may not be able to recognize the positives because of their negatively focused thinking. If you have a roof over your head, food on the table and someone to share it with, and you have most of your faculties, you won't need to score yourself a zero. Similarly, it would be very rare for someone to score 10 in all the departments. You also need to take into account that there are going to be daily fluctuations. We all have our good days and bad days. If this is the case, just take an average score. It does not need to be exact. It is just meant to be a guide.

If you aim, in the near future, to reach a score for example of 7 or 8 in each department, the shape of your wheel will look good and balanced in all departments. It is unrealistic to aspire to a score of 10 in all your departments of life, but it is always possible to achieve 10 in some of them.

Now enter your scores in the boxes on the chart on the following page. State the score you are today and your desired score in the future. You may want to create your own diagrams in your workbook.

Next, write your short- and long-term goals for each department. You may need some thinking time for this. If so, complete it on another day after you have slept on it. You can also put a target date by which you want to achieve each of your goals.

Your short-term goals should have a target completion date of between two weeks and two months (whatever suits you and your individual circumstances). Your long-term goals can have a date of up to two years, or even longer in some cases. For example, if your long-term goal is to become a director of the firm you are working for, this may take you a number of years to achieve. However, if your long-term goal is to achieve manager status, your target date will be sooner.

Once you move up to the next score point as a result of achieving your first goal (for example from a score of 4 to a score of 5), you will need to update your short-term goals in order for you to continue achieving and working towards your final destination, or achieving your long-term goal.

Read your goals on a daily basis and reassess them every two weeks. It is also a good idea to draw a new Wheel of Life every month. This will help you to see the improvements you have made and encourage you to continue on your new and positive journey.

Copy the Wheel of Life and the goal-setting chart, or create your own. You can find templates on the Internet if that is easier for you. Having your own copies will also make it easier for you to make any necessary changes.

Ideally your scores need to increase on a regular basis until you reach your target scores. However, it is possible that one of your departments will leap forward at a faster rate and may even reach your desired final score much sooner than you anticipated. It very much depends on the effectiveness of your goal. For example: if you score 3 in your work/career department, your short-term goal is to apply for the perfect job you have been seeking for a long time, and you subsequently get that job, your desired future score of 8 may well be achieved in just one big leap.

Life can be unpredictable, and often out of your direct control. You may be able to make improvements and positive changes to your life but you can't always change what happens in your life. For instance, if you become unwell and your progress is halted for a while, your score may reduce in one or more departments. Don't worry about this; it simply means that you are human. Life can be challenging and sometimes has a way of throwing up the unexpected. You need to accept, with strength and serenity, whatever life throws at you because the alternative is stress, imbalance and disharmony. If something is out of your control there is no sense in agonizing over it. Simply alter your scores, reassess, keep calm and carry on. The secret is to persevere. Keep going, keep achieving, and before long you will be back on track.

Goal-setting Table

Department	Short-Term Goal	Long-Term Goal
1. Mental Health Score: Future Score:	Target Date:	Target Date:
2. Physical Health Score: Future Score:	Target Date:	Target Date:
3. Attitude of Mind Score: Future Score:	Target Date:	Target Date:
4. Work/Career Score: Future Score:	Target Date:	Target Date:

5. **Home Environment** Score: Future Score:	Target Date:	Target Date:
6. **Finances** Score: Future Score:	Target Date:	Target Date:
7. **Family Life/ Relationships** Score: Future Score:	Target Date:	Target Date:
8. **Social Life/ Interests/ Hobbies** Score: Future Score:	Target Date:	Target Date:

Week 7, Day 7

» *RELAXATION* «

Soft Muscle Relaxation

This form of relaxation involves simply communicating silently with your muscles! When you are mentally and emotionally tense and stressed your muscles automatically pick up the message in your nervous system, and they too become tense. As you have learned earlier in the book, the mind and body work together. They are not separate. Whatever goes on in the mind manifests itself somewhere in the body.

The progressive muscle relaxation exercise in Week 5, Day 7 is extremely beneficial for muscle relaxation, but not everyone is comfortable with deliberately tightening their muscles. This soft muscle relaxation exercise, however, simply requires you to take your attention to your muscles and mentally give them an instruction and permission to relax.

159

If you have someone to read this out for you, ask them to read one line or section at a time and then pause, giving you enough time to repeat the instructions silently to yourself. If not, read the script several times until you have a full understanding of it and are able to remember the words. They don't have to be the exact words and it doesn't need to be word-perfect; feel free to change any of the words to suit your own individual preference.

If you are able to record the script remember to leave enough time for you to repeat the instructions to yourself. As with all the relaxation exercises, lie down in your usual place where and when you will not be disturbed.

Always begin by taking three deep abdominal breaths. Take your awareness to each part of your body as outlined below and say the suggested, or similar, words silently to yourself. You may repeat them as often as you choose.

My right foot is relaxing now. My right foot is soft and warm and loose and relaxed. My right leg is relaxing now. My right leg is soft and warm and loose and relaxed.

My left foot is relaxing now. My left foot is soft and warm and loose and relaxed. My left leg is relaxing now. My left leg is soft and warm and loose and relaxed. Both my legs are relaxing now. My legs are feeling soft and warm and loose and heavy now. My legs are now completely soft and relaxed, warm and heavy.

My back is relaxing now. The whole of my back is sinking into the floor and feeling soft and relaxed. The muscles in my back are spreading out against the floor and feeling warm and soft and relaxed now. I now let go of all of the tension in my back. My back is becoming more and more soft and relaxed. Soft and warm and relaxed.

My abdomen is relaxing now. My tummy rises and falls gently with each easy breath I take. My abdomen is soft and warm and loose and relaxed now. My abdomen is becoming more and more relaxed now. More and more soft and relaxed.

My breathing is easy now and my chest is soft and warm and relaxed. I allow myself now to sink deeper and deeper into relaxation with each breath I breathe out.

My right hand is relaxing now, and my fingers are becoming soft and loose and floppy and relaxed. My right hand is soft and warm and relaxed now. More and more relaxed. My right arm is relaxing now. My right arm is feeling soft and heavy and warm and relaxed.

My left hand is relaxing now. My fingers are loose and soft and floppy and relaxed now. My left hand is soft and warm and relaxed. More and more relaxed now.My left arm is relaxing now. My left arm is feeling soft and heavy and warm and relaxed. Both my arms are loose and soft and heavy and relaxed now. More and more relaxed.

My right shoulder is softening and relaxing now. My right shoulder is dropping downwards and I allow it to relax completely now. Completely soft and relaxed. My right shoulder is soft, warm and loose, and more and more relaxed now. My left shoulder is softening and relaxing now.

My left shoulder is dropping downwards now and I allow it to relax completely. Completely soft and relaxed. My left shoulder is soft, warm and loose, and more and more relaxed now.

My neck is relaxing now. My neck is feeling soft and warm and loose and relaxed. My neck is becoming softer and softer, more and more relaxed. More and more soft and relaxed now. My head is relaxing now. My head is completely supported and becoming more and more relaxed. Heavy and supported. More and more soft and relaxed. My scalp is relaxing now. I can feel my scalp becoming soft and loose and spreading out and more and more relaxed now. My scalp is completely relaxed. My forehead is relaxing now. My forehead is becoming wider and deeper, softer and smoother. My forehead relaxes more and more, and yet still more.

My eyes are relaxing now. My eyes are soft and comfortable and becoming more and more relaxed now. More and more relaxed. I allow my eyes to become completely relaxed now. My jaw is relaxing now. My jaw is becoming loose and soft and dropping downwards. My jaw is loosening more and more, more and more loose and relaxed now. My mouth is relaxing now and becoming more and more soft and loose and very relaxed. My tongue lies shapelessly on the bottom of my mouth, relaxing more and more.

My whole body is relaxed now. My whole body is soft and warm, and sinking into the floor. Completely supported and relaxed now. Completely soft, warm and relaxed. My whole body is now relaxed. Every part of my body is relaxed now. Every organ and gland, every muscle and bone is completely relaxed. My blood flows freely and effortlessly through my whole body. My mind is still and I allow myself to sink deeper and deeper, more and more deeply relaxed now.

Stay as you are for as long as you are able. Allow your body to feel as if it is floating. You may lose sensation in your arms and legs and perhaps even the whole of your body. This is completely natural. Enjoy the sensation of feeling weightless. Enjoy the way your mind drifts off. Simply let it come and go as it pleases. Remember this feeling and keep it with you for as long as you can.

When you are finally ready, open your eyes slowly and allow your attention to return to your body and the here and now, back into the present moment. Get up very slowly but only when you are alert and feeling refreshed.

Week 7
» RECAP AND REFLECT «

Tick the box when understood, practised and achieved

DAY 1

THERE'S NO SUCH THING AS A MISTAKE: Are you able to accept the philosophy of there being no such thing as a mistake? How does this help you?

DAY 2

ALTERNATE-NOSTRIL EXERCISE: Have you mastered this yet? Are you practising enough? Is it making you feel more relaxed? Don't forget to add this on to the sequence of exercises you've already learned. Think of a time when it could be useful to you.

DAY 3

RELAX YOUR FACE: Are you able to do this easily now? Are you practising enough? Are you able to do this at will when needed?

DAY 4

THE CONFIDENCE TRICK: Have you practised this exercise enough? Can you feel it working? In what way has it been effective for you? Have you applied the exercise when you feel that your confidence or self-esteem is low? If so, how did it help?

DAY 5

TAKE CHARGE OF YOUR THOUGHTS: Are you managing to be more aware of your negative thoughts? Are you going through the process of questioning yourself? Have you realized that you can take charge of your thinking? How easy is it to stop and change your negative thoughts? Are you committed to this now?

DAY 6

THE WHEEL OF LIFE: What are your thoughts regarding this exercise? Were you surprised when you saw the shape of your wheel? How will this help you? Do you understand that if you set and achieve goals on a regular basis your health and the quality of your life will improve?

DAY 7

SOFT MUSCLE RELAXATION: How does this relaxation method differ from the others you have practised? How much did you like this method? How did you feel when your relaxation ended? How many times will you practise this?

Now turn to your self-assessment rating scales and enter your scores for the end of Week 7.

Week 8

. . . .

Week 8, Day 1
» *AWARENESS* «

What is a Panic Attack?

ANXIETY OCCURS when stress is prolonged, continuous and not managed successfully, and it is inevitable if you don't have the necessary coping strategies in place. When anxiety reaches a very high level and you become anxious about being anxious, it is possible that a panic attack will follow. If you have no coping strategies and little support, panic attacks often become a greater problem than the original stress and anxiety. However, not everyone who has anxiety gets panic attacks. It tends to be people who experience symptoms of stress and anxiety in the respiratory and cardiovascular areas (breathing and heart) as opposed to symptoms in their muscles and digestive systems. (In women, panic attacks can sometimes also accompany other symptoms of the menopause.)

A panic attack is usually a symptom of severe stress and high levels of anxiety, but it is not always brought on by unexpected and severe anxiety, apprehension, fear or terror. It occasionally comes out of nowhere and for no apparent reason, and can even occur in the middle of the night while sleeping. The panic attack is usually accompanied by negative and exaggerated thoughts, and if it happens during sleep there is usually an accompanying anxiety dream or nightmare.

As well as the most common and alarming symptoms of a racing heart and rapid shallow breathing, there may be a sudden onset of further unpleasant symptoms such as:

- Confusion
- Disorientation
- Dizziness
- Shaky legs (jelly legs)
- Sweating
- Chest pains
- Trembling
- Nausea and vomiting
- Heightened senses, such as everything becoming louder and brighter

Not all these symptoms are experienced by everyone, but if you suffer with panic attacks I'm sure you will be able to identify with some of them. The important things to remember are:

> - All these symptoms are a direct result of the fight/flight response described earlier in the book. However, if you are tired and exhausted as well as highly stressed and anxious, a panic attack may occur very suddenly and without warning. With the build-up of unmanaged stress and anxiety over a period of time, the fight/flight response becomes oversensitive, meaning that your response is more easily triggered. In other words, if you are exhausted a situation where you would normally feel relaxed and in control could trigger a panic attack.
> - The symptoms and feelings are not harmful. A panic attack does not mean that there is something seriously wrong with you.
> - Even though you might think you are going to die, you're not. No one dies from a panic attack.
> - You might think you are going to faint, but you're not. Generally speaking you can't faint from a panic attack, because fainting is usually caused by the blood pressure dropping and panic attacks cause the blood pressure to rise.
> - You are not going crazy either! This is a common assumption but research shows that no matter how many panic attacks you have and no matter how severe they are, it does not mean that mental illness such as schizophrenia will follow.
> - Because panic attacks can be very frightening, you may become oversensitive about them too. This leads to further attacks of anxiety or panic, thus creating a vicious circle that is difficult to break.

The Vicious Circle of Panic

If you start to worry about your physical symptoms, as well as already worrying about having another panic attack, you will become super-vigilant and constantly on the lookout for anything that might trigger a further attack. If something feels wrong, or you think that you can't cope with a situation, or you become even slightly afraid, you will trigger the fight/flight response again, and once again you will experience overwhelming feelings of panic.

Finally, it is important to be aware that panic attacks are quite common and affect around 5% of the population. They are particularly common in people who have a high frequency of negative thoughts and beliefs and who have a negative attitude to life. When you constantly focus on the negative, your thoughts will tend to find more and more negative events, incidents and situations to trigger your highly sensitive fight/flight response.

Today, read this section over and over until you have a full awareness of why panic attacks happen, what causes them and what maintains them. Write down in your workbook how you personally relate to this information.

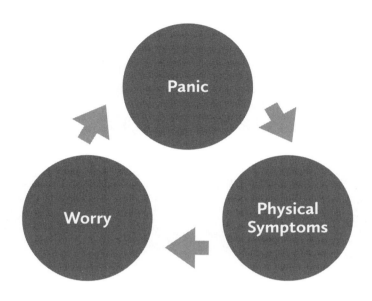

Week 8, Day 2
» *UNDERSTANDING* «

Understanding Panic Attacks

"Panic is a sudden desertion of us,
and a going over to the enemy of our imagination."
— *CHRISTIAN NESTELL BOVEE, author*

We have seen that panic attacks can occur when levels of anxiety are high and have been going on, untreated, for a long time.

However, as you have learned earlier, a feeling of panic can come on suddenly, out of the blue. It is difficult to understand how one minute you're feeling normal, and the next you are having a full-blown panic attack!

Even though everyone's situation is different, and every person is different, the symptoms and effects of a panic attack are very similar.

If you have been suffering with Generalized Anxiety Disorder for some time (feeling anxious all or most of the time), and you experience a sudden crisis or are faced with a threatening situation, this may too trigger a sudden *acute* attack of anxiety or panic attack.

Hyperventilation

This means *"over-breathing"* and occurs when you have a very strong emotion, like fear, or you have a sudden shock, and the fight/flight response suddenly kicks in. The sudden burst of oxygen is meant to be used for fleeing or fighting off the attacker. However, by staying still – as generally we no longer have to run away from threats – this extra burst of oxygen can be in excess of the body's needs. As you begin to breathe rapidly the result is that you breathe out too much carbon dioxide and the chemical balance of your body is disturbed. Your muscles probably do not require all this oxygen, so the effect of there being so much of it in your body can be severe and terrifying.

Below are some of the symptoms you may experience if you are hyperventilating:

- Very rapid and shallow breathing
- Palpitations or rapid heartbeat
- Sudden onset of sweating
- Tingling or numbness in the extremities
- Feeling light-headed or faint
- Blurred vision
- A feeling of unreality
- Muscle cramps

How Panic Attacks Happen

From the chart on the following page it is easy to see how panic attacks increase in intensity. If the first thought could be stopped and changed into a more realistic one, and a breathing exercise followed at this point, the panic would not progress and would be brought under control. If you focus on how bad you feel and how frightening it is, these negative thoughts will just pour fuel on the fire and the panic will become uncontrollable. However, trying to stop a panic attack is extremely difficult if it is full-blown and in the late stages. Catching it early – or better still immediately, as soon as you feel the first symptom – is vital for successfully bringing it under control. Running away to escape is not only unhelpful, it reinforces the behaviour pattern and prevents learning that a panic attack actually can be controlled, overcome and even prevented.

As you read earlier, when you are hyperventilating, it means you are breathing in too much oxygen and breathing out too much carbon dioxide. To correct this imbalance of gases you need to breathe in the air that you just breathed out.

To do this simply breathe in and out into a paper bag (never a plastic one), or cup your hands round your nose and mouth, keeping your fingers together and allowing no air to escape. Do this until you feel OK again.

Check with your doctor about this if you are asthmatic.

HOW PANIC ATTACKS HAPPEN

A situation occurs that
usually, for you, induces anxiety. Negative thoughts:
"I'm frightened, I don't like this at all!"

The fight/flight response kicks in.

"OH NO! It's happening again!"

Physical effects of anxiety become obvious –
sweating, heart pounding, shortness of breath etc.
"I'm having a panic attack!"

Symptoms increase due to the fear of a panic attack
"I can't cope." "I have to get out of here!"

Symptoms increase further –
tightness in chest, palpitations, feeling sick, trembling etc.

Hyperventilation.
"I can't breathe! I'm going to be sick,
I'm going to faint and make a fool of myself."

Dizziness, blurred vision.
"I'm going to pass out, I am going to die."

Runs away to escape.

Doesn't learn that the panic would have eventually
stopped if you had stayed in the situation.

Week 8, Day 3

» PHYSICAL HEALTH «

Yoga Stretches 1

Stretching our bodies is very important in reducing stress, as well as in keeping physically fit. Yoga's physical exercises, or *asanas*, are designed to stretch the whole body as well as stimulating all the internal organs and glands. Yoga keeps your body young, healthy and fit, and if I could recommend just one form of physical exercise, this would always be it.

Ideally, the physical elements of yoga should always be learned from a teacher; some of the exercises are complex and it is important that you don't harm your body by over-stretching or using excessive force. However, the gentle stretching exercises below will not harm you providing you only stretch as far as you can comfortably go. It is OK to feel a gentle stretch, but you should not apply any force at all, or feel pain.

If you practise them every day, the following stretches will help enormously with releasing stress in your body and keeping the muscles soft and relaxed.

Once you have practised them a few times, try to incorporate your breath control: Breathe in first, breathe out as you stretch and breathe in again when you are coming out of the stretch. Do them in the same order as they appear below.

1 · Sit on the floor with your legs stretched out in front of you, feet together and your toes pointing upwards. Have a straight back, shoulders back and look forwards with your head level. Place the palms of your hands on the tops of your thighs and, without bending your knees, slide your hands down your legs towards your toes. Only stretch as far as is comfortable. Once you feel a gentle stretch in your back and the backs of your legs, slide your hands back towards you. Repeat five more times, six in all.

2 · To counteract this stretch, draw your feet along the floor towards you, bringing your knees up close to your chest. Place your hands round your ankles and hug your feet close to your body. Then, keeping hold of your ankles, slide your heels along the floor until your legs are straight again. You may need to let go of your ankles before your legs are straight. This is to prevent you stretching too far.

3 · Place your hands on top of your thighs again, lean backwards a little, then slide your hands down towards your feet again, but this time, if possible, take them over the tips of your toes. Keep looking straight ahead. Do this six times in all. It may take some time for you to reach over your toes but you will get there eventually if you practise regularly. Remember – no force!

4 · Now counteract the stretch. Draw your feet towards you, with your knees right up, then take hold of your feet with your fingers underneath the soles and the thumbs on top of the feet. Slide your heels out along the floor, letting go of your feet whenever you reach your maximum stretch.

5 · The last stretch in this series involves sliding your hands this time down the sides of your legs and lowering your head towards your knees. You may eventually be able to touch your forehead on to your knees, but do not overstretch or force your body to do anything it doesn't want to do. You are just meant to feel a gentle stretch – never any force. Only a few very flexible people will be able to touch their knees with their forehead.

6 · The counteracting stretch is once again drawing your knees up to your chest, holding your feet as before and then placing your forehead on your knees. As you slide your heels out, just keep your head to your knees for as long as you can without forcing it. Bring your head up slowly when finished.

Now lie down flat on the floor for a few minutes and just relax. Practise this every day and watch your flexibility improve.

NOTE: I would advise you to do the above stretches before you begin your sequence of breathing exercises. If you do, carry out the next exercise in order to expand your lungs before you begin the breathing exercises:

The Chest Expansion Exercise

Place your arms across your chest, elbows out to the side, palms down towards the floor, fingertips touching. Draw your elbows backwards, keeping them close to your body. Your shoulder blades come together as you stretch. You will feel a slight rebounding as you return to the original position. Repeat six times.

Week 8, Day 4
» MANAGING STRESS «
Pick and Mix Coping Strategies

You have already learned many ways to manage your stress and anxiety, and I hope you are benefitting from putting them into practice. Here are some new ones, together with a few reminders:

1. Treat yourself to a massage every week or fortnightly.
2. Go for a walk in the countryside to breathe in fresh clean air.
3. Read a book (a novel is best for escapism and creativity) or a magazine.
4. Go out with friends.

5. Join a yoga or t'ai chi class.
6. Go to the cinema or to see a show.
7. Take up a new hobby.
8. Have a warm, relaxing soak in the bath.
9. Use aromatherapy oils in your bath or in a burner.
10. Keep everything tidy and in its place. De-clutter your home.
11. Do something to help someone else.
12. Listen to music: soft music to relax you, pop music to lift your mood.
13. Manage your time better.
14. Stop drinking energy drinks that contain caffeine and sugar.
15. Accept the things you cannot change.
16. Stop trying to be perfect all the time.
17. Trust someone to do something for you when you are under pressure.
18. Try reflexology, acupuncture or Emotional Freedom Technique (EFT).
19. Go to bed at the same time every night and get up at the same time every morning.
20. Cut down on caffeine – drink no more than four cups of tea or coffee a day.
21. If you smoke – give it up (get help if you need to).
22. Don't try to be responsible for everyone and everything.
23. Don't allow people to take advantage of your good nature.
24. Say no. You don't always have to agree to everything that's asked of you.
25. Try using Bach Flower Remedies to help with your emotions, in particular Rescue Remedy for anxiety (from health stores or pharmacies).

Week 8, Day 5

» *ANXIETY SOLUTIONS* «

Anchoring to Overcome Anxiety

This is a Neuro-Linguistic Programming (NLP) exercise that is extremely effective for overcoming anxiety and raising confidence when practised and perfected. The whole exercise takes place while you are in a state of relaxation. You will visualize the instructions in your mind's eye, practising them repeatedly and eventually transferring the therapeutic effects into your reality.

First, close your eyes softly, take three slow deep abdominal breaths and take yourself through one of the relaxations you have learned already. Once you are relaxed, visualize yourself sitting in a comfortable room in front of a large television. You are holding a remote control for the TV in your hand. Now think of a time when you were extremely anxious or having a panic attack. Press the start button on the remote control and imagine playing and watching a movie of yourself going through that distressing event on the

TV screen in front of you. Look at the screen carefully as you watch your distressing event from the beginning, before you became anxious, right up to the end when the anxiety had gone and you were feeling calm and safe again.

Now imagine the same event taking place but this time you have no anxiety at all; this time you are able to enjoy the event. You are relaxed and confident and totally in control. Imagine what you did differently. How you acted differently. What you said or didn't say before. Think about how the movie would look if you didn't have any anxiety at all.

Press the start button again on the remote control and watch the screen again, this time watching yourself coping really well, as you just did in your imagination with the same situation. See yourself on the screen smiling or even laughing. Hear yourself sounding confident and happy. Watch the other people around you. They look proud of you and happy for you because you are enjoying yourself. Watch the movie right up to the end point.

Now press the start button and watch the movie again. This time imagine the TV screen much bigger. Make the picture brighter and the colours more vivid. Make the sounds clearer and hear yourself speaking calmly and confidently. Play it right through to the end.

Press the start button on the remote control again, then put it down on a table beside you. Now imagine getting up from your chair and *stepping into the screen*. You are now starring in the movie, not just watching it. You *become* the you in the movie. Starting from the beginning, act out the scenes in the new way, with your new behaviour, feeling happy and confident. Feel, hear and see everything clearly as you go through the motions without even a thought of any anxiety. Fully experience everything and feel how good it is to have a happy ending. When you feel that you are experiencing everything to its full capacity and your new-found joy and confidence is the best it can be, place your right hand softly on the side of your face. As you do this, try to connect to the wonderful and perfect state of peace and joy that has taken over from your anxiety state. This action is called *anchoring*. Feel your hand becoming warm as it absorbs all the new feelings you are now enjoying. Leave your hand there as you continue to act out the scene's new ending – the successful ending with the new you! When the movie ends you can remove your hand from your face, step out of the movie on the screen and return to your seat.

After a few minutes, repeat the exercise again but using a different situation when you felt anxious. Having stepped into the screen, as soon as you get to the point where you felt anxious in reality, perform your anchor by placing your hand on the side of your face. Feel the anxiety slipping away. Feel yourself becoming calm and in control. See, hear and feel yourself being totally relaxed in that situation. Feel your new behaviour working well and feel the stronger, more positive new you, producing another happy ending.

If something doesn't feel right, simply change it. You are the director and producer of the movie. When you are fully satisfied and happy with the new you, you can step out of the imaginary screen, go back to your imaginary chair and press the imaginary stop button.

Finally, think about how you could use this new relaxed and confident behaviour when you are next in a situation where you would normally feel anxious. Think about your anchor and remember to use it as soon as the anxious thoughts or symptoms begin. Performing this action often enough will mean that you start to associate the anchor with confidence. In other words, the association of one thing in relation to another becomes effective.

If you rehearse this exercise (as you did on the screen, and then in the movie) with real events or situations that normally create your anxiety, when you face the situation in reality the anchoring will be more effective.

Although anchoring is used as an effective coping strategy here, you may be familiar with the fact that we often associate one thing with another and the associated feelings that come with the process.

For example, you may hear a song on the radio that instantly reminds you of someone and an associated feeling or emotion. Smelling a certain perfume may also remind you of a certain person and maybe, for just a moment, you are taken back to that time. You may also associate things you see with certain places or people or feelings. So try to put anchoring to good use; it can change a bad feeling to a good feeling on demand.

Week 8, Day 6
» *DIRECTION* «

Live Your Life With No Regrets

"Do not brood over your past mistakes and failures as this will
only fill your mind with grief, regret and depression."
— SWAMI SIVANANDA, *Hindu spiritual teacher*

You have already learned that to live in the present is absolutely essential if you are to gain peace of mind and manage your stress. You have also learned that there is no such thing as a mistake and that choosing not to dwell on the past or worry about the future brings balance and harmony into your life. However, there is one more issue that we haven't yet examined. That is *living your life fully*: taking each day as it comes and getting the very best out of it. When you live each day to the full, as if it were your first and your last, it ensures that you will have no regrets. Remember, you only get one day at a time and the really good news is that the rest of your life starts now, from today. As the old cliché says, *"This is the first day of the rest of your life."* Now imagine that it is your eightieth birthday and you are looking back over your life.

- What do you wish you had done less of?
- What do you wish you had done more of?
- Where in the world do you wish you had visited?
- What do you wish you had said to someone?
- Who do you wish you had seen more of?
- What do you wish you had done differently?
- What regrets do you have?

Now reflect for a moment on where you are now and what you are doing in your life right now.

- What changes do you wish to make now?
- What do you want to put more effort into?
- What goals have you set to ensure you don't have any regrets?
- What are you going to start to do today, right now?
- When you do actually reach a grand old age what would you like to be thinking?

Week 8, Day 7
» *MEDITATION* «
A Walking Meditation

This is not only one of the simplest forms of meditation but you get to take your exercise for the day at the same time! Walking is probably the best kind of exercise you can do if you are stressed and anxious; and here you are also engaging in meditation and mindfulness, so it is doubly beneficial.

Plan your walk to take about twenty minutes and for it to be in the countryside or a beautiful park or garden. Ideally, you will either be alone or walking with like-minded people who are doing the meditation with you.

This form of meditation involves being completely aware of, and being involved with, what you are doing, how you are doing it, everything you are feeling in mind and body and everything that is going on around you.

Before you start to walk, take a moment to become aware of your feet standing on the ground. How do your feet feel? Feel them taking the weight of your body. Feel them balancing you so that you don't fall over. Be aware of how your feet feel in your shoes. Feel the contact between your feet and the insides of your shoes. Feel the contact between the bottom of your shoes and the ground beneath you. Perhaps you can imagine the earth's energy flowing upwards through your feet and up through your whole body to the top of your head. As you do this, you may even imagine the earth's energy now mingling with the sky energy from above.

Now begin walking slowly. Walk normally; there is no need to change your walk. With each step you take, once again feel the contact between your feet and the ground. Notice how your heel touches the ground first, with the rest of your foot following. Be aware of when one of your feet is moving in the air as it moves towards the next step. Be aware of your legs moving with each step you take. Feel how they move. Try to be aware of the subtle changes in your body as you walk. Notice which parts of your body are moving and how they feel. Notice your ankles, knees, hips, back, neck, head, eyes, arms, hands and fingers, all moving together in harmony to help you as you walk.

Now focus on your feelings. How do you feel? Are you feeling happy about this walk, with this meditation? If not, what *are* you feeling? Examine your emotions and identify what it is you are feeling. Perhaps your feelings change as you continue your walk, or maybe your feelings change along with the changes of scenery.

How is your breathing? Be aware of your breath flowing in and flowing out. Be aware of how the flow of your breath changes as your emotions change.

Now focus on your thoughts. Has your mind strayed? What thoughts have crept into your mind? Is there one particular thought that keeps you occupied? Are you able to accept your thoughts and bring your focus back to your walking meditation? What do you think or feel when you become aware that your mind has strayed? Do not judge yourself harshly; simply acknowledge your thoughts and gently return them to the present moment, to harmonize mind and body.

Continue with the above until your walk comes to a natural end, after around twenty minutes. When you stop walking become aware of how it feels to be still. Bring your attention once more to your feet and your feet taking the weight of your body, and how your feet help to balance your body. Feel the ground beneath your feet, take a long, deep breath and gently come to the end of your meditation. Now reflect on your walking meditation and how it has affected you or changed you. What are your thoughts now? How do you feel now? How has your body responded to the meditation?

When you have mastered the walking meditation, you may wish to walk further and add a new aspect or dimension. Move the focus from your body, mind and emotions to your surroundings and be mindful of the following:

- The temperature of the air on your face and the quality of the air you breathe
- The trees, flowers, and plants
- The colours and textures around you
- The light, the darkness and the rays of the sun
- The smells and the atmosphere
- The many different sounds
- The sky
- The wildlife

Week 8

» RECAP AND REFLECT «

Tick the box when understood, practised and achieved

WHAT IS A PANIC ATTACK?: Does this apply to you? If so, are you able to recognize your symptoms from the long list? Are you aware of the reasons for your panic attacks? Do you know what triggers them?

UNDERSTANDING PANIC ATTACKS: Are you now able to understand what happens when you are having a panic attack? Do you now realize that it is your thoughts and beliefs that trigger the attacks? Do you understand that you can prevent, reduce or even stop an attack if you are able to control your thoughts and your breathing? How does knowing that you can take back control make you feel?

YOGA STRETCHES 1: Have you tried these stretches? How did you get along with them? Remember not to stretch too far. How many days of the week do you intend to practise them?

PICK AND MIX COPING STRATEGIES: Which of these are you using already and which of the rest have you chosen to try? Enter these as goals in the mental health section in the Wheel of Life.

ANCHORING TO OVERCOME ANXIETY: Have you been practising this? Practise as much as possible so that you are able to apply it whenever you feel your anxiety rising. Has it worked for you yet?

LIVE YOUR LIFE WITH NO REGRETS: This is something you need to keep reminding yourself about. Use the STOP Technique whenever any regrets from your past come to mind. Can you understand that, if you live your life fully and positively, you will have no regrets in the future and live your life without stress, anxiety and depression?

A WALKING MEDITATION: Have you had the chance to put this into practice yet? If not, write it down as a goal and do it as soon as possible. You don't necessarily have to be in the countryside; you can still meditate while you are walking in the town or city.

Now turn to your self-assessment rating scales and enter your scores for the end of Week 8.

Week 9

· · · · · · · · ·

Week 9, Day 1
» *PHILOSOPHY* «
Accept What You Cannot Change

IF YOU ARE AT A DIFFICULT TIME in your life, don't automatically think that this is the way it's always going to be. Each day of your life is different in some way, and if you look back over your life you will probably see a rollercoaster journey with highs and lows and twists and turns. What you are experiencing at this moment in time is simply a pause, not a full stop. Nothing stays the same for ever. You *will* come out of this low; hopefully you are in fact already part of the way there as you journey through the pages of this book.

Try your best to stay positive, be patient and keep a sense of proportion. Put all your energy into using your best endeavours to *Get Your Life Back*. You know it's worth it. If you were taking an exam that would ultimately change your life for ever, you would study hard, work hard and be determined to pass with flying colours. This book can also change your life for the better, but there is no examination at the end of it, so no need to worry about that! Just relax, do one thing at a time, take one day at a time, follow the advice and instructions and you will certainly get there.

Earlier in the book I advised you to change the things that you can, which are under your control, and accept the things you cannot change and which are out of your control. You already know that you cannot return to the past to change things, so don't spend valuable mental or emotional energy trying to figure out why you are where you are, and why this has happened to you. Why does anything happen? You may never really fully understand or find the answers you are looking for, so you simply need to ask yourself *does it really matter*? I know this sounds hard to accept, but on the other hand, it *has* happened and you *can't* turn the clock back. You can't make it *un-happen*. You are where you are and you need to deal with the present because that's all you've got. If something is troubling you from your past or you are worried about something that hasn't happened yet, stress is bound to follow. The past has gone – let it go. Regrets are pointless. Regrets are harmful. They fester and turn into something you will also live to regret. Regrets turn into stress, anxiety and depression; they make you ill. Regrets don't make any sense at all. So make the best of today in the best way you can. Live for today; the past has gone and it will not return. Seize the day!

Sometimes life does seem to go badly for us, even though we don't invite it. There are so many things that we are unable to control – but if we did have control over everything that happens, it would be a very strange life. Life doesn't always go the way we want it to, and that's a fact. There are also times when several things seem to go wrong all at the same time. However, I'm sure that if everything always went according to plan, some of you would still wonder what was waiting for you round the corner! In other words, we know quite well that life is not always a bowl of cherries, the sun doesn't always shine on us, and there is no such thing as a perfect life!

So why is it that we are shocked and dismayed when things do go wrong? Why do we say *"Just when I thought things were going well for me!"* or *"Why me?"* or even *"What have I done to deserve this?"* Well, I suppose generally speaking the answer lies in the fact that we often unrealistically expect things to go well, every single day of our lives. Some of us expect bad things to happen only to other people. We automatically think that we are immune to disaster and trauma. We never stop to think: *"Why not me!"* or, *"Well I suppose I've had it good for a while now, maybe it's my turn. Lots of other people go through much worse. I've been very lucky so far."*

Of course, I'm not suggesting that it's OK to expect things to go wrong! On the contrary, that would be a very negative and pessimistic attitude to life; unfortunately though there are negative and pessimistic people who *do* actually expect doom and gloom. They are of the mindset that life has dealt them a bad hand and that's the way it goes. But my answer to that is *It's not the cards that are dealt to you, it's the way you play them that makes the difference.* I fully understand that our lives are shaped by the attitudes, values and beliefs we develop as a result of our past experiences, but being philosophical I can only say yet again that:

> a.   the past has gone; let it go.
> b.   if we take the time to learn the necessary coping strategies to manage our misfortune, we can make positive changes and look forward to a better future.
> c.   if you are able to focus on the good things that happen to you and be grateful for your blessings, then your life will change for the better. It really is an attitude of mind.

So, where does *your* mindset belong and why? What kind of attitude do you have towards life? Are you an optimist or a pessimist? Why do you think that is?

Whether you are a positive or a negative thinker, you probably realize by now that what you focus on is what you attract. If you have experienced adversity, disaster, illness and bad luck in your life, and formed a negative belief about these issues, the chances are that you have become a negative thinker and a pessimist, which will undoubtedly lead you to experience even more negative outcomes. Whatever you perceive, you believe. It isn't *things* that cause your stress; it is more a matter of how you deal with them and what your attitude is towards them. For example: if two people were fired from their jobs, one might think that it was dreadful, worry about how they were going to pay the rent and subsequently slip into a state of anxiety and depression. The other, however, might think that it was a good opportunity for them to move into a different area of work that they have wanted to do for years, but not had the courage to change. They look forward to the challenge.

If you have experienced crises and disasters and somehow managed to overcome them, and have been philosophical about them, you will probably be a stronger person for it and will have developed a positive attitude. The likelihood is that, because you don't fear it, your future will be more favourable. If adversity arises, you will be able to cope with it because of your positive outlook on life.

Hopefully, you are learning to accept that life is not always easy. That there *will* be ups and downs, there will be mountains to climb, and there are sometimes mountains you will fall off! But that's OK. It *is* possible to climb right back up again. You *can* survive. You *can* move on and become stronger. We all possess an inner strength. All you have to do is try to connect with it. Believe in it. Know that it's there, that it has always been there and that sometimes, without even realizing it, you have drawn on it in times of need.

I believe that philosopher Friedrich Nietzsche's words: *"What doesn't kill you makes you stronger"* are actually true. Research into how people deal with trauma indicates that although traumatic experiences can be harmful, small amounts of trauma can actually make people stronger and better able to cope.

To sum up, when things go wrong and they are totally out of your control, accept them with calmness and fortitude. Deal with them the best way you can. Seek help, breathe, relax, exercise, put things into perspective, find the positives and do what you are able to do. *Focus on what you can do, rather than on what you can't do.* As time passes, even though things may not get any better, you will find you can come to terms with them more easily if you adopt a more realistic and accepting attitude.

Viktor Frankl was a victim of the Holocaust and was imprisoned in Auschwitz concentration camp during World War II. He describes in his book *Man's Search for Meaning* how he and others survived by identifying a purpose in life they could feel positively about, and being able to visualize the outcome of that purpose.

So the exercise for today is to take a good look at your general outlook and attitude to life and decide which kind of person you are. Where do you fit on the scale of negative to positive? Has what you have learned so far moved you further towards the positive side? I hope so. Now, how much further do you need to go?

Then, in spite of your adversities, make a list in your workbook of all the *major positives* in your life.

When you have done this, you can also make a list of all the *minor positives*.

I hope that by now you are realizing that despite things going wrong, there is always something that has gone right for you. It's time for you to focus on these now.

Remember, to overcome stress, anxiety and depression, accept the things you cannot change, or which are out of your control. Change what you can – and learn to know the difference!

Week 9, Day 2

» *PRANAYAMA* «

Exercise for Intense Emotion

This very effective breathing exercise can help to control severe distress and intense emotions, and also helps with palpitations. It may take some time to master but it is worth the effort. It involves holding the breath for over fifteen seconds throughout the whole exercise.

> Take a slow deep breath all the way in.
> Hold the breath for five seconds.
> Take the tummy right in.
> Hold the tummy in for another five seconds.
> Let the tummy out.
> After another five seconds, slowly breathe out and relax.

You will gain much benefit from the first stage and you may not find it necessary to progress further; however, if you do wish to go on, do so only when you have mastered the first stage.

> Breathe right in and hold for ten seconds.
> Take the tummy in in two equal steps and hold it in for ten seconds.
> Let the tummy out in two equal steps.
> Hold for ten seconds before breathing out slowly.

Week 9, Day 3

» *DIRECTION* «

Help Yourself by Helping Others

"Before giving, the mind of the giver is happy; while giving,
the mind of the giver is made peaceful; and having given,
the mind of the giver is uplifted."
— *BUDDHA*

Have you ever given a gift to someone and the gratitude they show actually makes you feel as good as they do for receiving it? Have you ever done something for someone and felt really good about it? How pleased did you feel that you were able to help? Did their gratitude cause you to feel that you were glad you could be of assistance, or that you would like to do even more?

The love and gratitude that people show when something is done for them is given back to you as a gift.

OK, not everyone is grateful, and some people don't show gratitude, that's true, but let's just focus on that old gratitude principle that *giving is receiving.*

If you work in the caring community or in employment where you are doing something to help others, you know what it is to feel that you have done a satisfying and rewarding job at the end of your working day. You don't just know it; you can actually feel it. It is a good feeling in your heart and soul, it puts a smile on your face and you feel contented. Imagine how this boosts your self-esteem and self-worth. If you don't work in a caring capacity, imagine how much better you would feel about yourself if you were able to do something equally rewarding.

If you don't experience this on a regular basis, perhaps today is the day you start the process so that you too can share in some of this appreciation and gratitude that is all around us.

Today do something for someone else. It doesn't matter that you are the one who needs the help; the object of this exercise is for you to feel better about yourself by helping others. As the sayings go, *what goes around comes around* and *you reap what you sow.*

If you have been experiencing this from the opposite point of view (as in, it is you that receives help), from today make sure that you show your appreciation and gratitude to the person who is helping you. They will be much more inclined and happier to continue to help you, and will also feel rewarded for their efforts.

If today you do help someone and they don't show their appreciation, instead of feeling resentful about it, accept that we are all different, try to change your attitude towards that person and learn from the experience. You will learn what it is like not to be shown gratitude and perhaps realize how important it is. But on the other hand, if they do thank you, try to be aware of any good feelings and the smile you have inside.

OK, so what can you do today to help someone? What kind gesture can you think of that someone would really appreciate? What can you do for someone that would help to make you feel good about yourself? It doesn't necessarily have to be something amazing, something big. Of course, it is your choice: you may decide you want to surprise someone you love by doing something really out of the ordinary. Doing something for them that you wouldn't usually do, such as cooking a meal, or helping with the housework, will be rewarded by the gratitude they show to you. It doesn't necessarily have to be *doing* something to help, either: it could be that you buy them a gift or take them out somewhere nice, maybe somewhere you know they love to go.

There are many ways and many people you could help. For example: you could offer to do someone's shopping or do some gardening for a neighbour, for no reason at all. Visit someone who is sick or old and maybe lonely. Let it be something different. Don't let it be something that you would normally do anyway, otherwise the gratitude might not be the same. We often take people for granted without realizing it.

If you are shown gratitude and the person you have helped really does appreciate it, notice in that moment how you feel. Perhaps you could make a conscious effort to continue in the same vein. Doing something for others is not going to help you to feel good for very long if it is a one-off gesture and just for one day. This needs to be an ongoing, more permanent arrangement. If you really want to feel good about yourself on a regular basis, then do something for others on a regular basis. If you want to have a continuous feeling of satisfaction and reward, see a consistent increase in your self-worth and a daily uplift in your mood, keep up the good work.

Volunteering is a rewarding experience for both the volunteer and the person or organization receiving it. When I worked in community mental health, once the patient was coping and functioning well we often arranged for them to do some volunteer work. Sometimes it was in a charity shop where they would also come into contact with the general public. This helped to increase their confidence as well as making them feel that they were giving something back to the community. This project was very successful for many reasons, but it was the patient who gained the most benefit. There are a host of ideas for volunteer work on the Internet and many of them include areas that you may have a specific interest in, such as working with animals in rescue centres, driving patients to and from hospital appointments, teaching literacy skills, mentoring, campaigning and fundraising, events and environment volunteering. A friend of mine who has a history of depression goes to a school two mornings a week to read to the young children. I don't know who enjoys it the most, her or the children!

This is about giving and taking in equal measures. Think about nature. If it wasn't for the trees and vegetation breathing out their oxygen, none of us would be here! Without us breathing out our carbon dioxide, there wouldn't be any trees, plants, flowers or crops. Living in peace and harmony with our planet isn't just about ecology; it is also about living in harmony with our fellow human beings. If we live our lives simply as takers, the chances are there won't be much harmony in our lives. Be a *giver* today and allow someone else to do the taking. It will enhance the quality of both of your lives.

Week 9, Day 4

» ORGANIZATION «

Organize Your Day With a Daily Planner

For part of this exercise I am going to assume that all your days are free. If this is not the case, if for example you go to work, then adapt it and tailor it to suit your individual needs. Make your Daily Planner just for the times you are free.

If you are going to manage your stress, eliminate anxiety and deal with depression, from now on your day needs to be organized and well structured. So far you have learned a number of exercises, relaxations and meditations as well as being given many directions, some advice and goals to set and achieve. It isn't surprising therefore if you become a little confused about what to do, when, and how many times a day or week you are expected to apply them.

Keeping a diary or using a large calendar for your daily tasks is very helpful, especially when you are depressed or you lead a very busy life. It acts as a reminder of what has to be done, helps you to focus on what you have achieved and lets you know how you are spending your time.

If you keep a diary you can continue to use that, but better still, you can use the Daily Planner below. You will be able to see at a glance how every day of your week looks.

On the Planner you need to list tasks, chores, goals and practising things like exercises and relaxations, but you can also enter your pleasurable activities and social events. Try to keep to your plan as much as possible, but remember, you will need to be flexible too, just in case something unexpected or unplanned occurs. Otherwise there is a danger that you may become frustrated, angry or stressed about it.

Often when you are depressed, you lose interest in day-to-day tasks and chores, or even more important things, putting them off until another time. As a result everything piles up, which causes you to procrastinate even more. Eventually you find yourself with a mammoth task ahead and, of course, become overwhelmed by it.

The Daily Planner is a good way of helping you to reduce the pile a little at a time. Remember, if you break the tasks down into smaller ones, you will be able to face them more easily.

Before you fill in your Daily Planner make a list of everything you feel you need to do. Then prioritize the individual items. If you find this task an onerous one, if possible ask someone to help you with it.

Daily Planner

	Mon	Tue	Wed	Thurs	Fri	Sat	Sun
9:00–10:00 am							
10:00–11:00 am							
11:00–12:00 noon							
12:00–1:00pm							
1:00–2:00pm							
2:00–3:00pm							
3:00–4:00pm							
4:00–5:00pm							
5:00–6:00pm							
6:00–7:00pm							

7:00–8:00pm								
8:00–9:00pm								
9:00–10:00pm								

The following example Daily Planner is meant only as a guide; you may need to adapt the times to suit you. For example, some people like to exercise first thing in the morning, but others may prefer to read the paper or do other non-exercise activities. Owls and larks behave differently, and that's fine. Just do what's right for you.

Example Daily Planner

	Monday	Tuesday
Wake–9:00 am	Practise breathing exercises and adopt a positive attitude before getting out of bed.	Practise breathing exercises and adopt a positive attitude before getting out of bed.
9:00–10:00 am	Do yoga stretches. Have healthy breakfast. Deal with post. Read paper.	Do yoga stretches. Have a healthy breakfast. Deal with post. Read paper.
10:00–11:00 am	Do housework until 10:30. 20 mins minimum current relaxation exercise.	Walk to the shop for bits & pieces. 20 mins minimum current relaxation exercise.
11:00 am–12:00 noon	Sort out washing & do necessary ironing.	Clear some clutter from kitchen drawers & cupboards.
12:00–1:00 pm	Prepare and eat a healthy lunch, then rest.	Prepare and eat a healthy lunch, then rest.
1:00–2:00 pm	Read today's instruction in book. Practise instructions, advice or direction from book.	Read today's instruction in book. Practise instructions, advice or direction from book.
2:00–3:00 pm	Take a 30 min walk in the park with Ray. Attend to Wheel of Life & write/review goals.	Exercise with keep-fit DVD. Rest with cup of tea. Make phone calls.

3:00–5:00 pm	Keep free to choose anything I feel I need to do	Keep free to choose anything I feel I need to do.
5:00–6:00 pm	Yoga stretches followed by breathing exercises. 5:45 pm. Prepare evening meal.	Yoga stretches followed by breathing exercises. 5:45 pm. Prepare evening meal.
6:00–7:00 pm	Eat & relax afterwards. Clean up kitchen. Call Danni & Sam to arrange lunch next week.	Eat & relax afterwards. Clean up kitchen. Check what is needed & make shopping list for supermarket.
7:00–8:00 pm	Complete Daily Planner for next week. Watch TV.	Practise current meditation exercise. Watch TV.
8:00–10:00pm	Phone Louise & Nikki. Read "today" in book again and do workbook exercises.	Watch TV until 9.30 pm. Practise Confidence exercise. Read "today" in book again.
10:00–11:00 pm	Get ready for bed. Read for half an hour. Do breathing exercises. Go to sleep.	Get ready for bed. Read for half an hour. Do breathing exercises. Go to sleep.

Week 9, Day 5

» *CORRECT THINKING* «

Thoughts that Incite Panic

There are certain thoughts and beliefs that induce feelings of panic. Remember, it is usually your perception, or how you interpret situations, that cause the panic attacks rather than the situation itself. If you are able to identify these thoughts and beliefs you can challenge them, change them and stop them. This will change the outcome and eliminate your panic attack. Similarly, if you can no longer make sense of or agree with your out-of-date beliefs, you can loosen and eventually release their hold on you. This in turn will help you to change your perception and prevent the fight/flight response becoming activated. You will take control instead of the inappropriate anxiety controlling you.

Here are a few examples of the thoughts and beliefs that ignite and fuel panic attacks. These thoughts can occur before, during and after a panic attack:

- I'm going to embarrass myself.
- I'm going to faint and be humiliated.
- I won't be able to move. My legs will turn to jelly.
- I think I'm going to die.

- I can never get my breath. I know I'll suffocate.
- I'm having a heart attack. I need an ambulance.
- Everyone is looking at me. They think I'm crazy.
- This is what happens when people have a nervous breakdown.
- I'm losing control. I'm hopeless. I'm stupid. I can't do anything!
- I can't ever go out again. I feel so ashamed. Nobody else has this problem, why do I have to have it?

I'm sure you might be able to add others to this list, but no matter what they are, they can all be disputed *because not one of them is true.*

Here are some questions you can ask yourself:

- Am I blowing this out of proportion?
- Am I being ridiculous?
- Am I being totally negative?
- Could I be exaggerating?
- How would my positive friends see this?
- Could I survive like I did last time?
- On a scale of 0–100, how bad is this really?
- Am I able to regain my control using my new skills?
- What is the worst thing that can happen?
- What is most likely to happen?
- Am I thinking in "all or nothing" terms?
- Am I being totally unrealistic?

Challenge your thoughts and beliefs while you are feeling OK. You don't have to wait until you are in a full-blown panic attack; it will be more difficult then. Just remember that there is always a different way of thinking about things and if you think in a positive or more realistic way, this will have a positive effect on your feelings and your actions.

Of course, if you practise your breathing exercises, relaxation, positive thinking and the STOP Technique, you won't need the above list because you will never have such negative thoughts again!

Week 9, Day 6
» *DIRECTION* «

Affirmations – It's All in the Mind

"Believe that life is worth living and your belief will help create the fact."
— WILLIAM JAMES, *philosopher*

Many of us will remember Muhammad Ali repeatedly saying *"I am the greatest!"* In the early days of his boxing career, people laughed at him and ridiculed him. They said that he was arrogant and big-headed. Their attitude was usually: *who does he think he is!* However, Cassius Clay, as he was known then, truly believed in himself, and that one day he would be a huge success, and sure enough, he *did* become the greatest. It is well known that people from all over the world came to love and admire him. He was – and still is – considered the most revered, iconic, legendary sportsman of all time. Muhammad Ali *believed* he was the greatest, and *indeed he did, in many people's estimation, become the greatest boxing champion in history.*

However, he achieved great success not only by his boxing prowess but also by believing in himself and by using the power of positive thinking, in particular, the power of *positive affirmations.*

A positive affirmation is a short statement, sentence or declaration that you repeat to yourself over and over again. The more you repeat it, the better. The stronger and more passionately you repeat it, the more chance there is of it becoming a reality. The most important ingredient, however, is *emotion.* The more emotion you put into it the greater the effect.

An *affirmation* is a message from your conscious to your subconscious mind, and if the thought is delivered with *feeling* the subconscious will accept it as an *instruction* or *command* or *directive.* You may be able to relate to this in a different way. If you tell yourself over and over that you are an anxious person and you *feel* anxious and *look* anxious and your body is *tense with the feeling of anxiety,* the very likely outcome is that you will become anxious. If you believe that if you put yourself in a certain situation you will have a panic attack, you most probably will have a panic attack. You have programmed your mind to be anxious. You will switch on the fight/flight response just by thinking about being anxious: it becomes a self-fulfilling prophecy. This sequence of events will continue until you reprogramme or recondition your mind.

Think about how a computer works. The computer will perform tasks if, and only if, it is programmed to do so. In order to change those tasks, the programmer needs to go back into the program and make the changes. Your brain similarly follows the instructions we give to it; if we want to raise our hand, the part of the brain that governs movement will receive a message and cause the hand to move.

If you tell yourself enough times that you are calm and in control, you say it with feeling and you relax and breathe slowly, your brain will obey the command in just the same way as it will obey your command when you tell yourself you are anxious. It is useful to remember that your subconscious mind does not know the difference between the truth and a lie! It will always obey your commands. You only have to have one thought that something terrible is going to happen and your brain will switch on the fight/flight response in just the same way as if you were actually being attacked.

When composing your affirmations they need to comprise the following ingredients:

POSITIVE · They must contain only positive words. For instance, it is incorrect to say "I am not afraid"; your subconscious mind will receive the word "afraid" and interpret it as being negative. The memory part of your brain will interpret that word as being threatening and immediately switch on the fight/flight response. A better choice is: I am strong, I am confident, I am now in control.

IN THE PRESENT TENSE · Your affirmations need to be said in the present tense. It is usual to begin the affirmation with the words "I am" rather than "I'm going to", and perhaps end with the word "now". This is because your logical mind only recognizes the present tense. If you say "I am going to be calm and confident", your subconscious will receive the order that at some unspecified time in the future you will be calm and confident, but it can't make sense of the future because it hasn't happened yet, and your mind cannot predict the future.

PERSONAL · They need to be *personal* to you. The words "I am" are bold and extremely powerful. It is a statement that acknowledges and accepts who you really are. Your subconscious recognizes that the affirmation is meant for you and is right for you and you alone. You cannot use a positive affirmation for someone else. You cannot mentally or psychologically influence someone else to do something you want them to do.

SPOKEN WITH EMOTION · Repeat your affirmation with feeling. So if, for example, you want to be confident, speak your affirmation with the feeling of confidence. If you want to be calm, say it with a feeling of calm and use your voice to convey that feeling.

You don't necessarily have to say your affirmation out loud, but it has more power in it if you do. Its power can also be increased by looking at yourself in the mirror and stating your affirmation with determination and conviction.

It is a good idea to repeat your affirmation as often as possible and whenever the opportunity allows it. For example:

- While waiting in a queue
- At the traffic lights
- When you are walking

- On the bus or train
- Before going to sleep
- Before getting out of bed

Repeat each of your affirmations as many times as possible. Say them with:

- Feeling
- Strength
- Conviction
- Belief
- Certainty
- Sincerity
- Passion

You can have more than one affirmation, but don't have too many at the same time. I would advise no more than three.

Emile Coué, the French psychologist and pharmacist, wrote the words "Every day and in every way I am getting better and better" on all his medicines. He instructed his patients to repeat the words many times every day. He called this "conscious auto-suggestion", but it is the same as what we today call positive affirmations. He found that the patients who followed his instructions recovered much more quickly than those who did not.

Here are a few more examples of positive affirmations to help you on your way:

- I am safe, I am strong, I am in control now.
- I am confident in being able to control my feelings now.
- I now choose to have only positive thoughts.
- I am able to make the right decisions today and every day.
- I now choose always to keep everything in perspective.
- I am now completely optimistic about my future.
- I now fully accept other people for who they are.
- I am now successful in everything I do.
- I easily achieve all my goals.
- I am now strong, positive and determined to do my best in everything.
- I change what I can and accept whatever is out of my control.
- I choose to be happy now and for always.
- Every day and in every way I am getting better and better.

- Every day makes me stronger and stronger in every way.
- I am safe and protected now.
- I live in the present and let go of my past.
- I enjoy being happy and healthy in every way.
- I love and enjoy life and give thanks for all my blessings.
- I am now filled with peace, love, joy and contentment.

Week 9, Day 7

» *RELAXATION* «

Creative Visualization

Creative visualization is not only one of the most popular forms of relaxation; it is also one of the most effective and most powerful, especially for depression. Many top sportsmen and women and other highly successful people use this method to achieve success. It is literally tapping into the power of the mind.

The relaxation below is aimed at releasing tension and stress in both mind and body. Ideally you will find someone to read this script out to you, using a soft gentle voice. Alternatively, you can record it for yourself. This relaxation can be found on the accompanying CD *Breathe and Relax* in Mary's own voice (see page 267). You will need to set aside at least half an hour and ensure that you will not be disturbed. Pause wherever you see ....

When you are comfortable, close your eyes softly, and allow a feeling of peaceful relaxation to come over you .... not trying too hard.......... just simply letting it happen.......... and allowing yourself to come into the present moment, letting go all thoughts of the past and future. Just listening to the sound of my voice, and telling yourself not to sleep.......... Give yourself permission to relax fully now.......... and feel yourself sinking softly into a feeling of serenity..

Now.......... take three slow deep abdominal breaths,.......... feeling your abdomen rise, as you breathe in, and your lungs filling with the warm softening breath.......... and slowly breathing out, letting your tummy sink down.......... and your chest release and soften.......... With each breath that you breathe out.......... release all tension from your mind.......... release any unwanted thoughts or feelings.......... allow a feeling of peace and relaxation to come over you .... Just simply watching the flow of your breath now.......... normal, gentle easy breathing. Simply allowing your body to breathe for you now.......... just breathing in.......... and breathing out ... . and with the next breath that you breathe out, completely allow your feet, legs and hips to soften and relax.......... feel them becoming heavy now as they rest against the softness of your support.......... Now allow your abdomen to soften.......... and your lower back to relax..

Just breathing easily and comfortably now.......... allowing your body to breathe for you ....

Now feel your back muscles giving way to a feeling of relaxation, spreading out and sinking down.......... softly and comfortably....................................... Feel your chest release all tightness and tension as your breathing now becomes easier and easier. Breathe in deeply once again now, and as you exhale, this time relax your shoulders.......... relax them more and more.......... and yet still more....................................

Let them drop downwards towards the floor.......... and allow your arms and hands to become heavy and warm and very, very relaxed now....................................

Free your fingers from all tension and tightness.......... feel them becoming loose and floppy, loose and relaxed, warm and free.......................................

Now be aware of the muscles in your neck loosening............softening.......... letting the tension melt away.......................................

Relax and soften your scalp.......... and the top of your head.......... Relax your forehead now.......... and all the muscles in your face.......... your eyes and temples.......... Loosen your jaw now.......... Deeply relax your mouth, and place a warm slight smile on your lips........... and send that smile to every part of your body..........and just know that all is well........... you have created this special time for peace and detachment................................... stillness................................ serenity.......................................

Allow your whole body to relax deeply now. Relaxing more.......... and more, sinking deeper.......... and deeper..........................and deeper still.................................... Now.......... let your mind wander.......... let it drift.......... let it float.......... like a bird.......... flying.......... gracefully across a clear blue sky.......................................

Find yourself, if you can.......... lying on a large, soft comfortable bed.......... in a beautiful room.......... Perhaps a room in a beautiful country home, surrounded by stunning scenery.......... perhaps mountains or rolling hills and forests or beautiful gardens....................................... Perhaps there is a lovely sea view from the window.......... perhaps there is a still calm lake.......... There can be anything you want there to be...........it all belongs to you...you are the creator, the designer.......... free your mind.......... but let it be a clear, bright room that you are lying in.......... a room without clutter.......... just a large, soft bed with beautiful drapes around the bed in the colours of your own making .... It has a soft, cosy cover.......... you can feel the comfort and the warmth beneath your now wonderfully relaxed body.......... Let your body sink.......... softly down into the bed.......... pleasantly sighing with contentment...................Relax.......... Deeply now.......... and deeper still.......................................

More and more relaxed now.....................................

In the room there is a table with a vase full of your favourite flowers.......... and their perfume fills the air.......... The sun streams in through a large open window. You sense an air of peacefulness..........stillness..................

Peacefully relaxed.......... without sleeping.......... Just soft, soothing thoughts of peace and stillness.......... Sinking.......... softly.......... serene and calm .... All is well.......... You are safe.......... contented.......... just breathing and sighing...... sinking softly into that part of you that knows you can give way.......... let go.......... be free.......... like the bird in the sky....floating on a breeze....................................

It is a warm summer's day.......... you can hear the sound of birds singing sweetly, as if.......... just for you.......... The rays of the sun now fill the room with a warm shimmering glow.......... and you are able to absorb this wonderful golden sunlight, as you lie there just taking it all in. Allowing the beauty, the clean, fresh air and the sweet-smelling fragrance of the flowers to permeate all the way through into your very being.......... Feeling the peacefulness of it all.......... soaking up the golden sunlight and directing it to all the tense and tight places in your body.......... and in your mind.......... feel all your stresses and strains melting away..................................... Just simply breathing in and breathing out.................................... your breathing hardly noticeable....................................

Letting the gentleness of the breath take you to a place of tranquillity.......... a safe place, deep in your heart, where you feel connected, steady, centred..................................... Just being able to accept fully who you are, as you are.......... now.......... in this present moment.......... in this present state.......... and just simply knowing that it is possible to feel joy.......... and soaking it up, this rich pleasant feeling.......... a feeling of utter contentment.......... and now allowing yourself to sink deeper.......... and deeper still..................................... Connecting now with your higher, true, self..........and just simply..................................... being....................................

And when you feel that you have absorbed as much as you can of the golden sunlight, and this peacefulness, this utter tranquillity.......... visualize yourself rising, very slowly off the bed.......... and walking across the room to the door.......... Go through the door and close it behind you.......... Walk slowly towards a staircase with ten steps going down. Stand now at the top of the stairs and hold on to the rail with your right hand. In a moment, you are going to walk slowly down the ten steps, and I will count them as you step on to each one, and with each count, and with each step down, you will become more and more deeply relaxed.

So.......... moving slowly now on to the first step, one.......... two, becoming peaceful now.......... three.......... relaxing more and more.......... four.......... five, more and more

relaxed.......... six, halfway down, feeling more and more deeply relaxed.......... seven..........
deeper still.......... eight, deeper and deeper.......... and nine, almost at the bottom..........
and ten, still awake but in a wonderful state of deep and peaceful relaxation.

Now at the bottom of the steps.......... feeling very deeply relaxed.......... but still awake,
and concentrating on the sound of my voice. You now find yourself walking across a
hallway towards a large oak door. Go through the door and close it behind you. And
there before you is a beautiful, special garden that belongs only to you.......... it is your
haven, your sanctuary.......... your place of peace and stillness. You step into it ....
and into the rich golden sunlight. Feel it warm on your face......................

Now walk down a path which leads you through this beautiful garden. As you walk
you are aware of a bright blue sky.......... You look all around you to see many trees,
some in blossom, some with brightly coloured foliage.......... There are many flowers
and their sweet perfume is all around you. You feel a warm gentle breeze on your face
now, and the sun warming your body.......... Continue to walk along the path, feeling the
ground firmly beneath your feet, feeling connected to the earth.......... feel the earth's
energy beneath your feet and flowing up through your body energizing you as you walk
forward.......... and stepping off the path now, you walk through a small wooded area.
The ground is carpeted with a magnificent display of beautiful bluebells. You find a
gently flowing stream and follow it until you arrive at a small, still lake. It is the Lake of
Tranquillity, glistening in the sunlight.......... calm and peaceful......................
still – with no ripples......................

Take a moment here, and find somewhere to sit down and rest. Look around you and
take in the beauty of this magical place.......... Notice how the sun shimmers on the
water.......... and you smile at your clear and happy reflection.

Close by a butterfly alights on a rock.......... you can almost hear the fluttering of its
wings.......... and you savour the moment.......... Everything in this peaceful special place
is just as it should be.......... and you are part of it, caught in a magical moment of perfection.......... time seems to stand still.........and you realize that you are exactly where you
are meant to be.......... now.......... in this moment.......... just as you are......................

Lifting your head towards the now bright orange sun, you marvel at the pink and red
mackerel sky, dappled with fleecy white and pink and lilac clouds as the sun begins
to set.
You stand slowly now. Stand straight, and tall. This amazing beautiful sight fills you
with a deep and profound sense of love and light.......... understanding, and belonging.......... You suddenly feel uplifted, recharged, empowered.......... strong.......... and
confident.......... loved.......... You stretch, raising your arms up towards the sky and
standing tall. You feel strong, happy and free......................

What else do you feel now? What else do you want now?..
.... When you are ready, slowly turn away from the lake and follow the stream, which takes you once again through the wood, carpeted with bluebells
....

Return to your garden.......... The large bright orange sun sinks down now to meet the horizon, creating a warm and welcoming feel to the garden.......... and, once more taking a last look around and soaking up the richness of the place......and knowing that you can return at any time, whenever you choose to, whenever you need to.......
....

You find yourself now once more at the large oak door to your beautiful house. You are able to open it quite easily.......... you glide in through the door and close it behind you. Walk through the now familiar hallway, towards the stairs.

Standing at the bottom step, place your left hand on the rail and begin to climb the steps slowly. As you climb, you will allow yourself to come slowly out of your very deep relaxation. And when you reach the top of the flight of stairs you will become much more aware of your physical body in the here and now. So, moving up the steps slowly now.......... ten.......... nine.......... eight.......... beginning to feel more aware.......... seven.......... six.......... five.......... more alert.......... four.......... almost there.......... three.......... preparing to come gently out of your relaxation.......... two.......... one..........
You are now at the top of the stairs.......... feeling alert and well and energized.

Walk along the corridor to the door of the beautiful bedroom.....................................
Go through the door and close it behind you.......... Once again lie down now on the large, soft, comfortable bed......................................

Take a slow deep breath and allow yourself to drift very, very slowly and gently back into reality, to the room where you are now.......... just as if you were floating softly on a cloud.......... back to the present moment.......... safe in the here and now. Harmonizing your mind and body, allowing your breathing to return to its normal rate and flow. And taking another deep breath, begin to move your fingers and toes.......... stretching your arms and legs.......... With another full breath, open your eyes softly, adjusting slowly to become completely aware of your surroundings. Roll over on to your right side, and curl up. Take your time. Sit up slowly only when you feel completely ready to do so. Don't get up until you are fully aware, wide awake and alert. When you do stand, move slowly..........

Take several minutes before you continue on as normal.......... then go about your day knowing that all is well – and you are better for this relaxation.

Week 9

» *RECAP AND REFLECT* «

Tick the box when understood, practised and achieved

 ACCEPT WHAT YOU CANNOT CHANGE: Are you aware of the things you cannot change? Are you able to accept them and let them go? Can you understand why, if you do this, your stress levels will reduce? Do you understand that if you refuse to accept the things you cannot change, your stress levels are bound to rise?

 EXERCISE FOR INTENSE EMOTION: Have you mastered this yet? Keep practising. Have you tried it out? Be on the lookout for any strong emotion you have and experience the exercise working for you.

 HELP YOURSELF BY HELPING OTHERS: What are your thoughts and reflections on this subject? Perhaps you were already doing this, but if not, have you started to yet? If so, how did it make you feel? Is it something you will continue to do? Have you had any further ideas on what you can do?

 ORGANIZE YOUR DAY WITH A DAILY PLANNER: Have you completed the plan yet? Reflect on how this will help you. When will you fill it in – on the night before or first thing in the morning? Perhaps you could do a week at a time. How could this benefit your life? What do you hope to gain from this exercise?

 THOUGHTS THAT INCITE PANIC: Have you been able to identify your negative thoughts? Are you managing to dispute them? How do you plan to keep on top of these irrational thoughts and beliefs? How many different ways could this exercise help you?

 AFFIRMATIONS - IT'S ALL IN THE MIND: Have you constructed yours yet? Reflect on what would work best for you. How will they help?

 CREATIVE VISUALIZATION: Have you found someone to read this out to you? Or perhaps you have my CD *Breathe and Relax* (see page 267). How did you like this method? Do you think it will help you? How many times will you use it this week?

Now turn to your self-assessment rating scales and enter your scores for the end of Week 9.

Week 10

. . . .

Week 10, Day 1
» *AWARENESS* «
What is Depression?

THERE ARE A GREAT MANY BOOKS written on depression and much research has been done on the subject over many years. It is a complex illness. There are many different forms and the word itself is often misused; many people will say they are depressed, when in actual fact they are feeling low in mood or sad or even just basically fed up.

Even if you have been diagnosed with depression you may not have been told what type of depression you have. Here is a brief description of some of the types:

Reactive or Situational Depression

This form of depression occurs when life gets you down and you have been under a great deal of stress or undergoing a crisis such as bereavement, loss of a job or divorce. The symptoms of sadness, worry and nervousness will often disappear without any treatment but it cannot be ignored, as in some cases it can lead to major depression.

Atypical Depression

This is one of the most common forms of depression and can occur as a result of a major depression in earlier life. Someone with this type of depression has an intense reaction and sensitivity to rejection, has increased appetite, weight gain, sleeps too much, has trouble with relationships and socializing, and often has a feeling of heaviness or being weighed down in the arms and legs. However, their mood can be lifted when something positive in their life occurs or when in a social setting. They can enjoy themselves despite having depression, but when the positives go, the depression returns. This is one of the reasons why relatives of someone with this condition sometimes find it hard to understand.

Chronic Depression or Dysthymia

This form of depression is not as severe or as disabling as major depression and usually takes the form of sadness over a long period of time. Its symptoms include fatigue, difficulty in concentration and sleep problems. There is also a risk of major depression following. This form of depression responds well to talking therapies.

Seasonal Affective Disorder (SAD)

This form of depression usually occurs in winter climates due to a lack of sunlight. The symptoms can include irritability, anxiety, daytime tiredness and weight gain. It can be treated with light therapy and it is generally recommended that the patient gets as much sunlight as possible.

The above forms of depression can all be overcome by taking all the advice in this book. With determination and the will to succeed it really is possible to *Get Your Life Back* and return to health and happiness.

The symptoms of the following forms of depression which are more serious can be alleviated by practising the coping strategies in this book but require additional professional guidance and supervision.

Major or Clinical Depression

This is the most common form of depression and causes severe symptoms of sadness, extreme fatigue, sleep problems, lack of appetite, lack of concentration, feelings of guilt, worthlessness, hopelessness and low self-esteem. There can also be physical symptoms such as pain and digestive problems. There may also be thoughts of suicide. For an official diagnosis the symptoms need to last longer than two weeks.

Post-natal or post-partum depression

This can occur up to two years after giving birth. It ranges from being mild to very severe and sometimes requires hospitalization. It is not only caused by a severe hormone imbalance but also by many other causal factors that need to be taken into consideration. For example: difficulties during pregnancy and delivery; a history of depression; massive major changes taking place in the mother's life; high levels of responsibility; a major change in daily routines; lack of support; relationship concerns; physical health problems following the birth; sleep deprivation and the inability to cope with a new baby.

Bipolar Disorder (sometimes referred to as Manic Depression)

Symptoms of this include extreme highs followed by extreme lows and are usually treated by a psychiatrist with medication called mood stabilizers. It can be very serious and often needs hospitalization. This illness has one of the highest risks for suicide.

Situational depression, atypical depression and dysthymia nearly always go hand in hand with stress and anxiety. When stress and anxiety are not managed well and a person feels overwhelmed by the pressures of life, these forms of depression often follow, which in turn may cause even more stress and more anxiety.

All forms of depression are often misunderstood. Unless you have suffered from depression yourself it is quite difficult to relate to it. No one goes around with a bandage tied round their head to indicate that they have an illness of the mind, unlike the plaster cast that tells everyone that you have a broken leg, and that it hurts, and that you cannot perform your duties as usual. Unfortunately sufferers of depression are still often told that they should "pull themselves together" or "get over it". A person with depression may wish that they had a physical illness so that people would understand, show compassion and help them in their recovery! Families and friends of people suffering depression often despair too because they feel they have "lost" the person they used to know and they just don't know what to do or how to help them.

As stated earlier, being sad is not the same as having depression. It is normal and perfectly natural to feel sad if you suffer a bereavement or lose your job, or experience any other kind of crisis or tragedy. Depression, however, is a severe and often serious illness. It affects us not only mentally and emotionally but also physically, behaviourally and psychologically.

The symptoms range from mild to moderate to serious and very severe. At its most severe, depression can be devastating. It can often mean a stay in hospital as well as being life-threatening; people with depression can feel that life isn't worth living, and have suicidal thoughts. Ultimately and tragically, it can actually lead to suicide.

Here is a list of some of the most common physical symptoms:

- **Digestive problems** such as constipation, bloating, nausea, loss of appetite. This is due to the fight/flight response causing the digestive system to slow down or even, in some cases, temporarily stop working altogether.
- **Immune system** slows down due to stress hormones in the bloodstream, and can cause you to have more infections.
- **Sleep problems** caused by introspection (dwelling on the negatives, over analysing, soul-searching, brooding).
- **Headaches** are very common in people with depression.
- **Muscle and joint pains**

- **Chest pain**
- **Exhaustion and fatigue**
- **Changes in appetite and weight**
- **Skin and hair problems**

People often wait a long time before visiting their doctor; they think they should be able to pull themselves together, or they see their illness as a weakness or think that nothing will help. It is often a relative who in the end insists they see a doctor. Deciding to seek help is the first, very important, step. With the right help most people recover from mild to moderate depression and in fact they often consider later that it was a positive experience, because it made them aware of important lifestyle changes that they needed to make, especially if their depression came about as a result of unmanaged stress. They also frequently learn the necessary coping strategies that will help prevent it from re-occurring.

Before your doctor can diagnose depression he or she has to ask a series of questions. This is necessary in order to be sure that there aren't any physical causes for your symptoms, such as thyroid problems, which can present similar symptoms.

The criteria for diagnosing a depressive episode can be found in the *Diagnostic and Statistical Manual of Mental Disorders.* The manual states that if you have five or more of the following symptoms (including either one or both of the first two from the list below), over a period of two weeks you will be diagnosed as suffering a major depression.

- Depressed mood
- Loss of pleasure or interest in usual activities
- Disturbance of appetite
- Sleep disturbance
- Psychomotor retardation or agitation (a slowing down of thought processes and physical activity, inability to carry out everyday tasks)
- Loss of energy
- Feelings of worthlessness and guilt
- Difficulties in thinking
- Recurrent thoughts of death or suicide

Children also suffer from depression. It is estimated that, in the UK, 4% of children between the ages of 5 and 16 are affected. The National Institute of Mental Health in the USA says that 9.1% of adolescents (ages 12–17) suffer with depression.

The contents of this book are based on my many years of experience working with patients suffering from depression, along with my own personal experiences of depression. Because depression is linked to stress, all the coping strategies found in this book will help you to overcome both. If you turn back to Week 4 you will be reminded of what stress is, how it affects you and how it develops and progresses. Depression is not only closely related to stress; it can be the result of *too much* stress, pressure and the inability to cope or the *perceived* inability to cope. A person diagnosed with clinical depression will have very high levels of the stress hormone cortisol in their bloodstream. If you manage your stress effectively, your stress hormones will diminish and your depression will reduce. However, there are additional treatments and therapies that will also help bring about a full recovery.

Medication

Depending on your form of depression one of the first things your doctor might do is prescribe an antidepressant. Because we are unique individuals, what works for one person may not work for another, and a period of trial and error over a number of weeks, or even months, will lead to you and your doctor finding the right one for you. Antidepressants help by lifting your mood significantly. However, it is estimated that up to a third of people are not helped by medication and many stop taking their medication because of the undesirable side-effects. It is not fully understood why antidepressants work, and there is a school of thought that suggests that it may even be the placebo effect that does the trick. (A placebo has no medical effect but if the unknowing patient believes it will work, then it can work.) Antidepressants are very powerful drugs and are not normally given to children, as a child's brain is not fully developed.

Medication alone is not always the answer and many people do recover from depression with therapy alone. Studies show that, in most cases, a combination of antidepressants and therapy is probably the best way forward.

Cognitive Behavioural Therapy

In the UK the NHS, and in particular NICE (The National Institute for Health and Care Excellence), recommends using CBT (Cognitive Behavioural Therapy) to treat depression. During my career, under the supervision of a clinical consultant psychologist I delivered a personally devised twelve-week course in CBT, which was very successful; many patients recovered from their stress, anxiety and depression before the course had ended. As well as CBT, the course used many of the other coping strategies and exercises that are covered in this book.

CBT is effective because it helps people challenge their limiting and self-destructive beliefs and behaviours. A person who is depressed is constantly focusing on the negatives in their life and will have many of the irrational thoughts and thinking errors described in Week 5, Day 5. In particular they are certain to be thinking in *black and white* or *all or nothing* terms. This means that there is no flexibility in their thinking. It is either one thing or another; there is nothing in between. They will be constantly analysing all their past mistakes or catastrophizing and imagining that everything that can go wrong will go wrong.

Week 10, Day 2
» *UNDERSTANDING* «
Understanding Depression

"The primary cause of unhappiness is never
the situation but your thoughts about it."
— *ECKHART TOLLE, author of* The Power of Now

Understanding depression is difficult. Even the experts don't fully understand the causes of depression, and those who suffer with it often find it difficult to explain. Having had bouts of depression in my own early life, both situational and post-natal, leading to a major depression, I can fully understand how difficult it can be for the onlooker to appreciate what it is like to suffer depression if they have never experienced it themselves. In my own case I suffered a whole gamut of symptoms, including many physical conditions and the added complications of psychosomatic (psychological) disorders such as limb pain and even globus hystericus (phantom lump in the throat!). Most of my family were sympathetic but didn't really understand or know how to help me. Medication didn't help me, and in those days counselling or stress management simply wasn't available, I just had to get on with it and allow time to pass. It was a few years before I joined my first yoga class and eventually made a full recovery.

When sufferers of depression are diagnosed and medicated it is rare that the doctor will explain what depression is, how it comes about, what to expect and how long it will last. It is even more rare for loved ones and relatives to be given any information on the subject; they are often left completely in the dark. Although the stigma of mental illness has now lessened and governments are trying their best to educate the general public, it is in many quarters still perceived as being a very embarrassing and unacceptable condition.

If you are a sufferer of depression and you feel your loved ones don't understand, set a goal for yourself to find a way of educating them. Reading these pages might be a big help.

If you are a relative or close to a sufferer and you are now reading this, here are some of the things that might help you to understand a little more about depression:

- Find out as much as you can about the illness
- Try to identify a support group for relatives or look online for support sites
- Be patient with the patient; they may be feeling guilty for having depression. They may be feeling helpless and hopeless and focusing on everything bad in their lives. This is a big part of the illness, a common symptom that is difficult (but not impossible) to overcome.
- Point out all the good and positive things in their life on a daily basis

- Involve them in some sort of activity – as much as possible
- Encourage them to take up a hobby or interest
- Go for long walks with them, at least half an hour a day
- Ensure that all their needs are being met
- Encourage them to socialize in some way.

Some of the Many Causes and Reasons for the Increase in Depression

1 · **A pessimistic perception and negative reaction to** major life events, particularly of loss, such as the death of a loved one, redundancy, divorce or the break-up of a relationship.

2 · **Insecurity** about employment can cause massive amounts of stress and depression. Years ago many more people had employment and, if they wanted it, a job for life. In more recent times job stability has become rarer and short-term contracts are more common. In this age of computerization and more advanced technology taking the place of people, worrying about staying in employment has major consequences. This is especially significant for young families, who are struggling with financial difficulties, and the over-50s, who may have been made redundant and find it difficult to find employment again.

3 · **Broken Homes.** Single-parent families are commonplace these days and it is not unusual in some schools to have more one-parent children than those with both parents living at home. Research has been carried out to highlight the effects on children who live with only one parent by comparing them with those who live with two parents. The findings show that children with both parents living at home are more likely to have fewer emotional and behavioural problems. They are also more socially adept and less liable to take drugs and adopt antisocial behaviour. In adulthood many of these children will have adapted well and be able to cope with the stresses and strains of life, but there are those who will cope less well and may be vulnerable to anxiety, depression and addictions.

4 · **Loss of the Extended Family and Decline of Community Spirit.** Research shows that where people live in tribal communities or extended family environments, depression is significantly less prevalent or even non-existent. This is most likely because when someone in the group has a crisis or a problem, or they feel unwell or afraid, the whole family or community gathers together to support them, help solve the problem or help them to overcome the adversity.

Unfortunately, this is less common today. People move away from the nuclear family for work, education or because of the price of property. They see their extended family less frequently, maybe only once or twice a year. There certainly isn't the opportunity to pop round the corner to offload your troubles or ask your grandmother for help or advice. Communication by technology can be a blessing, but it doesn't replace the importance and joy of human contact, support and stability.

5 · **Imbalance is a major cause of stress and depression.**

- If you have too much to do and not enough time, you are antagonized by this and, your fight/flight response will be set on permanent.
- If you have too much responsibility and not enough freedom from that responsibility, you will find yourself under pressure that you are unable to manage.
- If you work too long hours and don't take enough breaks, not only will you feel stressed, frustrated, anxious and even angry but, you will become physically drained, exhausted and possibly unwell.
- If you don't find time to relax or you choose not to relax – guess what? Yes, you will become mentally, emotionally and physically unwell.
- If you exercise too much and don't take periods of rest, your body will be screaming at you to give it a break!

6 · **Worry.** Having an excessive negative attitude about your problems, and the inability, or motivation, to seek solutions.

7 · **Feelings of Worthlessness.** During my career I came across a number of patients who felt that their life had no or very little meaning. For example:

- Mothers whose children had left home
- People whose partners had left them, or divorced them, leaving them alone
- The bereaved who had cared for a loved one over a long period of time
- People who had retired or been made redundant from a job they loved, and do nothing to replace it.

8 · **Too Many Major Changes Too Close Together.** We are all creatures of habit and generally feel comfortable with what we know, or are familiar with, and uncomfortable with the unknown. It isn't *actually* the changes that cause depression; it is the inability to adapt to change that causes the stress and subsequent depression.

Too many changes too close together is considered to be one of the four major contributing factors to stress and pressure.

I should also point out that the changes that we find difficult to adapt to don't necessarily need to be negative or unpleasant changes such as divorce or redundancy. *Any* major change can upset our equilibrium or balance. If, however, there are too many major changes too close together – for example, if a person gets married, takes on a new job, moves house and has a baby, all in the space of eighteen months – even though these changes were chosen, and they were happy changes, the stress they cause could be unmanageable.

This scenario is often misunderstood by the onlooker. Even the victim of the stress or depression themselves is often left mystified. You will hear them say "I've got everything I always wanted and dreamed of, I've got nothing to be depressed about. I can't understand what's happening to me." Retirement is a typical example of this. Someone looks forward immensely to their retirement but when it comes it is such a dramatic change to their routine and their life that it can ultimately lead to depression.

9 · **Introspection/Brooding.** If we fall victim to any of the above and feel unable to cope, we are in danger of focusing our attention inwards instead of finding ways to cope. It is then a very slippery slope towards depression. If this is the cause of your depression, taking action is extremely important.

10 · **Our Inability to Relax.** Relaxation is the exact opposite of stress. We cannot be stressed at the same time as being relaxed. When we are unable to balance our stress with relaxation, there is a danger that our stress levels will rise so high that we will become exhausted and overwhelmed with the pressure. Depression will often follow. Relaxation then becomes vital if we are to restore balance and return to good health. Relaxation, along with creative visualization, can be extremely therapeutic if practised daily. See Day 7 this week for an example of my specifically designed relaxation for overcoming depression.

11 · **Setbacks.** When a setback or a crisis dominates our life, causing worry, excessive negative thinking and an all-consuming pessimistic attitude, stress levels generally go sky-high. The fight/flight response remains switched on while we struggle through these difficult times. In addition, excessive introspection (focusing inwards) puts enormous pressure on us mentally. As a result we become physically, mentally and emotionally drained. And although we feel exhausted, sleep either eludes us or we experience intense dreaming or nightmares. The result is that we wake up still feeling tired, depressed, lethargic and lacking in motivation. One of the major symptoms and effects of depression is lethargy.

Lethargy can also be described as:

- Weariness
- Tiredness
- Exhaustion
- Fatigue
- Laziness
- Sluggishness
- Lifelessness
- Listlessness
- No *get up and go*!

It's no wonder then that people who are depressed find it extremely difficult to do anything at all! However, this is a great misfortune, because together with positive thinking, activity is probably one of the best ways of overcoming depression. So, I've got my work cut out here! I somehow need to persuade my depressed readers to get up, get moving and get active. This is *vital* if you are to overcome your depression. I know how that sounds – remember, I've been there myself – but I mean this most sincerely: I'm not telling you to *pull yourself together*, I am suggesting that from today you will make a conscious decision and a monumental effort to *Get Your Life Back* by finding things to do and returning to the things that you used to enjoy.

As you learned earlier, thoughts affect your feelings, your behaviour, your actions and your outcomes. However, you may not have realized that it works the other way round too. Your actions and behaviour affect your feelings and your thoughts. It follows therefore that if you do something that you enjoy doing, you will feel better, which will result in a happier thought. The happier your thoughts, the less depressed you are.

How to get out of the lethargy trap

1 · **Activity:** As outlined above, activity and exercise are vitally important if you are to overcome stress, anxiety and depression. When you exercise you release endorphins and serotonin (the feel-good hormones). However, there are further benefits:

- Distracts you from your negative thinking and worrying
- Helps you to achieve your goals
- Improves your self-esteem and self-worth
- Increases your social contact
- Increases your energy
- Makes you less tired
- Promotes sleep
- Promotes positive thinking

2 · **Completing a Daily Planner:** A Daily Planner like the one described in Week 9, Day 4 helps to ensure that you always have things to do to fill your whole day. If you have difficulty with developing one, ask someone to help you complete it.

3 · **Making an effort to achieve your goals:** The Wheel of Life exercise, Week 7, Day 6, will draw your attention to the areas of your life that need some improvement. Setting your goals and beginning to achieve them will lift your mood and raise your self-worth.

4 · **Visualization:** One of the most therapeutic tools you can use to overcome your depression and get you out of the lethargy trap is creative visualization relaxation. You may also have practised the visualization exercise from Week 6, Day 7 (A Powerful Encounter), in which you imagined or visualized meeting a person or persons who were there to help you to solve your problems and find solutions. It acts as a solution-finder by delving into, and exploring, your own inner resources, which in turn helps solve your problems. This of course is beneficial in many other ways too. It is a form of deep relaxation and will switch off the fight/flight response, balance out your stress, calm your mind and increase concentration, motivation and energy.

My last piece of advice for those of you suffering depression is to use
this book as a manual and do as much work with it as you possibly can
(just don't overdo it!).

Week 10, Day 3
» PHYSICAL HEALTH «
Yoga Stretches 2

"The yoga mat is a good place to turn when talk therapy
and antidepressants aren't enough."
— AMY WEINTRAUB, author of Yoga for Depression

I cannot emphasize enough just how beneficial joining a yoga class will be. More and more people are practising yoga now as we become more aware of its many and varied benefits. I found it to be both therapeutic and life-changing.

Yoga's physical exercises cannot effectively be taught from a book, but the gentle stretching exercises below along with the breathing exercises, relaxations, meditations and principles in this book are a very good start.

The first yoga stretches can be found in Week 8, Day 3. Return to these and go through them before attempting the following. They are best done in the morning and should ideally be followed by the breathing exercises sequence. This routine will leave you feeling energized, invigorated and motivated to go about your day with a fresh and positive perspective.

1 · Stand tall with your feet together. Place the palms of your hands flat on the top of your thighs, keeping your arms straight. For a slow count of six, slide your hands down the fronts of your legs, keeping the legs straight and knees locked. Only go as far as you comfortably can. Return to an upright position, again for a count of six. It does not matter how far you can reach down, but with time and regular practice you may be able to touch the floor with your fingertips and eventually place your palms flat on the floor.

2 · Keeping your feet together, legs straight, knees locked and your arms straight throughout, place the backs of your hands on the backs of your thighs and for a slow count of six, slide the backs of your hands down the backs of your legs, gently arching your back and allowing your head to drop backwards a little. Make sure there is no strain in your neck and open your mouth while letting the head fall back so there is no strain on your throat. Once you have reached what feels like your limit without strain, pain or shaking, return to an upright position for a count of six.

3 · Stand with your feet shoulder width apart and, keeping your legs straight, simply drop sideways to the right, your right hand reaching gently towards your right foot. Return to the upright position and then drop sideways in the same way to the left, and return to upright.

4 · Place the palm of your left hand at the base of your spine, fingers pointing downwards, and the palm of your right hand at the top of the right thigh. For a count of six, slide the right hand down the front of the right leg, as far as you can comfortably go, then return to an upright position. Eventually your fingertips or palm may reach the floor, in which case place the fingertips or palm at the side of your foot, fingers facing forwards.

5 · Repeat as above but this time with your right palm at the base of your spine and the left palm sliding down the front of the left leg as far as is comfortable, then returning to upright.

6 · Keeping your feet facing forwards, shoulder width apart, turn your body to look to your right. Place your right palm at the base of your spine and left palm on the outside of your right leg. Slide the left hand down the outside of the right leg, keeping the legs straight if possible (you may bend the knees slightly if necessary), then return to an upright position, still facing to your right. Hold this position for a moment, then turn to face your left.

7 · Repeat on the left side: place your left palm at the base of your spine, sliding the right hand down the side of your left leg, feel a gentle stretch and return to upright.

8 · Stand with your feet shoulder width apart and your arms down by your sides. Keep your arms straight and your fingers stretched out. As you take a deep breath all the way in, raise your arms out to the side and up, over your head until your palms touch above your head. Stretch as tall as you can go. Keeping your arms straight, lower them down again as you breathe all the way out. Repeat twice more.

9 · You can do this next stretch sitting, or standing with the feet apart. Place your fingertips on your shoulders with your elbows pointing downwards. Keep your fingertips on your shoulders while you circle your elbows three times forwards and three times backwards.

10 · Standing tall again, with the feet shoulder width apart, face front, take a slow deep breath in, then drop your head back loosely, open your mouth and breathe out through your mouth (so as not to strain the throat), and gently arch the back with your hands and arms dropping loosely behind your back. You should feel a gentle stretch in the middle of your back and the front of your body; don't overdo it. When you are ready, breathe in again and return to an upright position. Move immediately on to the next part.

11 · Keeping the feet shoulder width apart, take a full deep breath all the way in. This time as you breathe out drop your body forwards towards the floor (you needn't do this slowly). Let your hands, arms and head drop forwards very loosely. At this point you may bend your knees a little. Imagine you are a rag doll, very loose and floppy. Let go completely and feel all the tension draining out of you. Make sure you are not holding your arms stiffly or straight out in front of you; they should flop very loosely down from your shoulders towards the floor. Let your fingers also be loose and curled. Let go more and more. Check that your neck and head are also loose and floppy and relaxed. Let all your tension flow out and away. Stay for a few breaths and when you are ready, breathe in, slowly return to an upright position and breathe normally.

I call this last exercise "The Rag Doll". It is more of a letting go than a stretch and can be performed without having to do all the others first. It is very useful for whenever you are feeling stressed or wound up. Try it when you get home from work, or after a day's shopping and you're feeling exhausted.

Week 10, Day 4
» MANAGING STRESS «
Fulfilling Our Emotional Needs

Emotional needs are feelings that we all have in order for us to feel good about ourselves and which are vital for good mental health. We all have essentially the same needs, but they can vary from person to person depending on personal circumstances. We all possess the resources and ability to achieve all of our basic human emotional needs. However, when these needs are not met there is the potential to suffer mental distress and mental health problems such as high stress levels, anxiety and depression. It is therefore essential that you identify any needs not being met and acquire the motivation and solutions to attain them.

Below is a brief description of ten of the most important emotional needs.

1. **Security** – a safe place in a healthy environment in which we are able to progress through life without fear or threat.
2. **Attention** – to be able to give and receive it in order for us to feel respected, loved and cared for and to receive feedback that we are valued as a person.
3. **A sense of autonomy and control** – having the ability and freedom to make choices for ourselves and to be independent from others.
4. **Being emotionally connected to others** – to feel safe in a relationship; able to trust one another and able to communicate our feelings freely to each other.
5. **Feeling part of a wider community** – to have a sense of belonging, whether it is in a small or a large group, in a social setting or work environment.
6. **Friendship and intimacy** – to know that at least one other person accepts us totally for who we are, with all our faults and weaknesses.
7. **Privacy** – having time, space and freedom to ourselves in order to reflect on our experiences.
8. **A sense of status** within social groups, and to feel valued by our peers.
9. **A sense of competence and achievement** – from learning, achieving and having the ability to apply our abilities and skills, thus maintaining our self-esteem.
10. **Having meaning and purpose** – which comes from being stretched and tested; having the ability to use our resources and skills to our full potential in what we do and think. This ensures self-worth.

Read through these needs carefully and systematically. Identify how your needs are being met and write each one down in your workbook. If you find that you are not achieving any of them, think about each need and what must happen in order for you to fulfil it. Write it down as a goal to achieve as soon as you possibly can.

NOTE: There is an excellent website where you can do an online emotional needs audit and receive the results via email: www.enaproject.org.

Week 10, Day 5
» *ANXIETY SOLUTIONS* «

Thinking About Things in a Different Way

"The mind is everything. What you think you become."
— *BUDDHA*

However your stress manifests or expresses itself, whether it is in physical ailments, anxiety, panic attacks or depression, many of your thoughts will probably lead to unpleasant feelings and negative behavior, resulting in a negative outcome or consequences.

You will have seen in Week 5, Day 5 that there are many ways in which you can deal with your thinking errors. We have addressed some of these methods already and I expect that you are continuing to follow the advice and practise the skills. However, another productive way to overcome these harmful negative thoughts and beliefs is to challenge them in a way that leads to a more balanced and reasonable view or perception. Remember, it is not the situation that causes your distress, but the way you *perceive* the situation.

Socratic Questioning

Some of your negative thoughts can be challenged quite easily in order to help you recognize that there is another more rational way you can think about things. However, with more severe forms of anxiety disorders and depression you can tend to have thoughts, beliefs and assumptions that are more resistant to change. Socratic questioning is a technique that helps to challenge the most rigid of these beliefs and can therefore result in a more balanced, rational and reasonable perspective.

Have you ever thoroughly questioned someone else about their problems and difficulties? The chances are you have. When someone comes to you to offload, or you are having a chat to someone close to you and they talk about their fears and worries, you probably ask one or more of the following questions:

- *Is it really that bad?*
- *Wherever did you get that idea?*
- *Have you tried talking to him/her?*
- *Are you sure you've got that right?*

But do you ever ask *yourself* questions like that? Have you ever stopped to examine what the real truth is?

The aim of Socratic questioning is to examine, challenge and attach logic to our cognitions (thoughts and beliefs) and to identify any evidence that discredits them. This can result in a more balanced and logical viewpoint. Many people who are anxious are not always exactly sure what their fears actually are and their beliefs or assumptions about a situation may not be relevant to the person they are today and the circumstances they are in. For example: someone may be anxious about flying but may not be able to pin it on anything in particular. They might say they would have a panic attack, but don't really know why. It could be possible that their real problem is claustrophobia because they were once locked in a cupboard when they were six years old. Their fear is not necessarily about the plane crashing – they may not even think about the fear of the plane crashing; they probably don't have a phobia about driving their car and the car crashing, even though that risk is greater. Many phobias are borne out of an incident that happened a very long time ago and which doesn't apply or make any sense today.

Similarly, a person suffering from depression may dwell continuously on the fact that they didn't get the job they went for ten years ago and still perceive themselves as being useless, hopeless and that they are a complete failure in everything they do. This may prevent them from moving forward with their life and realizing their full potential.

So Socratic questions help to identify what the *real* fear is – and then pick it apart!

Below are some examples of Socratic questions that challenge your irrational thoughts, beliefs and assumptions. Identify one of your self-defeating beliefs, such as: *No matter what I do it's never good enough*, or *I can't eat vegetables because I will be sick* or *I can't go on holiday because I will be ill* and subject it to the following questions. Get someone to ask you the following questions or write the questions and answers down in your workbook.

- What are the actual facts, the actual truth?
- How do you perceive this now?
- What evidence is there to support your perceptions?
- What evidence contradicts your perceptions?
- How is this belief helpful to you?
- How would you feel if you didn't have this belief?
- When did you become aware of this belief?
- Who else was involved? Is this person still part of your life today?
- Is your belief based on an event that happened when you were a child?
- Is it still true now?
- Is it always true?
- Could you give me an example of when it hasn't been true?
- Could you be assuming something?
- What could you assume instead?
- What would you say to someone else who had the same belief?
- What would they think?

- How would they react to it?
- Do you think that will definitely happen or only possibly happen?
- How can you think about this in a different way?
- What conclusions can you draw now?

What you need to do next

1 · Think about the results or discuss them with someone else. This exercise will have more impact if someone asks you the questions and you answer them out loud.

2 · Thinking about your example of a self-defeating belief, formulate a new belief: "I now believe.. because...................................... ."

3 · Write it down. Repeat it often throughout the day, or use it as one of your positive affirmations, and use it especially when you are aware of having the irrational thought.

4 · Repeat the process for any other thoughts, beliefs and assumptions that are causing your anxiety or low mood.

Week 10, Day 6
» DIRECTION «
Complementary Therapies

Many towns or cities have at least one complementary therapy centre. I have been a member of the Solihull Natural Health Group for over twenty years and was its Assistant Co-ordinator for many of those years. As a result, I must have attended hundreds of talks, seminars, courses and workshops on most of the therapies that are available; I have benefitted from a great variety of therapies in my time and would thoroughly recommend that you try some from the ones listed below. I am including those that are particularly helpful for treating stress, anxiety and depression and all related conditions.

Yoga

One of the first things I did for myself when going through a bout of depression many years ago, after a friend recommended it, was to join a yoga class. I was very reluctant to do this at the time, but I will always be grateful to that friend because it changed my life and I never looked back. It was the best thing I could have done to set myself on the road to a new and healthier life.

The form of yoga I studied was Pranayama Yoga (introduced in Week 3, Day 2). It involves not just physical exercises (asanas) and breathing exercises but also the philosophy of yoga. This is a simple philosophy and is accessible for everyone; its principles and influence can be found in many pages of this book along with its unique breath-control exercises, relaxations and yoga stretches, which you are already practising.

To learn more and enjoy and safely perform the physical postures, you will need to find a class because you cannot easily learn these from a book. There are many forms of yoga taught in the West, hatha and Iyengar yoga in particular being very popular. They will all lead to the same end – you will become healthier, happier and stronger in mind, body and spirit. You will enhance the quality of your life and gain peace of mind and tranquillity.

Emotional Freedom Technique (EFT)

This is one of the most effective forms of therapy I ever used in my career as a stress management consultant and therapist. It works by stimulating acupuncture points, mainly on the face and hands, by tapping on them using the fingertips. No needles are involved! It is painless, non-invasive and usually works quite quickly. The technique can help to overcome, or greatly reduce, a large variety of mental health issues including: anxiety, panic attacks, phobias, OCD (Obsessive Compulsive Disorder) and even auditory hallucinations (hearing voices). The results were so good that I easily persuaded many of my colleagues to train too. It is a result of this that the UK NHS Mental Health Trust I worked for now approves the use of EFT.

Reflexology

This ancient Chinese practice also uses energy points, which correspond to the organs and glands of the body, but in this discipline they are mainly on the feet and hands. As a slight pressure is applied to the points it simultaneously stimulates the corresponding parts of the body in order to create balance and for them to work more efficiently. It can also be used as a diagnostic tool: while feeling the points, a practitioner can tell if there is a problem in that area. It is extremely good for relieving stress and anxiety as well as for physical ailments.

Massage

Another one of my favourites. There are many different types of massage but the most common are aromatherapy, deep muscle, Swedish, sports, Thai, hot stone and shiatsu. I can recommend them all!

T'ai Chi (or T'ai Chi Chuan)

This is actually a type of Chinese martial art, which developed in the thirteenth century but has evolved more recently into a meditation in movement. It incorporates slow, deep breathing along with very gentle slow, flowing movements of the whole body. It is wonderful for releasing stress and anxiety and inducing a feeling of inner peace. It is obviously extremely popular in China but can also now be found in many countries across the world.

Week 10, Day 7
» *MEDITATION* «
A Guided Visualization for Depression

There are many ways of treating and overcoming depression, the main ones being positive thinking, visualization and being active. We have covered the positive thinking part and examined the importance of activity; we have also already done some visualization. So here is a specific guided visualization exercise that can help bring you out of your depressed state. You don't have to be suffering from depression to benefit from this; it is good for everyone.

Go to the usual place where you do your relaxation. Lie down comfortably and close your eyes. Take three slow deep abdominal breaths.

When you are ready, try if you can to visualize yourself in the middle of the countryside on a cold winter's day. You are walking along a tree-lined country lane, but all the trees are bare. You are walking slowly and sluggishly, feeling the hard ground beneath your feet. The sky above is cloudy, grey and dismal with no sunshine, but you don't really notice it; your head is down and you just keep walking, not really knowing where you are heading. There is no smile on your face and you are feeling tired and cold, but you are determined to carry on because it is expected of you and you know you have to keep going, no matter what.

After a little while you reach a wooden gate, to your right. It seems like a good idea to go through the gate so, placing your hands on the rough wooden bar, you open it and go through, closing it behind you. You find yourself in a bare and empty field with nothing in it but rough patches of grass and the dry scorched earth. It's also a little bumpy as you walk across it towards a hill in the distance. For some reason you have the feeling that you need to climb this hill and get to the top. Walking with some difficulty across the field, you stumble once or twice, but you are able to pick yourself up and keep going. Once you reach the other side of the field you find you have to walk through a small, dense, dark forest.

Once again there are no leaves on the trees. The trees are so close together you are forced to take the narrow winding path through the darkness of the forest. You feel a little crowded, cold and alone, but eventually you see a clearing where the sun is just beginning to break through the clouds. You can see clearly now how the rays of the sun filter through the tops of the trees. You quicken your pace a little, eager to escape the dark, dismal, gloomy forest. It doesn't take long for you to reach the clearing, where you find a small lake at the foot of the hill. The lake looks a little gloomy too but there is promise that it will shortly be illuminated by the now bright-golden sun.

As you walk along the path round the lake, the hill is now very close and seems much higher than it was when you were still in the field. At the foot of the hill you take a long deep breath before beginning your climb. Surprisingly, you find a burst of energy from somewhere deep within you and the climb now doesn't seem so arduous. You suddenly find yourself in the midst of the sun's golden rays, which light up your way – your journey to the summit. You feel stronger, you have more energy than you've had in a long time and a slight smile is forming on your lips.

The top of the hill is now in sight. It seems as if it is summoning you, encouraging you to reach it quickly. Birds are now flying high above and you can hear them singing to you as if calling out to you – *you can do it, you're almost there*! As you look up to acknowledge their presence you notice that the sky is now a rich deep blue without a cloud to be seen. The large golden sun is now shining directly on the top of the hill and suddenly you're there – at the top, flooded with golden light, feeling warm; feeling contented, exhilarated, and feeling as if you have conquered Mount Everest!

You stand tall and breathe in the fresh clean air. You know you have reached your goal and begin to experience a feeling of joy, a sense of achievement and satisfaction. You feel like a brand new person. You raise your arms and lift your head to the clear blue sky and let the rich golden rays of the sun envelop you. You absorb all its energy and take whatever you need from it. Whatever you are lacking, whatever you have been without for so long. Your body, mind and spirit become enriched now as they soak in everything they need to return to full health, happiness and contentment.

Then at the top of your voice you shout "*I am strong, I am happy, I am free, I am me again!*"

Now, incredibly, you begin to fly! You soar like an eagle flying effortlessly on the thermals in the air. The landscape all around you looks so beautiful it takes your breath away. From this perspective everything seems so small, so insignificant, and you feel so large and powerful. You are able to look down at your life and realize that everything is manageable, uncomplicated, attainable and surmountable. You have the power now to overcome all obstacles. There is nothing that you can't do or achieve. You are bigger and stronger than all of your problems; your struggle has ceased. *Your life is back!*

You now become *you* again, standing tall at the top of a hill that has become a mountain. As you look below you, you notice that the land has now become green and lush and beautiful. It has become a bright summer's day. You are ready now to face your reality with renewed strength and fortitude. You race down the mountain with ease and vigour. You are soon at the bottom and make your way along the path round the now lovely clear, still, tranquil lake surrounded by trees in full bloom and flowers of every colour. You smell their sweet perfume and hear the evening birdsong. You notice the wildlife all around you, the animals coming to walk with you.

Reaching the now summer-leaved and brightly lit forest, you take the same path as before, but it now has a crystal-clear stream running beside it. You bend down and cup your hand to drink the sparklingly fresh and healing water. You feel a clearing of your mind and a peace within your soul you have never felt before. It has calmed and quietened your mind. It has refreshed every cell in your body.

Reaching the field you crossed earlier, you now find that it is a field of lush green fresh grass and abundant with beautiful yellow, red and blue wildflowers. You run through the field now with your renewed energy, happiness and excitement. You can't wait to get back to your new life, to enjoy it, cherish it and live it to the full. Go through the gate, close it behind you and find yourself back on the road where you began your journey. The road of course is now flooded with golden sunlight and lined with trees in full blossom.

Take your time now to return gently and slowly to the room where you are relaxing.

Allow your breathing to return to its normal rate and flow and find yourself back in the here and now.

Reflect on this visualization and make notes in you workbook. *Practise every day.*

Week 10

» RECAP AND REFLECT «

Tick the box when understood, practised and achieved

WHAT IS DEPRESSION?: Are you clear about what depression is and how it affects you? Do you have any of the physical symptoms? How many symptoms on the list of criteria do you have? If you have more than five, including one of the first two, have you been to the doctor?

UNDERSTANDING DEPRESSION: Do you understand more about depression now? Have you identified the type and cause of your depression? What are you doing to help lift it? Have you increased your activity? Are you using your Daily Planner? If not, start today. Were you aware that your thoughts are mostly negative? What do you intend doing about your negative thoughts? What else do you need to do?

YOGA STRETCHES 2: Have you tried these? How did you feel afterwards? Do you intend to do these every morning?

FULFILLING OUR EMOTIONAL NEEDS: Do you meet all your emotional needs? If not, what can you do to correct this? What difference would it make to you if you fulfilled all your emotional needs?

THINKING ABOUT THINGS IN A DIFFERENT WAY: Which of your thinking errors have you put under this scrutiny? How does it change your thinking? Does this exercise help you to think in a different way about your negative thoughts and beliefs? How does it help you?

COMPLEMENTARY THERAPIES: Have you tried any of these? If not, which would suit you most? Find out where your nearest complementary therapies centre is and which therapies they offer. Try your local community centre for yoga or t'ai chi. You may want to go with a friend who will support you.

A GUIDED VISUALIZATION FOR DEPRESSION: How did you like this? How many times will you practise it this week? Are you able to remember the instructions? Can you get someone to read it out?

Now turn to your self-assessment rating scales and enter your scores for the end of Week 10.

Week 11

. . . .

Week 11, Day 1

Our Inner Resources

*"Look well into thyself; there is a source of strength which
will always spring up if thou wilt always look."*
— *MARCUS AURELIUS, Roman emperor and philosopher*

Think of a difficult time you went through in the past, perhaps a crisis or a trauma.

> • Did you think at the time that you might never get over it?
> • Did you wonder whether you would be able to cope?
> • Did you feel that nothing could ever be as bad?
> • Perhaps you thought your world had come crashing down around you.
> • Perhaps you did not believe that things would ever feel normal again.

LOOKING BACK AND REFLECTING on that crisis now, how do you perceive it at this moment in time? Did you get over it? Have you come to terms with it? What helped? How would you cope if you had another difficult time or crisis now?

Many of us have been through great adversity; it is very difficult to escape pain and sorrow in the world in which we live. I'm sure we have all been told at some point that time is a great healer, but like everyone else, you may have thought on hearing it that it was just a cliché, and that you would never feel OK again. However, time passing *can* be a great help. Time puts a distance between us and the pain, the present and the past, and it is this distance that does the healing. For some, the pain never completely goes away, but with their inner resources of strength and peace together with the passing of time, they can still learn to cope.

Think about the times you have coped or been strong, either for yourself or for someone else. There are times when we all have to be strong. We may have no choice in the matter. Often, when we are responsible for another human being and something bad happens, our light shines through, we take control and we do what we have to do. We can be strong when we have to be strong. However, we often sit down when it's all over and think *"Wow! How on earth did I do that? Where did that come from?"*

There may also be other times in your life when you have been struggling and had to dig deeply, but you got there in the end. You may realize that there was something inside you that got you through, and it wasn't just time passing: it was instinctive, automatic, intuitive. It motivated you to get out of bed in a morning. It may have got you to work, or helped you to get through normal everyday tasks, even if you seemed to be in a dream, or you felt that it was happening to somebody else and you were just observing from a distance. You must have eaten, you must have dressed, had normal conversations, even though you didn't feel up to it at the time. The reason you were able to do all these things is that we all possess an amazing, unconscious ability to draw on this inner resource of strength even if we didn't know we had it.

Once you know this inner strength is there, you will be able to summon it up whenever you need it. Sometimes you just need an extra boost of strength to get you through the next few minutes, or the next hour, or the next situation. Sometimes, when you think you can't carry on, it naturally kicks in anyway. Have you ever stopped to take a long deep breath, intuitively knowing it would help? Your breath is the link between your body, your mind and your spirit and it is the spirit where your inner resources reside. Just taking a deep breath can sometimes help you to connect to your inner resources. Being in a state of peacefulness also helps with this connection, and being able to empower yourself so easily at such difficult times is very comforting and rewarding. It's almost like having a best friend by your side all the time, giving you the support and encouragement you need to soldier on.

Some people are aware of their inner strength and are able consciously and deliberately to draw on it in times of stress or distress. Just by looking inside themselves they are able to feel stronger and empowered, and ready to face the challenge. You too can connect with that inner power simply by being quiet and looking inwards for a moment.

Others may need to reconnect with their true self. This means bringing your awareness to who you truly are. Remember that every life experience you have had has made you who you are today. Of course you will have had both good and bad experiences in your life, but each of these can be strengthening and fortifying. Every time you have achieved something or overcome adversity, every time you have met head-on something that was challenging or demanding, and every time you have felt proud about an accomplishment, you have been building up your deposits in your own bank of inner strength.

You have already done some exercises in self-awareness (Week 2, Day 2 and Week 3, Day 4). Go back to these exercises now and remind yourself of all your unique qualities, skills, abilities, talents, gifts and strengths. This is who you really are, inside, the human spirit part of you. This is the essence of you. However, over the years, as life goes on this spirit sometimes gets covered up with layer upon layer of stressful living. It is easy to lose sight of your strengths when coping with life is proving difficult. Directing a negative focus outwards onto your burdens and demands leads you away from your true inner and stronger self.

What you need to do therefore is to peel away these layers; this will enable you to connect once again with the very positive Inner You. Being mindful will help, and you have already started to do this without even realizing it, because whenever you relax, meditate, do your breathing exercises or involve yourself completely in the moment, you are removing the layers, little by little, one by one, just like peeling an onion. If you continue to do this, along with cultivating a positive frame of mind, you will arrive at the core.

Your core is physically located in your solar plexus. You find it just above your navel and below where your ribcage comes together in the middle. It is an energy centre deep inside you. Yoga practitioners may know this as the solar plexus chakra.

Try this exercise to connect with your inner self:

When you are fully relaxed, take your attention to your core, the centre of yourself. Imagine it as a light or a flame that never goes out. Imagine yourself breathing in the light and strength that emanate from there. Now fully connect with the essence of who you are, the strong and powerful self that never sleeps. Draw on the power that lies within you and let it empower you, with whatever it is you need to be able to cope with the difficult situations you are facing.

As well as the inner self, you also have a higher self. Your higher self is all-knowing, full of wisdom and knowledge and is the utterly positive and truthful side of you. Some say it is part of your subconscious mind, or the awakened aspects of yourself. The higher self is there to give you help and guidance whenever you seek it. You can reach your higher self in deep relaxation, meditation or simply being quiet and peaceful, at one with yourself. You can ask your higher self a question; if you just listen and stay patient you may hear the answer.

Go back to Week 6 Day 7: A Powerful Encounter. This meditation uses the higher self to assist you in finding answers. Do this meditation again soon.

So, going back to the time when you coped even though you thought you wouldn't be able to, you probably realize now that your inner strength came up through the layers of difficult everyday life to help you out, even though you had not summoned it. Sometimes, it will just kick in of its own accord in order to protect you and others, to keep you safe and help you cope.

We have all heard stories of people being suddenly empowered with amazing physical superhuman strength; for example, being able to lift a car up to free someone trapped underneath it. This is the effect of the flame of inner strength igniting and delivering physical strength when needed in a time of crisis.

Today, think about how strong you actually are. Try to recall the times when you have succeeded even though you thought you would fail. Tell yourself how well you did. Pat yourself on the back and be happy with who you really are. Read your list of achievements over and over again, and know that deep inside there is a part of you that is stronger than you ever realized.

Week 11, Day 2
» PRANAYAMA «
Exercise for Depression

This exercise, when perfected, can control, reduce and even eliminate some forms of depression. As this is an advanced exercise, and depression can affect the breathing quite seriously, it is imperative that you have mastered all the previous breathing exercises in the book before you attempt this one. As always, concentrate fully on what you are doing and harmonize mind and body.

I am going to break it down into two parts to make it a little easier. The first part can be done as an exercise in itself: if done at a normal pace it relaxes the mind; if done very slowly, it induces sleep.

> Begin by taking a deep abdominal breath all the way in and all the way out.
>
> Next, divide the full breath into two equal divisions:
>
> Breathe in halfway, pause, breathe right in.
>
> Breathe halfway out, pause, breathe right out.
>
> Then, divide the breath into three equal divisions:
>
> Breathe in one third, two thirds, and right in.
>
> Breathe out one third, two thirds and right out.
>
> Continue, when you are able to do so comfortably, to divide the breath into four, then five and six divisions.

With practice you will be able to make the divisions equal and be able to achieve a full breath. This means that your lungs are full at the end of the in-breath divisions, and empty at the end of the out-breath divisions.

Once you have mastered dividing the breath you can move on to the second part, which involves dividing both the breath and the tummy into equal divisions.

Begin by breathing out a little and stopping the breath there. Then:
Take the tummy right in and hold it in while you:
Breathe right in and right out.
Then let the tummy out smoothly.

Now divide both tummy and breath into two equal divisions:

Breathe out and hold there. Then:
Take the tummy in halfway, pause, then right in. Hold it in while you:
Breathe in halfway, pause, then right in.
Breathe out halfway, pause, breathe right out.
Let the tummy out halfway, pause, then right out.

Now divide into three divisions, always breathing out a little and holding there before you begin:

Take the tummy in one third, two thirds, and right in and hold.
Breathe in one third, two thirds and right in.
Breathe out one third, two thirds and right out.
Let the tummy out one third, two thirds and right out.

When you feel able, move on to four, five and six divisions.

Only increase the divisions when you feel comfortable enough to do so. Aim for six within two weeks by practising at least three times a day. Eventually you may be able to go on to achieve twelve divisions, but this may take quite some time.

Add this exercise on to the sequence of the other exercises you have learned so far.

Week 11, Day 3

» DIRECTION «

Is Your Personality Causing Your Stress?

*"True wisdom comes to each of us when we realize how little
we understand about life, ourselves, and the world around us."*
—SOCRATES

There are many personality types, but it is important to recognize those that may be causing an increase in your stress levels. Characteristics of your personality may actually be a contributing factor to your inability to cope effectively with the pressures in your life.

There is one particular type that most probably would be one cause of your stress: the A-Type Personality. It could also be described as "self-imposed pressure".

It is very important that people displaying A-Type Personality characteristics make urgent positive changes to balance their lives and manage their stress.

A-Type Characteristics include:

- Highly competitive
- Does more than one thing at a time
- Doesn't make plans
- Often needs recognition and approval from others
- Can be very impatient
- Does everything at a fast pace, including talking, walking, driving and eating
- Is a perfectionist and expects perfection from others
- Can't delegate easily
- Works too long hours
- Has few interests outside of work
- Finds it impossible to relax and thinks it's a waste of time
- Can sometimes feel agitated, irritated and hostile

If you have all or most of the characteristics above it is imperative that you make some changes *now,* today. Your stress levels will be high and if you are not ill already, you are heading that way at a fast pace of knots – unless of course you have been applying all the exercises and other material in this book, in which case you will have addressed and reduced some of the issues already.

If you have half of the characteristics, it is still very important that you make adjustments – again starting today.

What you're aiming for is to work towards acquiring the characteristics of a B-Type Personality. I say "work towards" because that type of personality is probably too relaxed for you and you may find the pace too slow.

An A/B-Type Personality would be perfect for you to aim for and achieve because it is somewhere in between an A and a B. The person with an A/B personality is still driven and works hard, but usually has a more balanced lifestyle, is more flexible and is able to relax easily when needed.

Reducing or completely eradicating some of your A-Type characteristics will result in a much more organized and hassle-free life. Making these important changes will not only make you much healthier and happier; the changes will also benefit the people you share your life with. Among other benefits your blood pressure will reduce and you are less likely to suffer from a stroke or heart disease. You will probably also live longer and you will certainly start to enjoy life more! Here is what you need to do to create more much-needed balance in your life:

- Where possible, delegate tasks to others, even if it means spending time coaching them. Completely let go some of your responsibilities.
- Slow down (driving, eating, talking etc).
- Do one thing at a time and in order of priority.
- Learn some time management skills and stick to these plans.
- Reduce your commitments. You don't *have* to be all things to all people.
- Take breaks and holidays without feeling guilty.
- Use your breathing exercises and relax every day.
- Learn to be more patient and manage your hostility.
- Go out with friends and/or family on a regular basis. Take up a new hobby or find a new interest. You need to balance your work with rest and play.

- Consider whether your deadlines and targets are unrealistic and, if you set them yourself, think about what needs to change.
- If someone else is setting your deadlines and targets, talk to them and be honest about your stress levels.
- Talk to someone about your feelings.
- Challenge your perfectionism.
- Challenge your irrational, self-defeating and outdated beliefs. You may have some beliefs that belong in the past but which still affect your stress levels now.

It's not easy to change the habits of a lifetime, but doing something about it every day, no matter how small, can get you there in the end and it is well worth it. Try putting a big notice on your desk, or somewhere where you will see it often, that simply says "SLOW DOWN!"

Week 11, Day 4

» SELF-ESTEEM «

Boosting Your Self-Esteem

What do you do when someone praises you or shows approval or admiration? How do you respond when someone says "You look nice today"?

Maybe you completely dismiss a compliment, disregard it or feel embarrassed by it. You may even argue, saying "Huh! *No I don't!*" If this is you, you may have low self-esteem. Perhaps you have never interpreted it as that, but think about it carefully now. Is it that you simply don't agree with them? Is it that you think they are patronizing you or, even worse, lying to you? Are you just so self-critical that you could not possibly agree, and think that they are right? That they must be wrong because their comments do not coincide with your own thoughts and beliefs about yourself? Perhaps you don't value yourself enough. Maybe you don't have a very high opinion of yourself. Maybe you have been put down for so long by someone in your life that you truly believe you *deserve* to be criticized.

Why would it be so wrong or feel so alien simply to agree with them and just say "Thank you"? Perhaps you think that you could never agree with them because it would make you go against your own core beliefs about yourself. Your beliefs may tell you that you are not good enough, stupid, bad and not worthy of praise, but it could be that these beliefs are irrational and totally out of date. Maybe they were put there by someone who was being deliberately hurtful, someone who didn't value or respect you. They may not even be in your life any more. Why would you hold on to their opinions? Why believe that person and not believe the people in your life now who you value and respect? It doesn't make any sense – does it?

Don't hang on to the negative past and the people from your past who shouldn't be affecting your life now, in the present. Don't let them harm you today. Don't allow yourself to hurt because of untruths spoken in your past. If however, that person is still in your life, and they continue to criticize you and put you down, don't empower them by believing their hurtful comments. Stand up for yourself, walk away, ignore them, because by listening to them and conversing with them you are allowing them to win. You are giving them the power to control you. Remember who you are today. Value yourself just as others do. Remember your achievements, strengths, skills and abilities.

Many of your negative or irrational beliefs about yourself are possibly due to earlier experiences, events, relationships or messages from parents, teachers, partners, other adults or even other children. You simply believed what you were told at the time and the message got stuck, like a broken record. When we are very young we do tend to believe everything adults tell us, even though they may not be being truthful at all. (Think of Santa and the Tooth Fairy!)

We very often believe what adults, especially people in authority, say to us because we hold them in high esteem and don't always have the confidence to question them. Have you ever stopped to think about *why* someone criticized you or put you down? Have you challenged their words? Have you used Socratic questioning to dispute the beliefs that were generated as a result of that criticism? (Week 10, Day 5). Have you ever thought that the people who criticized you might just have been in a bad mood, tired and irritable, maybe even jealous of you? Were you in the middle of an argument that provoked them to say things in the heat of the moment that they later regretted? Were they bullying you? Were they insecure and needed to control someone else just to make them feel big? Perhaps they felt inadequate and projected their failings and weaknesses on to you? Or were they just plain and simple horrible people who took pleasure in putting you down? Whatever the reason, you don't have to believe their words now, and you never did have to believe them. Remember, they were just opinions, and opinions can always be discounted and rejected.

Nonetheless, it is easy to understand how we can grow up to believe the things we were told and therefore go on, often into adulthood, basing our own opinions about ourselves on an untruth. For example: if we are told by a teacher that we are stupid, and we are not able to argue with them, it is easy to believe that we are actually stupid because they are telling us that we are, and they must be right because they are a teacher and teachers must be believed. Therefore we might find it difficult to believe that someone could praise us. How can we be praised for something we've done if we are stupid? Of course we don't knowingly go through that thought process: it happens automatically, unconsciously. Our lives are shaped by our beliefs whether they are true or false.

If we are bombarded by negative and critical comments over a period of time it is more than likely that we will suffer low self-esteem. The opposite applies too: if we have only experienced being praised, loved and complimented, and told that we are clever and wonderful, we are likely in adulthood to have much higher self-esteem. Too much of anything can be a bad thing, though; if we are praised too much as children, it can be a nasty shock to be criticized when we reach adulthood and the real world!

So how do you feel now? What are you thinking now? Is this the first time you have thought about, and been able to rationalize your low self-esteem and low self-worth and where it came from? Did it actually come from someone else? Have you allowed another person to control your thoughts and beliefs? Are you still holding on to destructive and hurtful words you heard from someone years ago, even though they are totally inappropriate and unacceptable today?

If you have a low opinion of yourself and you do not accept that you are a unique and valuable human being, equal to everyone else, then maybe it's time to question some of those old beliefs about yourself and start to think about yourself in a better light. After all, all those people who love, admire and respect you can't be wrong! There are more of them, anyway, than that one person long ago. Why should they influence how you feel today?

So today, and from now on, whenever you get a compliment, force yourself to smile and say "Thank you." It may feel very uncomfortable at first, but just persevere. Do not be tempted to say "Oh, this old thing" or "Well, I got a lot of help" or whatever else you usually say! It's OK for people to admire you or your work, or your kindness, or your hair, or what you're wearing. You *are* good enough. You are *not* stupid, you *do* look good, you *are* a valuable human being and equal to everyone else. You are no different, and you deserve to believe the truth when someone is admiring you.

Another point to consider is that not accepting someone's compliment could be seen as disrespecting their opinion. It's a little bit like refusing a gift: you should show that you are happy that they are showing you some affection and approval. Cherish it. Try to understand why they are showing affection or valuing you in some way. Start to *value* their opinions rather than reject them. They are entitled to have them and might feel put down themselves if you disrespect or disregard them. Remember who you *really* are and that your negative, irrational old beliefs no longer suit you. Live in the present, not the past.

Remember, you need only value opinions if they are complimentary about you. Never ever place any value or respect on a put-down or an insult. Go back to Week 2, Day 2 and Week 3, Day 4 now and read your list of qualities, strengths, skills, abilities and achievements and why people like you and love you. Copy that list and add some more to it today. Carry the list round with you and read it often.

Take Pride in Yourself

Write down in your workbook everything you can think of that has made you feel proud of yourself in the past two weeks.

You may need a little time to think about this; maybe you don't often think that you have done anything to be proud of. If you find this difficult to do, try to imagine what someone else would suggest. But, for every occasion you can recall feeling proud or perhaps pleased with yourself, your self-esteem, self-worth, self-confidence and self-belief will all be increased. As this happens, your stress, anxiety and depression will all be reduced and before long you will be thinking of yourself in a completely different light. Don't forget to use your positive affirmations – they will help enormously!

Week 11, Day 5

» *CORRECT THINKING* «

It's the Thought That Counts

"The happiness of your life depends upon the quality of your thoughts."
— MARCUS AURELIUS

Sometimes it can be quite difficult being positive all the time. In fact, I doubt that anyone remains positive for twenty-four hours a day. However, we can strive to be positive as much as we possibly can, because it is certainly worth the effort. You have so far learned a great deal about how positive thinking can lead to living a more positive life. After all, your thoughts affect almost everything you experience.

Your thoughts affect	
your feelings	what you do
how you behave	your conversations
your interactions	your attitudes
your values	your standards
your outcomes	your success
your failures	your physical health
your mental health	your emotional well-being
your relationships	your achievements

So that's pretty much everything! *Everything* begins with a thought, even what you have just read. OK, I know it's difficult, but surely the above list will encourage you to strive for positivity and motivate you to think more positively. There is something else you can do to help and remind you every day to strive for positive thinking – which will in turn lead to peace, harmony, good health and happiness. Below is a list of questions that you should ask yourself every morning as soon as you wake up:

- What three things am I grateful for today?
- What could make me proud today?
- What will make me happy today?
- What will I enjoy doing today?
- What will I succeed in doing today?
- In what ways could I be positive today?

Every night before you go to sleep, ask yourself the following questions:

- What made me proud today?
- What did I learn today?
- In what way did I help someone today?
- What made me happy today?
- What did I do today that made someone happy?
- In what way was I successful today?

These questions can make a real difference. Instead of waking up with a negative attitude because you have got a whole day to get through, you will start your day thinking about how good your day is going to be. You could perhaps even look forward to feeling good about yourself. You might think about the possibility of achieving more than you could ever imagine.

Instead of going to sleep with negative thoughts in your mind and finding it impossible to drop off to sleep as you dwell on them, you will have a peaceful and restful night's sleep knowing that you have had a good and successful day and have another one to look forward to tomorrow.

If you find any of the above questions difficult to answer, keep trying until you come up with something. There is always something, but maybe your focus is not fully in positive mode yet. If you can really recall absolutely nothing, use the word *could*. For example: "What *could* I be grateful for today?" (There are many things in our lives that we take too much for granted; maybe you could explore these.) Being positive will make you happier. That stands to reason. Below are six things that are sure to help you get there.

1. BE ENTHUSIASTIC · Be enthusiastic, excited, eager, passionate and animated about things in your life. Or find something that you can feel excited about. Always make sure that you have something to look forward to. Arrange to meet friends more often, or find a new hobby or interest that you could feel enthusiastic about. Maybe return to something in the past you used to love doing and looked forward to. Maybe just go out for the day and do something lovely, especially if it's something you don't usually do.

If your mood has been low for a while it might have made you lethargic and listless or dispirited, so you need to *change your mind* – change your thinking and your attitude. Let your thoughts count. You might be saying "That is easier said than done", but imagine this scenario:

You are feeling down and miserable but there's a knock on your door and your best friend, who you haven't seen for ages, comes marching in. She/he is laughing and appears to be full of fun. They want to tell you all about what they've been doing. You have a choice about how to react, but you haven't seen them in such a long time and they don't know you have been depressed. You don't want to upset them or worry them or dampen their mood, so you put on a happy face and pretend that you're OK.

It's the *pretending* that often does the trick. It *will* work and you *will* feel better for it. If your life depended on it you *would* be able to act as if you felt fine. When you pretend to feel happy you actually fool your body; it will react according to how you think and feel, even if you are faking it. Your stress hormones will reduce, your fight/flight response will switch off and you will feel more relaxed. Remember the Confidence Trick (Week 7, Day 4)? This demonstrated that when you stand the way a confident person stands, you actually feel more confident! Mind and body work as one. If you act as though you are happy and well, your mind, body and spirit get the message and before long it will feel like second nature.

2. SET GOALS · Set goals and visualize yourself achieving them. When you have achieved them you should definitely feel much more positive. You will also feel more enthusiastic about setting further goals.

3. MANAGE YOUR STRESS · We have already addressed this, so just a reminder – stress makes you miserable, anxious, depressed and negative. Continue to manage your stress and watch yourself becoming more positive by the day as you work through your many newly acquired coping skills.

4. DO SOMETHING DIFFERENT · You never know what you can achieve until you try. Negative thinking will stop you doing things, but positive thinking can free you from the confines of your limitations. Be daring, take a risk, go ahead and do something you have always wanted to do and prove to yourself that being positive can help you to do things you never even imagined being able to do before. Positive living can motivate you to completely transform the quality of your life.

5. FOCUS ON THE POSITIVE · I have met a lot of people who, at the beginning of their treatment, focused only on the negatives. However, it wouldn't usually take long before I managed (albeit, sometimes with difficulty) to change that. I ran classes in positive living: at the beginning of the course I would, as I have done here, teach about the drawbacks of thinking negatively. In the second week I would put a notice on the door saying "THIS IS A NEGATIVE-FREE ZONE" in very large and colourful letters. It made my class laugh and see the funny side of it – but not only that; it also worked! Whenever anyone was being negative everyone else would laugh and refer them to the sign.

I started a new job in a mental health centre and one of my first tasks was to co-facilitate the group therapy sessions. There were usually about six or seven people, who would sit around and tell us all how terrible their week had been, After everyone had had their turn they would simply all go home looking and sounding worse than they had when they arrived. It wasn't surprising – they had just spent an hour and a half listening to everybody's tragic stories. However, they did return the following week and go through the same procedure all over again.

Naturally I was very concerned about this; I was happy that the patients were being encouraged to talk about their worries and express their feelings, and I could see the benefit in that, but I wasn't so happy that everybody went home feeling just as miserable as when they first arrived. I soon changed that! We turned the group into a solution-focused group where everyone had a chance to talk about their week and how they felt about it, but the other members of the group would each have to offer advice or come up with a suggestion on how to solve the problem. It made such a difference; it worked wonders. Not only did they go home with some answers but they had also used their own insights and experience to help other people. Just one simple change created a therapeutic and beneficial reward for all the members of the group – including the staff!

Change your focus and only focus on the following:

- What you can do, rather than on what you can't do.
- What you have got, rather than what you haven't got.
- What you have been successful with, rather than what you failed at.
- Your strengths and qualities rather than your faults and weaknesses.
- The people you have in your life, rather than the people you don't.
- How much money you have, rather than how much footballers earn!

Never underestimate the power of positive thinking!

Week 11, Day 6
» *DIRECTION* «

Change

*"Progress is impossible without change, and those who cannot
change their minds cannot change anything."*
— *GEORGE BERNARD SHAW, dramatist*

We humans are creatures of habit; on the whole we don't get on very well with change. When changes are forced upon us and they are out of our control, we can suffer the effects of stress. When we have too many major changes occurring too close together, the stress can be severe. Those changes don't necessarily need to be unpleasant changes, either; even if we got promoted, or married, or moved to a nicer and bigger house, we still have to cope with the adjustment to a new set of circumstances. It is that adjustment we find the most difficult to cope with rather than the change itself. The inability and failure to adjust to these changes is what actually causes the stress.

Adjusting to change can be very difficult for some people. Some may find it easy or even exciting, but remember, we are all different, and even though some changes might be exciting, we still have some adjusting to do.

Take moving house, for example; it may be a great new house with more space and much better accommodation and environment, but if we perceive the change and the newness to be stressful – then it is.

All our senses are being fed new stimuli, and the brain has to adjust to what it's seeing and hearing and smelling and touching, every day, all the time. It has no memory of these changes, so it has nothing to refer to or latch on to when making an assessment of the new circumstances and whether or not there is danger here. This newness can induce the stress response, as at some level we interpret the new information as being threatening because it is unfamiliar to us. Of course over a period of time everything becomes more familiar and once we adapt to the changes, and our brain has completed its evaluation, we eventually adjust to our new circumstances and are able to perceive the change to be something that we are able to cope with – we have *learned* that there is no danger, no threat.

Adaptability varies from person to person. We are all different and therefore some people cope more easily than others. It can sometimes be linked to life experiences: a person who has experienced a lot of change in their life will probably cope better than someone who has experienced very little or no change.

Although we may not realize it, change is constant in our lives. Change is a reality for everyone and no two days are ever the same. However, if we lack the ability to cope due to our stress levels being very high to begin with, too many major changes can push us over the edge. The need to adapt to too much change will therefore be much more difficult to cope with than usual, and stress management becomes essential.

Reasons why people find change difficult

- Lack of awareness that a change is necessary
- Lack of self-belief
- Low self-esteem and lack of confidence
- Fear and anxiety
- Dislike of change
- Not enough information
- Lack of experience of change
- No or little support or advice
- Indecisiveness
- Fear of failure
- Fear of success (it might bring more responsibility, more stress)
- Practical issues such as lack of funds, being too busy, moving away from family and a support system
- Change can threaten our security
- We feel uncomfortable with the unfamiliar

Try to identify why you find change difficult and make a list. Next identify solutions to these difficulties, taking into account that you may have some irrational or negative beliefs that need to be challenged. The following advice will help, but you can also seek help from others. If you know someone that finds change easy and maybe even actively invites it, speak to them about what helps them. Try to identify what kind of attitude and beliefs they have towards change and what skills they have that you could learn. They are most likely to be a very positively focused person who looks ahead rather than dwelling on the past or being stuck in a rut. Follow their lead and take their advice. Let them become your role model on the subject of change.

What Helps With Change

Because change is inevitable and constant, it is impossible to escape it. There are times when changes occur that are totally out of our control and without the necessary skills to help to cope with the change it would be easy to feel helpless and afraid about this. Even if we have ourselves decided to make a change, it can still be difficult to adjust to. You can prepare for planned changes, and for unplanned ones, by acquiring the skills to cope before you make your decision to change something.

When we are faced with unexpected or uninvited change it is sometimes very difficult to know just how to start adjusting. We flounder about, trying our best to muddle through and cope, perhaps making mistakes along the way. So here are some guidelines to help:

- First of all use all the coping skills you have learned such as breathing exercises, meditation, relaxation and positive thinking.
- Speak to someone who will listen to your concerns and in whom you trust.
- Find out all the relevant information before you make the change (this is essential!).
- Discover what the change will actually mean to you personally, as well as to any others it will affect.
- Focus only on the facts, not hearsay or rumours.
- Accept that your skills will help you to cope with adjustment but accept your limitations too.
- Set realistic goals and discuss them with the other people involved.
- Don't expect too much of yourself too soon.
- Challenge any negative thoughts or beliefs you have about the change.
- Be assertive with yourself and others.
- Review your progress and reassess goals.
- If things do go wrong put them into perspective, breathe and regroup.
- Persevere – in time, it will get easier.

- Accept the inevitable and those things you have no control over.
- Practise change. Start by deliberately making small changes that are well within your control. For example: take a different route to work, move the furniture round, change your routine, shop in different places or eat different foods.

Week 11, Day 7
» *RELAXATION* «

Relaxation Using Your Breath

As with the previous methods of relaxation, lie down on the floor in your usual room at your chosen time of day when you will not be disturbed. Make yourself warm and comfortable. Allow at least twenty minutes for this relaxation.

Take three slow deep abdominal breaths. When you are ready to begin, allow yourself to become aware of your breath flowing in and out of your nose. Focus only on this. If your mind wanders off, acknowledge it and gently bring your focus back. Feel the air, perhaps cool as you inhale and warmer as you exhale. Stay with the breath in your nose for a few minutes.

Next, imagine if you can that there is a channel that extends from your nostrils to the back of your throat. Now be aware and feel your breath as it flows from your nostrils to your throat. Become aware of the breath as it enters and leaves your throat. Focus on this for the next few minutes.

Imagine now this channel extending from your throat downwards to the centre of your chest. If it helps, place the tips of your fingers on a point in the middle of your chest, on your breastbone. Now breathe down to that point. Feel your breath flowing down to the bottom of the channel in your chest and flowing back up again and out through your nose. Keep your focus there for another few minutes – or as long as you wish; there are no hard and fast rules in this relaxation. Just go with the flow.

Now your channel opens up and extends downwards to your diaphragm (just under your ribcage). Place your fingertips there. Again take your breath down to the point where your fingertips touch the body and let it flow back up to escape through your nostrils. Keep your focus on that for a few minutes or more.

Move your fingertips down to your navel now and imagine the channel of breath moving down to that new point. Focus all of your attention on your breath flowing all the way down the channel to your navel and all the way back up and out through your nose.

Again, move your fingers down a little more to below your navel, on your lower abdomen. As you breathe gently in and gently out through this imaginary tube all the way down to where your fingers are gently placed, feel your abdomen gently rising and falling. Stay as you are for a little while and then, when you are ready, remove your fingers and place your hand comfortably on the floor by your side, but continue to breathe down to that point, up the channel and out through your nose.

After a little while, and by now, you are probably very deeply relaxed, imagine your breath being a colour, of your choice perhaps a colour you feel you need. Imagine the colour of your breath healing your body and healing your mind. Let the colour now become brighter and let it permeate the whole of your body. Feel your body lighting up. If the colour changes just go with it, let it happen, feel it relaxing you more and more. After a little while longer or whenever you are ready, return your thoughts to your breath gently flowing in and flowing out.

You can end your relaxation whenever you are ready to. Bring your mind into the present moment and acknowledge the relaxed state in which you find yourself. Just allow yourself to come very slowly out and allow your breathing to return to its normal rate and flow. Roll onto your right side and stay for a little while. Only when you are ready, sit up slowly.

Week 11

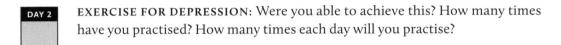

» RECAP AND REFLECT «

Tick the box when understood, practised and achieved

DAY 1 **OUR INNER RESOURCES:** Read this again and reflect on the message. Were you already familiar with your inner resources? How could they help you in the future?

DAY 2 **EXERCISE FOR DEPRESSION:** Were you able to achieve this? How many times have you practised? How many times each day will you practise?

DAY 3 **IS YOUR PERSONALITY CAUSING YOUR STRESS?:** Are you able to relate to the list of characteristics of A-Type behaviour? If so, have you worked out a plan and set your goals to make the necessary changes? Have you started to work on them yet? If not, when?

DAY 4 **BOOSTING YOUR SELF-ESTEEM:** Does any of this apply to you? Have you begun to say thank you when you are being complimented? Can you identify where and when your low self-esteem developed? Have you started to take pride in yourself? How did you feel when you identified all those things you were proud of?

DAY 5 **IT'S THE THOUGHT THAT COUNTS:** On a scale of 1–10 how positive were you before you started working on this book? Where on the scale are you now? Which of the suggestions do you think you need to follow in order to reach a higher score? Find something to remind you to be more positive. Make a sign or choose an object such as your phone or a plant; this will act as a reminder to think positively whenever you see it.

DAY 6 **CHANGE:** How many major changes have you been through in the past year? How did they affect your stress levels? How do you cope with change? What do you need to do now in order to help with future changes?

DAY 7 **RELAXATION USING YOUR BREATH:** How many times have you practised this? How well did you relax using this method? Will you use this method again? If you haven't used it, do so today or as soon as possible.

Now turn to your self-assessment rating scales and enter your scores for the end of Week 11.

Week 12

· · · · · · · · ·

Week 12, Day 1
» *AWARENESS* «

Sleep Awareness

*"It is a common experience that a problem difficult at night is resolved in
the morning after the committee of sleep has worked on it."*
— *JOHN STEINBECK, author*

HAVING DIFFICULTIES dropping off to sleep at night is a clear sign that you are worrying or anxious about something, and maybe not able to talk to anyone about your problems. It is often a symptom of stress, anxiety or depression, particularly if you are also waking up early in the morning and are not able to go back to sleep. However, sleep problems can also be a sign of an underlying physical condition, so a visit to the doctor is the first thing you need to organize.

Good quality sleep is vital to good health in mind and body. Although we don't know the full extent of the precise functions of sleep, we do know that during sleep our bodies continue to work for us, keeping us healthy, especially our immune system, nervous system and thought processes. Sleep also restores balance and recharges our energy levels. If we miss out on good quality sleep there will be a decline in alertness, performance, normal functioning and memory. Chronic insomnia is associated with stress and depression and can also *cause* depression and mental impairment.

When sleep deprivation goes on for some time it can lead to more serious complaints. It is well known that in some countries controlled sleep deprivation is used as a form of torture.

Sleep also affects how we perform our daily tasks, so lack of sleep can potentially affect our efficiency at work as well as our and others' health and safety. Sleep has an impact on how we look, how we feel and how we think and behave. In other words, it has an impact on all aspects of our lives including quality of life.

One of the many adverse effects of poor sleep is having difficulty getting up in the morning. After a good night's sleep we wake up feeling refreshed and alert and feel able to face the day's demands. However, when we don't sleep well or don't have enough quality sleep it is likely that we will wake up feeling tired, lethargic and low in mood. As the day goes on we can become exhausted, stressed and irritable, and any physical ailments can also become worse. This sometimes leads to a vicious circle where our anxiety about poor sleep causes us to sleep less well. When our worry button automatically switches on as soon as our head hits the pillow, we quickly induce a state of high alertness as the fight/flight response switches on. The more we worry about not being able to get off to sleep, the less likely we are to fall asleep. This scenario can go on and on, worsening, night after night, and before very long we form the belief that we are becoming an insomniac.

Of course, if you relaxed and used your breathing exercises you would drop off to sleep without allowing the worry to take over. You will find a very effective breathing exercise for inducing sleep, in Week 11, Day 2.

The reasons why we need to sleep and the effects of sleep have been studied for around two and a half thousand years, but we still don't know everything there is to know about it. It was only in 1928 that the EEG machine (electroencephalogram) was first used to measure and record brain activity during sleep. As a result, researchers were able to measure four different stages of sleep, which are detailed below.

STAGE 1 · This occurs when we are very relaxed and is where sleep begins. It is a relatively light sleep. Our brain produces very slow brainwaves: theta wave, which lasts for only five to ten minutes. Stage 1 is also recognized as a transition period between wakefulness and sleep, or consciousness and unconsciousness. These types of brainwaves can also be found in a state of meditation. It follows, therefore, that if we use a form of relaxation as we get into bed we will soon be in a state of consciousness where sleep comes easily.

STAGE 2 · This stage lasts for approximately twenty minutes and the brainwave activity here is sometimes referred to as *sleep spindles.* This is when the heart rate slows down and the body temperature drops – just as it does in relaxation.

STAGE 3 · The brainwaves are slow and are known as delta waves. Noise and activity will usually not waken the sleeper. It is also the transition time between light and deep sleep.

STAGE 4 · This stage is known as REM sleep or rapid eye movement sleep and it is here that most dreaming occurs. Brainwave activity and respiration is increased.

Sleep does not progress through these stages in sequence: it begins with stage 1 and progresses to stages 2 and 3. After stage 3, stage 2 sleep is repeated, then there is a period of REM sleep. Once REM sleep is over, you go back to stage 2 sleep. These cycles can be repeated four or five times during a night.

We generally enter REM sleep around ninety minutes after falling asleep. We continue to go in and out of this stage and it increases in length as the night progresses, sometimes lasting for an hour.

If you go to bed feeling anxious it will take quite some time to drop off to sleep, unless you counter the anxiety with relaxation. This is why I strongly recommend that you use your breathing exercises and relaxation techniques as soon as you get into bed or just before. Also before getting into bed, write down any worries or anxieties that are on your mind, set your goals and complete your Daily Planner for the next day. This will get them out of your mind and onto paper.

It follows then that the more you practise your relaxation, meditation and breathing exercises on a daily basis, and throughout the day, the more easily you will achieve a good-quality night's sleep. If you have twenty to thirty minutes of physical exercise every day, this too will help a great deal.

Recent research has also shown that positive thinking and a positive attitude help to reduce brainwave activity throughout the day, thus encouraging better quality sleep. You have also learned that positive thinking reduces and controls stress and anxiety, so adopting a more positive attitude will help too, especially if you are having problems with sleeping.

Try to adopt a new belief that you are a good sleeper. Repeat positive affirmations to yourself during the day, such as "I sleep well and peacefully each and every night." Also try to focus on all the positives in your day, and use the STOP Technique whenever you catch yourself having a negative thought. To go to bed thinking that you are going to spend all night tossing and turning or that you will wake up too early in the morning is only setting yourself up to have a sleepless night. Stop creating the self-fulfilling prophesy about poor sleep and challenge any negative beliefs you have about sleep.

Some frequently asked questions about sleep

Q · **How much sleep do we need?**

A · One of the many myths about sleep is that we all need eight hours of sleep every night. In fact, although this is the average, each and every individual will need a different amount of sleep based on what their body needs and how they lead their lives. The National Sleep Foundation says the average amount of sleep we need is somewhere between six and nine hours. However, I have heard of people managing very well on only between three and five hours sleep each night.

Q · **Do teenagers really need all that sleep?**

A · Contrary to popular opinion, teenagers aren't just being lazy! They do actually need a little more sleep than the average – between nine and ten hours, as opposed to the adult average of eight hours. Experts say that adolescents and teenagers have a slightly different body clock to adults because their bodies manufacture the sleep hormone melatonin later at night. This makes it more difficult for young people to fall asleep, which has the knock-on effect of making it more difficult for them to wake up in the morning. Parents of young teenagers will know just how difficult it is to get a teenager up out of bed and out to school and that they are often tired, lethargic and moody in the mornings. It is not surprising, then, that it is possible for their school work to suffer.

At Monkseaton High School in the north-east of England, teenagers are allowed to start school one hour later than the younger pupils. Early results from this experiment, which is being overseen by scientists, including Oxford neuroscience professor Russell Foster, indicate that general absenteeism has reduced by 8% and persistent absenteeism by 27%.

Mr Paul Kelley, head teacher, said it was now medically established that it was better for teenagers to start their school day later in terms of their mental and physical health. He added that by simply changing the time of the school day, pupils will be less stressed and that it could help in creating "happier, better educated teenagers".

Q · **Do older people need less sleep?**

A · At the other end of the age scale, it is a common myth that older people need less sleep. It is true that the quality of their sleep might lessen and they may have more disturbed sleep, but this is usually due to chronic health problems such as osteoporosis and diabetes. Older people also tend to nap during the day, which perhaps means they need less than a normal quota of sleep at night.

Q · **Can we catch up on lost sleep?**

A · The sleep experts say *No you can't.* Recent research in the United States shows that having one long night's sleep or sleeping in at the weekends after a week of late nights and early mornings doesn't do you any good. In fact it can severely impair your performance the next day, especially later at night. Basically, you cannot recover from a build-up of sleep loss after just one or two good nights' sleep.

Q · **Is it OK to watch television to help me get off to sleep?**

A · No! Definitely not! You may think that it helps you to take your mind off the pressures of the day, but in actual fact it is harmful. For a start, if the programme you are watching is action-packed it will only increase your brainwave activity, keeping you awake and alert rather than relaxed. Research has shown that watching TV can actually contribute to numerous health problems including depression. One of the most damaging effects is the flickering blue light that the television emits; this interferes with the production of the sleep hormone melatonin, which not only damages our internal biological clock but also keeps us awake and alert. You may well fall asleep if the programme is boring, but you will probably wake again shortly afterwards.

Q · **Drinking alcohol at night helps me to get to sleep; is this OK?**
A · No. Although alcohol is known to be a sedative and will indeed help you to get to sleep quickly, it may actually cause you to wake up in the night because your sleep will be lighter as the alcohol is broken down in the body. Alcohol can also have an adverse effect on you if you drink regularly because it increases light sleep and reduces the amount of deep restorative sleep. The other obvious side-effect is the potential of dependency.

Q · **Will eating cheese before going to bed give me nightmares?**
A · No. This myth has been around a very long time, but there is no scientific evidence that cheese gives you nightmares. However, it is suggested that if you overeat foods that you are not used to, especially rich foods, you may suffer from digestive upsets overnight.

Q · **It is said that we dream during REM (rapid eye movement) sleep. Is this the case?**
A · Although we do dream during REM sleep, dreaming also occurs during other stages of sleep. It is also common to have dreams as we move from sleep to wakefulness.

Q · **Will drinking warm milk help me to get to sleep?**
A · No; at least not on its own. Although milk may contain tryptophan, an amino acid responsible for the body making serotonin, which is vital for healthy sleep, drinking milk alone will not produce this effect; you need also to eat some carbohydrate-rich foods. You would, for example, be better off having a slice of toast or some cereal with your milk. Romaine-type lettuce contains tryptophan, so a lettuce sandwich might be a good idea too. There is a school of thought that suggests that warm milk induces sleep due to a psychological effect – the *association* of milk with sleep.

Q · **Is it OK to drink coffee before going to bed?**
A · Coffee contains caffeine, which is a known stimulant and increases adrenalin and other stress hormones, which in turn keep us alert. Coffee just before bed, or for some people in the evening or afternoon, should be avoided. However, you don't necessarily have to give up drinking coffee completely; the effects of caffeine last for only four to six hours, so you can still enjoy your early-morning coffee.

Q · **Is it better to take herbal or over-the-counter remedies for insomnia?**
A · Always consult your doctor before taking *anything* that induces sleep, including herbal remedies. Even these are not always safe. Prescription drugs (sleeping tablets or tranquilizers) should only be taken as a last resort or in an emergency, and for a very short period of time. It is possible to become addicted to or dependent on some of them if taken for long periods of time.

Week 12, Day 2
» UNDERSTANDING «

Good Night – Sleep Tight

THE DO'S

- DO go to bed and get up at the same time every day (this is the most important piece of advice).
- DO take exercise early in the day, definitely not before going to bed.
- DO try having a warm bath immediately before going to bed, to relax you.
- DO use lavender, either fresh in a vase or the dried kind in little bags, or drops of lavender oil on your pillow to help you relax and sleep.
- DO always try a relaxation or breathing exercise to help you to get off to sleep.
- DO make sure you are warm and comfortable when you go to bed.
- DO try to remove all clutter from your bedroom and keep it tidy.

THE DON'TS

- DON'T sleep with too many or too-high pillows.
- DON'T exercise too late in the evening or just before you want to go to sleep.
- DON'T go to bed hungry as this will keep you awake; have a light snack if needed.
- DON'T eat spicy or rich foods or a large meal before going to bed.
- DON'T eat processed foods if you have a sleep problem, as the chemicals in them can keep you awake.
- DON'T drink caffeine or alcohol before going to bed if you have difficulty sleeping.
- DON'T watch television just before going to or when in bed.
- DON'T use computers of any kind just before going to bed or while in bed.
- DON'T read a thriller or action-packed book just before trying to go to sleep.
- DON'T go to bed if you are not tired or sleepy.
- DON'T stay in bed tossing and turning, if you are awake for over half an hour – get up.
- DON'T lie in bed worrying about something; write it down instead.
- DON'T worry during the day about not sleeping well at night.
- DON'T automatically think you are not going to be able to sleep well.
- DON'T rely on sedatives.
- DON'T have the window open if it is very cold or foggy outside.
- DON'T continue to sleep on an uncomfortable or old mattress (over eight years old).

Pranayama Breath-Control Exercise for Insomnia

This is the same exercise as the one used at the beginning of the exercise for depression in Week 11, Day 2.

For help with falling asleep you need to do this exercise very slowly.

> Take a very slow deep breath all the way in and all the way out.
>
> Breathe in halfway, pause, then breathe right in.
>
> Breathe out halfway, pause, then breathe right out.
>
> Breathe in one third, pause, two thirds, pause, then right in.
>
> Breathe out one third, pause, two thirds, pause, then right out.
>
> Continue with four, five and six divisions.

There is no need to divide further. If you do not fall asleep on reaching six divisions, go back to the beginning and repeat the sequence.

Meditation Exercise For Insomnia

> - Lie comfortably in your bed, ready to go to sleep.
> - After taking three slow deep abdominal breaths:
> - Focus your mind on the day's events as if you were looking at photographs, but don't start from the beginning of the day – instead go through the events backwards, starting with what you just did before getting into bed.
> - Create a mental image, like looking at a photograph, of what you were doing just before going to bed, then an image of what you did just before that, and just before, and so on.
> - Keep the images in your mind for just a few moments.

This meditation exercise is very effective, much more so than counting sheep, because it keeps you focused and you are not likely to allow your mind to stray.

Week 12, Day 3

» PHYSICAL HEALTH «

Taking Care of Yourself

There are many things we can do to keep physically healthy in times of stress and adversity. It is especially important to look after our bodies during these times because stress lowers our immune system, makes us tired and exhausted, interferes with our sleeping patterns and has an adverse effect on all our organs and glands.

Below are a few things you can do to maintain good physical health:

EXERCISE · We have already discussed the importance of exercise, so this is a gentle reminder. You must take at least twenty minutes of exercise at least four times every week. Walking, cycling and swimming are recommended but as long as it isn't a high-impact, competitive sport, any kind of exercise is fine. Read over the benefits of exercise again in Week 2, Day 3.

HAVE FUN · Another aspect of physical health in relation to stress, anxiety and depression is *having fun.*

It is often the case that when you are stressed, anxious and depressed one of the first things to go is your social life. Although in the past you may have had an activity-filled social life, you fall into the trap of thinking you haven't got the time or energy for it any more. Generally speaking, when your mood is low it is difficult to motivate yourself to go out and have fun. However, it is actually more important to continue with fun activities when you are stressed or low in mood; having fun is a major balancer for stress because it (like exercise) switches off the stress response and encourages the relaxation response.

Make a list of all the things you used to enjoy, or like the idea of trying now, and make a conscious decision to start some of them as soon as possible.

EAT A HEALTHY BALANCED DIET · Stress can cause a change in eating habits. This is due to the stress response causing the digestive system to slow down, become sluggish and even stop altogether when panic mode sets in. Loss of appetite is quite common when people are anxious and low in mood. They may not feel like eating much at all and will often not eat enough to stay healthy. On the other hand, some people when anxious or low will overeat or eat all the wrong things. Nice-tasting food may make them feel better in the short term but this good feeling won't last, particularly if what they eat are products like cake and chocolate that contain a lot of fat and sugar. After the initial sugar rush the body will crave yet more sugar – the person may eat more and then the guilt sets in. In response to this feeling of guilt, in order to feel good again, people will eat more sugary, fatty food . . . and so it goes on, round and round. This is called *comfort eating.* I'm sure most people recognize this habit; and many people have experienced it themselves in some form.

Certain other habits can also increase when there is anxiety or low mood, like smoking or drinking alcohol or caffeine-rich drinks such as tea, coffee, cola drinks and high-energy drinks. A dependency on these leads to an unhealthy lifestyle, as well as inducing anxiety and anxiety-related issues.

If you think you have any unhealthy eating habits, record your intake for around a week; it may shock you into making some urgent changes. Begin to cut down or replace the unhealthy food with something that is good for you such as fruit and vegetables. Try drinking just plain water. If you begin to crave something do some breathing exercises, use positive affirmations and take a walk or some other exercise. You can also try analysing your craving. Ask yourself why you think you need that food. Is it because you feel comforted by it? If this is the case, think about why you need comforting. Then find a healthier way to fulfil that need. I can almost guarantee that your craving will be nothing to do with being hungry.

In order to stay healthy your daily diet should include the following six basic nutrients:

1. **CARBOHYDRATES** (rice, pasta, potatoes, bread, cereal)
2. **PROTEIN** (meat, fish, eggs, cheese)
3. **VITAMINS** (fruit, vegetables, fish oils, eggs, dairy products, liver, grains)
4. **MINERALS** (mainly fruits and vegetables)
5. **ESSENTIAL OILS** (nuts, fish oils, seeds)
6. **UNSATURATED FATS** (vegetable oils, nuts, avocado, flax seed, and some oily fish, such as mackerel, salmon and tuna)

These essential nutrients if eaten every day will create a balanced diet, a healthy body and therefore a healthy mind.

Many people eat mostly carbohydrates, protein and fats, often forgetting about or completely missing out the other healthy nutrients that come from fruit and vegetables, fish, nuts and seeds. If you recognize yourself here, start working on improving your health now by making a very important change to your eating habits.

I have already addressed the fact that the mind affects the body a great deal, but it must not be forgotten that the body affects the mind too; it is not a one-way street. Whatever you put into your body will affect every part of you including how you think, how you process thoughts, energy levels and your stress levels.

When you next go food shopping put some healthy food into your shopping trolley. Buy lots of fruit, even if it is just one kind that you like. The same applies to vegetables. Fresh is good, but frozen is often just as nutritious, and is certainly better than not buying any at all.

Grill, steam or oven-cook your food rather than frying it. If you do fry, use olive oil or vegetable oil and use a griddle pan so that the fat drains away.

Don't overcook your vegetables otherwise you will destroy their vitamin and mineral content; try steaming or roasting them in the oven. This is much better than your vegetables sitting in water; the nutrients will end up there and be poured down the sink.

Processed and Ready-Made Foods

These are full of preservatives, colourings and flavourings that are made from chemicals. These are harmful to your body and therefore to your mind.

Cut Down on Salt

We should not be eating more than six grams of salt a day. We all need a little salt as it helps maintain the right concentration of fluid in the body. However, too much salt raises the blood pressure, which in turn contributes to or causes other health problems like heart disease and strokes.

Beware! Salt is very often hidden in foods and can be found in all kinds of processed foods, ready-made meals, crisps (chips), olives, bacon and other processed meats, and even sweet foods like cake, biscuits and cereal.

Cut down on sugar

Sugar is your enemy. It not only causes weight gain: it can cause or contribute to many physical conditions such as diabetes, osteoporosis, liver problems, gallstones, high cholesterol and even cancer. Refined sugar contains no nutrients at all. It has no proteins, no fibre, no minerals, no essential fats and no enzymes. It contains just calories. It also makes your body take vital nutrients from your healthy cells and depletes your reserves of calcium, sodium, potassium and magnesium as well as B vitamins. Cut down as much as you are able. If you must have sugar, buy the unrefined variety. Note that many foods contain sugar hidden in the ingredients list under different names. These are many and include: sorbitol, caramel, anything ending in -ose and anything containing the word syrup.

Drink More Water

This is essential. The human body is mostly made up of water, so it stands to reason that without water we become ill. To stay healthy we need to replace the water we lose when we breathe, when we sweat and when we urinate. We get some of the water we need from our food, but mostly it comes – or should come – from what we drink. Advice on how much we need varies, but a lot of research suggests that on average women need to drink 1.6 litres and men 2.0 litres per day. Beware also of drinking *too much* water – your kidneys can only cope with so much. Keep a bottle or glass of water with you throughout the day. It's best if you don't put ice in your water, because the sudden coldness in your stomach can be a bit of a shock to the system. Don't think that you can count your water in other drinks such as squash or juice; they are usually full of sugar. Sorry! Tap water will do just fine.

If you are not accustomed to drinking much water, make sure you increase your intake gradually as your kidneys will take time to adjust. Start by drinking just two glasses a day and gradually, over a period of two weeks, increase to around six or eight glasses. On very hot days and when you exercise, you may need more as you will sweat more.

Week 12, Day 4
» MANAGING STRESS «
Perfectionism and Stress

"He is a man whom it is impossible to please,
because he is never pleased with himself."
— *G O E T H E , writer and statesman*

Perfectionists always have to get things just right, otherwise they believe they are a failure, and to fail is just not acceptable to them. Their belief system tells them something like "Unless I get everything perfect, I am no good, I am a failure." Or maybe "I should do everything perfectly otherwise people won't like me or respect me." It's easy to understand how this irrational, self-defeating belief may have been formed. Probably in childhood when a parent or teacher put repeated pressure on them to do well "or else".

Of course it could also have evolved as the result of enjoying great success in the past, earning praise, respect and admiration and a great feeling of achievement. Wanting to continue to be admired and respected, a person might put themselves under so much pressure all the time that they have simply "evolved" into a perfectionist.

Perfectionism can also be borne out of having many of the characteristics of an A-Type Personality as described in Week 11, Day 3.

A perfectionist is guaranteed to feel like a failure. Because of the exceptionally high standards they set themselves, nothing is really ever good enough; there is always going to be something else they can do (they think) to make things better. Of course, like beauty, perfection is in the eye of the beholder. What is perfectly OK for one person, the perfectionist will find fault in and continue to work on and on, not knowing when to stop.

A perfectionist is often constantly tired, frustrated and anxious due to their fear of failure. They are never satisfied with their achievements, thinking only that they should continue to strive for further success. To work for a perfectionist is also difficult because nothing is ever good enough. Because of the extremely high standard they set for themselves, a perfectionist often expects everyone else to have the same exacting standard. To live with a perfectionist can be exasperating. A child who is put under pressure by a parent who is a perfectionist may be constantly struggling to meet their parent's demands and live up to their rigid high standards, principles and expectations. The child may subsequently suffer anxiety and stress themselves and ultimately become depressed or develop low self-worth, or become a perfectionist themselves.

However, there are some advantages to being a perfectionist:

Advantages

1. A high quality of work is produced.
2. Clients/customers can depend on quality.

3. Employers will most likely approve and respect the quality of work and effort put in.

Generally, though, they are far outnumbered by the many disadvantages:

Disadvantages

1. Inability to accept that mistakes are normal and that we can actually learn from our mistakes.
2. Very high stress levels due to self-imposed pressure and exceptionally high standards.
3. Living under constant fear of failing.
4. Fear of showing vulnerability or losing control.
5. Fear of doing anything in case they are not able to do it perfectly.
6. Fear of taking risks.
7. Constantly critical of other people who don't live up to their standards.
8. Working long hours due to self-imposed pressure to get everything right.
9. Never knowing when to stop, which can lead to burnout.
10. Irritating other people.

If you are a perfectionist what else could you add to the above list?

How to reduce your perfectionism

1 · Accept that everyone makes mistakes and that's OK. Just because you make a mistake, or you can't do something, it doesn't mean to say that you are a failure; it simply means that you are a normal human being. We all have different strengths as well as faults and weaknesses. You must know people who make mistakes and who have weaknesses. Try to accept that not everyone always gets everything right, and under most circumstances, that is OK.

2 · Ask yourself *"Does it really matter?"* (Week 5, Day 3). In the scheme of things and bearing in mind the fact that life is short, try to put things into perspective. Ask yourself if you are really sure that what you have done so far needs more effort put in. Could it actually be acceptable just the way it is? Will anyone complain that it isn't good enough? Will anyone notice?

3 · Turn your attention to what you are really trying to achieve. Is it a good job well done or is the request that you do it perfectly and produce a perfect result, working above and beyond your limits and duty, spending hours and hours extra until you feel perfectly satisfied?

4 · Focus on what you can do rather than on what you can't do. Think positively about your skills, your strengths and the experience you have, rather than dwelling on your faults, weaknesses and doubts.

5 · Define and outline your goal and put a time limit on the task. If you are *exact* about the details you will know when you have reached your goal and know when to stop.

6 · Strive for excellence according to your own judgement rather than worrying about what other people will think.

7 · Challenge your self-defeating beliefs. If you do something for someone else's approval it can cause worry, anxiety, low self-esteem and a lack of self-confidence. Do things for yourself and learn to be happy with your end result and your achievements. Ask yourself: "Am I really a failure if I feel happy that I've done a good job? Does it always matter if others don't approve?"

8 · Don't procrastinate. Set a goal to start the task at a certain time and stick to it. Putting things off because you are afraid you won't do it well enough is pointless, because you will never know until you try. Even if it proves difficult, that's still OK. No one is good at everything, and learning to do something by making mistakes is perfectly normal and perfectly acceptable.

9 · Deliberately lower your standards by setting rigid time limits. For example: set yourself a limit of half an hour to tidy the house. That means that you only have ten minutes each in three rooms. Stop when the half hour is up, no matter what. Do not chastise yourself for not doing everything. Nothing terrible will happen, and if you do feel anxious about it, do some breathing exercises to calm your mind.

10 · Be mindful: fully concentrate on what you are doing. Be in the moment and stop yourself from worrying about the outcome. If you focus on the job in hand you will do a better job.

11 · Deliberately stop doing what you're doing even when you feel uncomfortable about not having finished it or it not being *perfect*. Walk away from it and do your breathing exercises. Also notice what other people say or do. Have they noticed? Do they care? Is it something that other people do as a matter of course anyway? You can always return to the task later if it isn't complete, but do not return to it if it isn't perfect in your eyes. Leave it as it stands and see if anything terrible happens. (Of course, brain surgery, or flying a plane, don't count!)

12 · Finally, think about what is more important to you, your health or your perfectionism. If you are damaging your health due to the pressure, stress and anxiety you put yourself under by being a perfectionist, is it really worth carrying on the way you are?

Week 12, Day 5
Put Your Problems in a Box

*"We cannot solve our problems with
the same thinking we used when we created them."*
— ALBERT EINSTEIN

If you are practising living in the moment, this shouldn't be a problem! But here's a little help if you need it.

Problems can invade your thinking, which in turn prevents you from living in the moment. They can grind you down; make you feel miserable and helpless or worse. If you focus on your problems instead of the job in hand you are more likely to make mistakes and take much longer to complete a task. It may lead to you having even more problems at the end of the day and the original problem you started with may become worse because you still haven't done anything about it or found a solution.

As a problem pops into your mind when it doesn't belong there, "put it into a box" and take it out later when you have the time, space and energy to think about it seriously and find a solution.

The Chinese language does not have a word or character for "problem": they use a character that means "opportunity". What does this say to you? Does it mean that Chinese people don't have problems? Well, according to their language they clearly don't! They only have opportunities or, at worst, situations that need to be solved. Finding solutions means drawing on your strengths, skills and abilities and also offers the opportunity to apply your strengths, to learn and add to your positive experiences and achievements.

That all sounds very philosophical but it also tells us that there is another way to think about our problems. The word "problem" conjures up negativity. It's almost heart-sinking. If someone comes to you and says they have a problem, how do you respond? Perhaps inwardly you say to yourself *"Oh no!"* or *"I've got enough of my own, thank you very much!"* So just hearing the word "problem" can actually switch on the stress or fight/flight response because we perceive it in a negative way – unlike the Chinese, for whom the connotation is positive. With a more positive perception we will suffer less stress and feel more confident about ourselves and our lives. With a positive attitude towards our *problem* we are much more likely to find a solution.

So, I wonder how your subconscious responds when you go around all day with a "problem" on your mind. Constantly worrying about your problems actually creates more of a problem! Negative thoughts breed more negative thoughts, and negative thoughts create negative feelings.

Wouldn't it be more effective if you thought about your problems in a different way? A more realistic or positive way? You would actually feel much better, have a clearer mind and focus more on how you are going to overcome them or solve them.

As suggested earlier, putting your problem into the imaginary box is a positive way. You only take it out at a more appropriate and convenient time, when you are able to do something about it. You can then search your bank of skills and abilities, or even other people's, as well as your past experiences. Calming and clearing your mind in order to find an answer will also serve you well. With a calm and relaxed mind you can also tune in to your higher self and your inner resources. When you find your solution just think how clever, how skilled and how experienced you are. This in turn will raise your self-esteem, increase your self-confidence and reduce your anxiety.

Always write your problem down in detail so you are clear about what the actual problem (opportunity) is. Sometimes we can try to solve the wrong problem, wasting time and energy. For example: if the problem is that you are becoming angry with everyone, the problem probably is not the fact that all those other people are doing something wrong – the problem could be that you are tired and stressed and you need to find a solution to that; to manage your own stress.

I suggest that you enter a specific solution-finding timeslot into your Daily Planner – see Week 9, Day 4. Also, try doing the meditation from Week 6, Day 7 (A Powerful Encounter).

A Guide to Problem-Solving

1 · **Define the problem**. First, spend some time discovering what the actual problem is. So for example, if you are driving a car that keeps breaking down, the problem might not be the car itself; it could be that you haven't enough money to replace it or get it repaired.

Secondly, ask yourself if there really is a problem. It could be that you perceive something as being problematic while others don't see it that way at all. Find out what others think and how they perceive it.

Thirdly, define the problem in as much detail as possible. Ask yourself what the nature of the problem is and the *who, why, what, where and when* questions. This way you will understand the problem more fully and therefore find the solution more easily.

2 · **Define the goal.** If there is a problem, there has to be a goal. What outcome do you want? What outcome do you need? For example: if the problem is that you are stressed and not coping very well, the goal would be related to what you want or need instead of being stressed, such as wanting to feel calm and more in control in your new job.

A way of defining your goal more precisely is to use the SMART acronym:

- **Specific** Put in as much detail as you can. For example: if it's a new car you want, *specify* and be clear about your budget, the make, the model, engine size and even the colour.
- **Measurable** How will you know when you have achieved the goal? If your goal is to achieve peace of mind, you need to have a good idea of how that might feel for you. Will you be able to recognize peace of mind when you have attained it? What will it feel like? How will peace of mind change your life? What will be different?
- **Achievable** There is no point setting a goal to fly to the moon (unless of course you are an astronaut!).
- **Realistic** You may not be able to afford a Lamborghini, so work out how much you can afford to spend.
- **Time-Limited** Write down your target date. This will motivate you to take action and ensure that you will achieve your goal within a specified period of time.

3 · **List all the realistic possible solutions.** Write down everything you can think of that will help to solve the problem. Ask others for their ideas. Have a brainstorming session (now commonly called a "thought shower") with several friends or colleagues. Don't discount anything, even if it sounds ridiculous. List everything and be willing to try as many as possible. Your list might look something like this:

- Practise relaxation every day
- Go to weekly yoga classes
- Go for a walk every lunchtime
- Put things more into perspective
- Go to bed earlier
- Ask colleagues for help
- Book a holiday for July
- Make lists and prioritize

4 · **Make a decision.** Decide which solution you are going to go with, or prioritize and decide which you will try first. Consider which are the easiest to implement and which are the most realistic. You can also score all the suggestions and see which one comes out on top.

5 · **Make a plan.** If the solution needs to be broken down into manageably sized pieces, you will need a plan. Again this is something you could enter into your Daily Planner.

6 · **Reward your achievements.** Once you have achieved your goal and solved your problem, it is important that you recognize it and reward yourself in some way.

Week 12, Day 6
» *DIRECTION* «

Laughter is the Best Medicine

"Laughter is a tranquilizer with no side-effects."
—*ARNOLD H. GLASOW, author*

Try to laugh more today. This is another great balancer for stress. Laughing makes you breathe in such a way that it increases the flow of oxygen and switches off the stress response. There is even something called Laughter Yoga, which encourages you to laugh deliberately. In other words, you make the sounds of laughter and just simply laugh at nothing and for no reason. A forced laugh will eventually cause you to start laughing spontaneously, and before long you won't be able to stop laughing. (I know this to be absolutely true because I have attended a laughter workshop!) Laughing is so good for you they even have classes in it. Give it a try. Go on, it won't hurt. You might even enjoy it, despite maybe feeling a little foolish to begin with. It's also a good idea to do this with others: it doesn't take long for everyone to be laughing uncontrollably for quite some time.

You deserve some fun. Everybody does. You're no different, no matter what your circumstances are. When was the last time you went out and had some fun? Maybe the last time I suggested you do that! When did you last have a really good laugh? Have you lost your sense of humour? Are you depressed? If so, go out with someone who you can laugh with. Put on a film or TV show that makes you laugh. Get someone to tell you some good jokes.

Buy one of those DVDs of comedians telling jokes for an hour. Get your favourite, and try it out.

When you laugh your body releases more endorphins, the feel-good hormones. So the more you laugh, the better you feel.

Now try to remember a time when you did have a good laugh. It doesn't matter if you have to go back a long time, just bring it to mind. Try to relax and cast your mind back.

- In your mind's eye, what are you seeing?
- Where were you?
- Take yourself back there now.
- Who was with you?
- What were they saying?
- What were you saying?
- What were you laughing at?
- Who else was there?
- What were you doing?
- How were you doing it?

- Now see the colours in the picture you are creating in your mind's eye.

- Taste what you were eating or drinking.
- What were you listening to?
- How did you feel?
- Why did you feel it?
- How are you feeling now, in this present moment, and why?
- Now come back into the present moment.
- What did you learn from that?

Were you able to laugh and feel good again, even though this happened long ago? You probably were; it is entirely possible to reproduce feelings that make you feel good or happy or content just by thinking about them. Perhaps lately you have spent more time recalling sad times, bad times, times when you were unhappy. How do they make you feel?

Have you ever realized that you cannot feel angry without first thinking about something that makes you angry? Have you ever realized that you cannot feel afraid without first thinking about the thing that makes you afraid? The same is true for happy feelings. If you want to feel happy, think about something that makes you feel happy. If you want to laugh, think about something that makes you laugh.

So, then, isn't it better to recall the good times? Can you see how they can change your mood and even make you laugh out loud?

Patch Adams is an American film made in 1998 starring the late Robin Williams. It was based on the true story of Dr Hunter "Patch" Adams. The doctor, who was a bit of a comedian, set up a comedy film show for his patients because he knew the therapeutic affect it would have on them. He used to dress as a clown and visit the children on the children's ward he worked at regularly and the children he visited appeared to recover more quickly than expected. Nowadays, in many hospitals across America laughter is considered an important part of therapy, and patients are encouraged to attend comedy film shows in the hospital, set up specifically to induce well-being and a quick recovery.

A number of years ago a psychologist, Robert Holden, set up a laughter clinic in Birmingham, England where he taught many people how to feel good again. It became a huge success because of the clinic's excellent results. The endorphins flowed and people who were depressed began to laugh and live again. Robert went on to become very well known for his work in positive psychology and his innovative Happiness Project. He is now Britain's foremost expert on happiness.

> *To finish: I have a joke for you –*
> *How many psychiatrists does it take to change a lightbulb?*
> *Answer: Only one, but the lightbulb has to want to change!*

Week 12, Day 7
» MEDITATION «
Meditation on Your Journey So Far

In her book *The Lotus and the Rose: The Art of Relaxation,* the yogini Sunita talks about man's aspirations. These include self-sacrifice, compassion, diligence, perfection, detachment and enlightenment. As a yoga student, and in particular when training to teach, I was encouraged to meditate on each of these in turn. It is amazing how, when we contemplate these qualities for any length of time, our minds throw up whole narratives on each of them. This practice demonstrating our ability to seek out the wisdom and knowledge from our subconscious mind, our higher self, was preceded by a two-hour long programme of yoga philosophy, mental relaxation, breath-control exercises and an advanced sequence of yoga asanas (physical postures). We would then spend half an hour in deep relaxation of mind and body, after which we were given our subject on which to meditate.

I appreciate that not everyone has the opportunity to follow such a lengthy, intense programme, but you can still practise the art of meditating on some of these themes. I would suggest that you go through the process of stilling your mind by focusing on your breath, or being mindful of your breathing, followed by practising the whole sequence of pranayama yoga breath-control exercises and the yoga stretches you have learned here, and of course any yoga exercises you may have learned from your own yoga class. Follow these with a minimum of twenty minutes in deep relaxation. Once your mind has wandered off into a state of deep relaxation where you have perhaps "lost" your body, introduce the subject on which you would like to meditate. (I suggest you decide this before you begin your programme.) Of course you don't *have* to follow this sequence. If you prefer, simply start to meditate whenever you are ready.

I am now going to suggest something slightly different. Instead of meditating on any of the subjects above, I would like you to meditate and contemplate your whole experience and journey through this book. The knowledge, skills, philosophy and directions you have learned and practised, and hopefully mastered, and how you have benefitted from your encounter. Open your mind and just wait to see what comes up for you. You may find that you have learned something that wasn't actually in the book at all! Maybe you have learned something about yourself that you hadn't realized before. You may be given further insight into the knowledge you have acquired. You may even connect with your higher self, which may have additional messages and guidance for you. Whatever arrives, enjoy it and accept it.

And finally, last but not least, once you have achieved peace of mind don't make the mistake of giving up everything you have learned. You are in that tranquil state because of what you have experienced, what you have done, what you have thought about and what you have learned and practised and achieved. Keep it that way. Continue to apply all the skills that have helped you to get from where you were to where you are now. Keep up the good work now that you have **Got Your Life Back** and enjoy it forever more.

Week 12

» RECAP AND REFLECT «

Tick the box when understood, practised and achieved

DAY 1   **SLEEP AWARENESS:** Do you have any difficulties sleeping? What is the cause of them? Do you now have a better understanding of sleep? Do you realize the importance of good-quality sleep?

DAY 2   **GOOD NIGHT – SLEEP TIGHT:** If you have difficulty sleeping, what do you need to start doing? What do you need to stop doing? What will you do to ensure you have enough quality sleep? Keep a record of the quality of your sleep on a scale of 1 to 10 to build up a picture of what needs to change.

DAY 3   **TAKING CARE OF YOURSELF:** Do you take enough care of yourself? Do you fully understand how the mind and body work together and how important it is to monitor both? Set any necessary goals to ensure that your health is improving.

DAY 4   **PERFECTIONISM AND STRESS:** Do you recognize yourself as being a perfectionist? Can you understand how it could cause or increase stress levels? If so what do you need to do about it?

DAY 5   **PUT YOUR PROBLEMS IN A BOX:** Are you able to think about your problems in a different way now? When will you begin to work on them? Start with the easiest to solve.

DAY 6   **LAUGHTER IS THE BEST MEDICINE:** How many times have you laughed since reading this page? Have you arranged any further opportunities to laugh some more? If not – why not?

DAY 7   **MEDITATION ON YOUR JOURNEY SO FAR:** This meditation is different to the ones you have done so far. Can you understand how it is different? If you haven't yet tried it, that's OK but do so as soon as you are able. Write down your thoughts and reflections or discuss them with someone.

Now turn to your self-assessment rating scales and enter your scores for the end of Week 12.

In Conclusion

· · · · · · · · ·

1. Reflection

YOUR JOURNEY to overcome stress, anxiety and depression and *get your life back* has not quite ended, even though you have come to the end of the book. You will still need to keep up the good work you have done in order to make further improvements or maintain your progress.

In the last meditation you did, you were asked to reflect on your whole journey as you advanced through the book. I hope this helped you to encapsulate everything you have learned, put into practice and achieved. It may also have given you some insight into how you have changed and evolved throughout your twelve-week journey.

Take a few moments, either now or later when you have more time, to reflect further on:

- what you have achieved
- how you have changed
- what you need to do next
- what you will do in the future based on the learning and understanding you have acquired while reading this book
- what you found the most helpful
- what were the most enlightening things you learned
- what was the most important thing you learned and why.

Finally, turn back to the beginning of the book and reread the page on "Your Creation".

- How close have you come to becoming your creation?
- Have you *Got Your Life Back* yet?
- What else needs to happen?
- If you are not there yet, when do you think you will be there?
- What will you do to ensure this?
- If you *are* there and you have achieved your goal, and become a new and healthier and happier you, then *Very Well Done! Congratulations! I knew you could do it! Now go and celebrate!*

2. Reassessment

Turn to the beginning of the book and the page on your *Self-Assessment.* You will have already entered your scores for your ability to cope and your stress levels, for the end of Week 12.

Did you meet your targets, or is there still work to be done? If there is still work to do, create a new, similar chart and continue to enter your scores on a weekly basis. Set appropriate goals in order to increase your scores and move up the rating scales until you reach your desired scores.

Turn to Week 7, Day 6 and assess how your Wheel of Life looks today. You may have been creating new wheels in your workbook or elsewhere, so today enter your new scores for all the departments of life and create a new wheel.

How does it look? Is it more rounded than in the past? How do you feel about the progress you have made? You may have been focusing your attention on the departments that had the lowest scores, so perhaps you still have work to do and improvements to make in other departments. This is a lifetime exercise, so do not despair if your wheel is still a bit out of shape! There is plenty of time to expand and progress in all departments.

Today is only the first day of the rest of your life!

3. Where do I go from here

"What you do today will determine your future."
— CATHERINE PULSIFER, author

Well done on all the achievements you have made so far. I hope very much that you feel proud of yourself and that your self-esteem, your self-worth and your confidence have all risen immensely. I hope also that your stress is under control, your anxiety has diminished and your depression has eased considerably, if not completely disappeared.

When you were reflecting on your journey so far, you may have realized that you have made many changes and achieved many goals. Your *mission* now, of course, is to maintain your progress and/or to continue to make further progress.

I occasionally used to have clients who were re-referred to me because they had relapsed, sometimes months after they had been discharged. Although they had made a complete recovery, or made such significant progress that they no longer needed my guidance, I could often guess why they needed to see me again. This doesn't happen very often, but it can. What happens is that people begin to feel perfectly well, even better than they were before they became ill, but they then think that they don't need to keep up their relaxation or practise other coping strategies, or they begin to take on more and more demands. They think that they will be able to cope with them now that they feel so much better.

However, they slip back into their old habits and find that they no longer have any time to maintain their progress. They falsely believe that it doesn't matter if they don't relax or exercise every day. They forget to practise their breathing exercises and positive thinking, and so they become unwell again.

To avoid this situation the secret is to continue to use your coping strategies, maintain your progress and regularly monitor your stress levels and your ability to cope. Do this by filling in a chart every week – or fortnightly if you prefer. Follow a plan that is designed to keep you at the level of high scores you achieved at the end of Week 12. If you see your stress levels getting higher, do something about it, immediately! You will have found out which strategies work best for you as you worked through the book. Plan to use them, remember them and build them into your weekly timetable or Daily Planner.

The main thing to remember is that you need to build them into your life and allow them to become second nature.

To remind you, **The Four Major Coping Strategies** are:

RELAXATION

EXERCISE

SLOW DEEP BREATHING

POSITIVE LIVING

4. My Top Ten Coping Strategies

1. RELAXATION · Always the most important and needs to be considered compulsory if you are to manage your stress effectively. It is impossible to feel anxious at the same time as being relaxed. Find a method that suits you and one that you really like. Try to relax at the same time every day for around twenty minutes or longer.

2. EXERCISE · Exercise for a minimum of twenty minutes four times a week. Walking is the most effective and beneficial form of exercise for stress, anxiety and depression. Swimming, cycling, dancing or other forms of exercise that increase your heart rate and breathing are also good. If you are over forty-five and/or unwell always check with your doctor. Always begin slowly, warming up the muscles, and slow down the pace at the end of the exercise.

3. SLOW DEEP BREATHING · Often, throughout the day, take three slow, deep abdominal breaths. This will switch off the stress response, slow down the heart rate, lower blood pressure and increase concentration, energy levels and positive thinking. Breathe deep into the abdomen, allowing it to rise or expand, and then the chest to expand fully. Exhale slowly, causing the abdomen and chest to sink down. Concentrate and imagine that you are breathing in peace, and breathing out tension. Try also to make time to practise the pranayama breath-control exercises once a day, if not more.

4. POSITIVE THINKING · Negative thoughts create negative feelings, which lead to a negative outcome. Be aware of your thoughts. If you catch yourself being negative, stop, challenge and change. Repeat positive affirmations as often as possible. They can empower you and help you to win, achieve success and calm your mind. They will switch off the stress response and change unhealthy negative emotions into positive, vibrant, powerful feelings. Remember – "As you think, so you become." If you think you can do something – you probably can!

5. BE AWARE · Get to know yourself – your limitations, your strengths and your weaknesses. Know just how much pressure you can take, but know also that every day brings something different. Be aware of what is going on around you. Stay focused and be aware of what is real and what is imagined. Recognize what needs changing and change it. If it can't be changed accept it, but most of all, know the difference. Recognize what you have control over and what you don't. Be aware of, and accept, other people's needs and limitations and be aware that they may be different to yours.

6. DO NOT IGNORE THE SIGNS · Accept the need to do something about your stress levels. Know that if you continue to push beyond your limitations you are pushing yourself too hard and you will possibly feel worse later. Rest, take a break and relax.

7. BE ORGANIZED · It is better to spend time in order to save time, energy and effort. Make lists and prioritize whenever possible. Finish one task before beginning another. Concentrate all of your energy and be mindful of what you are doing. Detach from it when it is completed. *Make* time for rest, breaks and fun! Always make time for relaxation. Make sure you find the correct balance in all things.

8. STAY ACTIVE AND KEEP PHYSICALLY FIT · As well as exercising several times a week, in order to stay healthy in mind and body you need to remain as active as you can. If you are unable to exercise outdoors or away from home, find something you can do indoors. Sitting down for long periods of time not only causes lethargy and boredom; it can also lead to physical ill health and can accelerate the ageing process. Exercise is also one of the best things you can do to prevent dementia. Balance your exercise with rest and make sure you are not functioning at a hundred miles an hour.

Eating a healthy balanced diet is also essential: eat at least seven portions of fruit and vegetables a day and make sure you are drinking enough water.

9. LIVE FOR TODAY · Live each day as if it were your first and your last. Live in day-tight compartments. Let go of the past, learn by your mistakes, have no regrets and move on. Plan for your future and set realistic goals. Do not worry about the future: if you have made reasonable plans, there is no need. You have no control over the past or the future; you only have today and you only have it once. Make it the best it can be. Put things into perspective and focus on solutions, not problems.

10. PERSEVERE · Whatever you do, never give up. Persevere, doing the best you can and being the best you can be. You are a unique and important individual and equal to everyone. No one is *better* than you. We are all the same, as well as all being different. Let your light shine in order that others may shine their light. Be grateful for all your blessings, every day and every night.

"When I let go of what I am, I become what I might be."
— *LAO TZU*

About the Author

· · ·

FOLLOWING AN EPISODE of post-natal depression, Mary was advised to take up yoga. She did so reluctantly, but very soon recognized the benefits as she recovered and became stronger. She continued to attend two or three classes every week for three years until being invited to study and train to teach pranayama yoga and relaxation.

She subsequently spent two and a half years studying on a one-to-one basis with her teacher and mentor and, having successfully completed her training, held her first yoga class in 1983.

Seeing her students reduce their stress and anxiety, Mary developed an interest in stress and stress-related conditions. Subsequently, over the next few years she gained qualifications in stress management, counselling, life coaching, Emotional Freedom Technique and energy field healing.

Mary is also trained in many other areas including Cognitive Behavioural Therapy, solution-focused therapy, understanding bereavement, The Fast Trauma and Phobia Cure and how to lift low self-esteem.

Using the skills she acquired, Mary worked in one of the UK Priory Group of psychiatric hospitals and in the UK National Health Service in community mental health for over twenty-five years.

She was also a successful stress management consultant, counsellor and life coach, delivering talks, seminars, workshops and courses as well as applying a wide variety of skills, therapies and techniques on a one-to-one basis. After retiring in 2010 Mary devoted her time to writing *Get Your Life Back*, with the aim of helping as many people as possible to overcome their stress, anxiety and depression in the same way as she has helped her patients and clients during her career.

Born and brought up in a small Lancashire village, Mary now lives in Solihull in the West Midlands with her husband.

Learn more about Mary and Get Your Life Back at *www.maryheath.co.uk*

Acknowledgements

. . .

FIRST AND FOREMOST I would like to thank my dear husband Ray. I am especially grateful for all the hours and all the days and weeks he spent endlessly and painstakingly proof-reading my manuscript, and then having to do it all over again with my next draft! I cannot thank him enough for his expert eyes meticulously seeking out my grammar and punctuation errors. He also put a great deal of time and effort into the I.T. side of things so that I could focus on the writing of my book.

Ray also worked hard to seek out an appropriate website designer and, using his abundance of skills and experience, was able to contribute much to the design and content. His help and advice, his support, encouragement and his love were invaluable. I shall also be forever grateful for his firm belief in my book. It gave me the heart-warming motivation and incentive to keep going.

I would also like to thank my lovely daughters, Louise and Nicola, for their love, their constant support, praise and reassurance. They have both inspired me by their inner strength, determination and dedication to achieve great success in their own chosen careers in the caring profession. I am immensely proud of them.

I am especially grateful to Sabine Weeke of Findhorn Press for believing in me right from the start. Thank you so very much for all your guidance, support and most especially for making it happen and my dream come true!.

Many thanks go to Damian Keenan for the design of my book. With all the tables, charts, diagrams and endless lists he deserves a medal for his skills, efforts and patience.

Much gratitude also goes to Jacqui Lewis my copy-editor, for her expertise, skills and guidance, patience and advice.

Many thanks also to Carol Shaw of Findhorn Press. Your knowledge and advice on publicity, marketing, websites and social media was invaluable. I didn't really have much of a clue about these before I spoke to you.

A big thank you also goes to Mak and Ben at Creative Astro who designed my website and helped with my blog and Facebook. I would have been completely lost without them.

Many thanks go to Ken Cabral, son of the late yogini Sunita, for granting his kind permission for me to include the pranayama yoga breath control exercises from his mother's book *The Lotus and the Rose.* They have been instrumental, not only in helping me overcome many of the adversities in my life but also in helping my numerous students, clients and patients.

My special thanks go to my friend Ruth Lawton for her proof-reading and offering to be my first guinea pig. Also for her continued support, encouragement and advice, especially as it was mostly conferred during our lovely afternoon teas!

My love, thanks and immense appreciation go to the late Mary Peacock, my yoga teacher for many years, who not only taught me everything I know about pranayama yoga but who was also influential in changing my life's path, which ultimately led to me writing this book.

Without the foresight, discernment and wisdom of Ann Harper, my dear friend and founder member of the Solihull Natural Health Group, I would never have embarked upon my journey of discovery of alternative and complementary therapies. I learned so much and gained an incredible amount of insight and knowledge from the countless talks, lectures and workshops she organized and coordinated for over thirty years. My book would never have been written had I not found this wonderful, extraordinary and inspirational group in 1991. I extend my sincere gratitude to Ann and everyone connected to the group who has inspired me over many years. Without them this book would simply not exist.

Many thanks and much appreciation goes to Sarah Withnall, my dear friend and ex-colleague. We worked closely together on many successful projects for almost ten years, our aim always to be the best we could be in helping our patients to cope, recover and to "get their lives back". Thank you Sarah, for your unswerving love, support, encouragement and undying friendship.

I would also like to acknowledge and thank Benita Jones, another of my ex-colleagues in mental health. Always supportive of my incessant ideas for new groups and courses for the psycho-educational day support team, Benita gave me free rein to devise, develop and deliver my courses, which, fortunately for me (and of course the patients) went on to be successful and therapeutically beneficial.

Last but not least, and very importantly, I extend my sincere thanks and gratitude to all my students, patients and clients, from whom I have learned so much.

Discover the companion CD to *Get Your Life Back*

Breath and Relax to Overcome Stress, Anxiety and Depression

by Mary Heath

IF YOU ARE AFFECTED BY STRESS, anxiety, depression or any stress-related condition, conscious breathing and visualization can be very effective in bringing relaxation and relief to a busy mind and body.

This CD offers you a powerful and unique sequence of breath control exercises from Pranayama Yoga, which supports you in calming the mind and controlling your emotions. Following on, a 25-minute creative visualization takes you softly and gently from relaxation to realization of your full potential. Guided imagery enables you to empower yourself with thoughts and beliefs of what you are capable of achieving, generating and encouraging personal growth and positive change.

Using these techniques you can expect to:
- Create a feeling of relaxation in mind, body and spirit
- Calm and clear your mind, promoting positive thinking
- Control your emotions
- Prevent, control and overcome anxiety and panic
- Relieve palpitations, hyperventilation and tension in the respiratory system
- Reduce and overcome nervousness and mental tension
- Relax and soften muscular tension
- Improve digestion, concentration, circulation, energy levels and sleep
- Build confidence and self-esteem

978-1-84409-673-2

FINDHORN PRESS

Life-Changing Books

Consult our catalogue online
(with secure order facility) on
www.findhornpress.com

For information on the Findhorn Foundation:
www.findhorn.org